Paul Lyons

Class of '66

**Living in
Suburban
Middle
America**

Temple University Press

Philadelphia

Temple University Press, Philadelphia 19122
Copyright © 1994 by Temple University. All rights reserved
Published 1994
Printed in the United States of America

Library of Congress Cataloging-in-Publication Data

Lyons, Paul, 1942–
    Class of '66 : Living in suburban middle America / Paul
Lyons.
       p.   cm.
    Includes bibliographical references (p.   ) and index.
    ISBN 1-56639-213-6 (alk. paper) — ISBN 1-56639-214-4
(pbk.)
      1. United States—Social conditions—1945– —Case studies.
2. Baby boom generation—United States—Case studies.
3. Middle class—United States—Case studies.   4. Suburbs—
United States—Case studies.   I. Title.   II. Title: Class of
1966.   III. Title: Class of sixty-six.
HN58.L96   1994
306'.0973'0946—dc20   93–50899

To Jennifer, Nate, and Max
who embody my hope in the future

Contents

Acknowledgments

In writing this book, I have benefited from the support and criticism of many friends and colleagues whose faith in my efforts remained firm even when at times it seemed that this book would never see the light of day.

I would like to thank Richard Stockton College of New Jersey for funding much of my research through several Research and Faculty Development stipends, through one Distinguished Faculty Fellowship, and through a sabbatical. A personal thank you goes to Vera King Farris, our college president, for establishing both the fellowship grants and for finding ways to assist faculty in making sabbaticals more financially feasible.

I am also indebted to those who have served as deans of the Division of Social and Behavioral Sciences, John Searight and David L. Carr. Deep appreciation also extends to our extraordinary office staff, whose dedication and graciousness make faculty life run so smoothly: Anne Glapion, Gail Gregson, Debbie Joseph, Theresa Steinke, Patti Williamson, and the divisional adminstrator Barbara R. Rosenblatt.

My students have been most helpful, literally serving as a catalyst for the inception of this book. They helped teach me about the complexities of defining both the 1960s and the Sixties generation.

The following Stockton colleagues either read all or parts of the book or participated in the Works-in-Progress Seminars during which I presented on my research: Patricia Reid-Merritt, David Emmons, Joe Rubinstein, Laurie Greene, Bill Gilmore-Lehne, Bill Sensiba, Joe Walsh, and Stephen Dunn. I thank them all for their thoughtful criticisms.

The Stockton Library—special kudos to Mary Ann Trail—has always provided me with all the assistance I have requested and then some.

Kali Tal, publisher of *Vietnam Generation,* and the poet W. D. Ehrhart have provided me with perceptive criticism and comradely support.

I have been fortunate to be part of a Philadelphia-area seminar that has been in operation for more than a quarter century. Its members, on many a Sunday morning, between bites of bagels and cream cheese and sips of coffee, have always been there to push me to greater clarity in my work. I feel great pride in calling such people my friends. Particular gratitude extends to Isadore Reivich, Albert Silverman, Vince Pieri, and Eva Gold. A special thank you goes to Josh Markel, a dear friend and seminarian, for his critical comments and warm support.

I must thank Jay Mandle and Joan Mandle for keeping me focused on the essential qualities of the scholar—the determination to state the truth and the commitment to have that truth serve the establishment of a free and democratic society.

Louis Ferleger has been a steadfast supporter in the creation of this book. His commitment to the value of *Class of '66* has sustained me over the past several years.

I wish to thank members of my family both for tolerating my single-mindedess and for being my most loyal supporters. My wife, Mary, my partner for more than twenty years, remains my North Star. I have found particular pleasure in having two adult children whose intelligence and humanity inspire me to keep at my work. And Max, well, I hope that he finds this book worth reading in about five years.

I am most grateful to Michael Ames, editor-in-chief of Temple University Press, for his enthusiasm, his firm hand, and his thoughtfulness in guiding this book to publication.

Finally, I must express my gratitude to the graduates of Coastal High School who allowed me to enter their lives and to tell their stories. Their graciousness, their hospitality, and their openness will always remain with me. They taught me a great deal about the essential decency of middle-class Americans.

Pomona, New Jersey

Class of '66

I'm not finding any real Sixties people. None
of the people I'm interviewing were into drugs or
protesting.

   —a student engaged in an oral history of the 1960s

Introduction

This is a story about white, middle-class American baby
boomers who came of age during the 1960s. Is it possible that
an essential part of the story of the Sixties generation has not
been told—and retold—given the procession of movies like
The Big Chill, television shows like *thirtysomething*, nostalgic
retrospectives in magazines like *Rolling Stone*, documenta-
ries, and memoirs?

During the nearly twenty years that I have been teaching a
course on the 1960s, I have become fascinated with the
distorted views my students hold about the meaning of terms
like "baby boomers" and "60s generation." They assume,
often based on popular cultural experiences, that baby boomers, with few, if any, exceptions, went to or wished to go to
Woodstock, protested against the Vietnam War, and engaged
in the rites of passage, including drug experimentation, of the
hippie counterculture. Indeed, they are often quite shocked to

discover, when engaging in oral history projects, that many of their baby-boomer subjects do not fit their presuppositions.

The story my students tell, which, I believe, reflects a view held by a majority of Americans, goes something like this: The Sixties radical hippies raised holy hell as they grooved on acid rock, smoked grass, dropped acid, and fought against authority in general and the Vietnam War makers in particular. Then, in the Seventies, they awoke with hangovers—those who didn't overdose and die or forever make mush of their brains—and, somewhat liberated from old-fashioned, repressive behaviors, especially regarding sex, reentered the mainstream. The story has a certain rhythmic charm: of hippies becoming yuppies, of materialism unleashed, of a nervousness about a betrayal of one's youthful past. As a character in the movie *The Big Chill* asks, Was it all just a passing fad, a fashionable and youthful moment?

In my students' story of the 1960s, the electoral shift from Gene McCarthy and George McGovern to the Reagan Revolution reflects a doubling back of "doing your own thing" from the marketplace of ideas to, simply, the marketplace, a transformation of hippie into yuppie. But, of course, the story contains several glitches. For one, several recent studies suggest that a surprising percentage of activists have held to their values and remain marked by their youthful ideals as they approach middle age.[1] Of perhaps greater significance, the dominant story excludes from baby-boomer credentials those not of the middle class: nonwhites and poor and working-class people.

The people my students often discovered in their oral histories were baby boomers whose lives seemed relatively unaffected by the 1960s, who had stayed within the mainstream of what Herbert Gans calls middle American or popular individualism.[2] As much as possible, they went about their lives as, at best, spectators to the tumultuous events of the 1960s and early 1970s, for example, civil rights, Vietnam, cultural rebellion. Such were most of the 1966 graduates of Coastal High School.

Coasters range from upper middle to working class, with a heavy concentration in the middle middle. They are suburbanites. We too often conflate suburban residence with an upper-middle-class affluence. Many social critics write as if "affluent" and even "rich"—as well as "white"—are the appropriate adjectives to precede the word "suburb." Such assumptions, especially characteristic of liberals and radicals, simplify the complexities of suburban America and make it more difficult to recognize, not to speak of respect, the struggles of middle-income families seeking to achieve and maintain, in the face of cultural deterioration and economic stagnation, if not decline, what historian Loren Baritz calls "the good life."[3]

To tell the story of a particular graduating class, I have needed to clarify the problematic categories within which it must be listed. These *are* middle-class suburban baby boomers. One might call them "silent majority" baby boomers, not because they are a majority within their generation—that remains to be determined, although my hunch is that they are—but because they were not, for the most part, involved in any of the vocal challenges, both political and cultural, associated with the 1960s. Their essential posture was conservative and, given the times, cautious. Most of them voted for Richard Nixon in 1972, their first presidential election. But in heeding Nixon's call for a silent majority to stand up against the various challenges of the 1960s, Coast baby boomers also were affected, characteristically at some distance and indirectly, by most of those challenges. They remained conservative but in a variety of ways had to come to grips with the questions concerning race, gender, morality, and patriotism that had driven the social movements associated with the Sixties.

I have alternated thematic material with profiles of Coast graduates. The chapters begin by describing the social, cultural, and historical context of the area—what it was like to grow up on the Coast. The portraits give flesh and blood to that context and to the themes that begin with Chapter 3.

One recurrent theme is that of a "warming" of a generation. Let me use a recent event to make my point. In the debate over gays in the military, there has been a tendency to minimize the advances that have led to the very fact of the controversy. Barry Goldwater has come out unequivocally for inclusion. The New Left and counter cultural segments of the Sixties generation may have "chilled"—although I believe that has been much exaggerated—but more significant is the warming, the gradual acceptance over time by mainstream people, especially more apolitical baby boomers, of what were once radical challenges. Coast graduates have incorporated core "Sixties" values, for example, greater toleration on matters of race and gender. In the 1992 presidential election, nearly half my sample voted for Clinton. Interestingly, such a shift from lifelong Republicanism was more notable among women, several of whom mentioned that their disillusion with Bush focused on his antiabortion position. A cautionary note: My own sample showed no greater tolerance regarding homosexuality.

This book challenges the argument that baby boomers went from activists to yuppies; instead, it focuses attention on the less spectacular developments among what I believe to be the larger segment of the Sixties generation. We've heard all too much about yippies and yuppies. Too many of those writing about the Sixties, having themselves been part of the more visible and vocal activist and hippie wing, analyze themselves. The picture one receives from a mix of the academy, the Beltway, and Hollywood, from the networks and PBS, tends to ignore the more mainstream experiences of baby boomers.[4]

Regarding Vietnam and the Sixties movements, discussed in chapters 3 through 6, Coast boomers confound the prevailing dichotomy that divides a generation into those who protested the war and those who served in it. In fact, most of those who found ways to avoid service in Vietnam did not join the marches and vigils against the war; rather, many of them supported it or were ambivalent, sometimes even oblivious. Coastal baby boomers looked to the National Guard or the reserves to resolve the contradictions between their mainstream values and their self-interests.

Their private lives inform another central theme of this book: the ways in which suburbanization allows middle-class people, mostly white, to construct cocoons to fend off what they perceive as threats to their families, their work, their communities. Too many observers have contempt for their struggles; they reduce them to stereotypes, for example, conformists living in "ticky-tacky" suburban tracts or racists in flight from cities, or they fixate on a segment of their most affluent members, for example, the professional, upper middle class, the "yuppies." This book examines the actual lives of a middle-class suburban generation that does not fit such stereotypes.

I have changed the names of the towns, the high school, and the graduates and have obscured a variety of situations to protect, as much as possible, the privacy of those who cooperated in the making of this book.

Americans are in the habit of
never walking if they can ride.
　—Louis Philippe, 1798

Home Life

It wasn't until after the Korean War that the Garden State
Parkway extended down to the South Jersey shore area. At
the time, Atlantic City's decline, accelerated by commercial
air traffic to Florida, was becoming apparent. The offshore
communities of Wilbur, Channing, and South Bay presented
attractive options to many of those fleeing both the urban
decay and the increasing black presence in Atlantic City and
nearby Pleasantville.[1] By 1965, as the decline approached its
nadir, Elwood G. Davis, in a report on poverty commissioned
by Atlantic Human Resources, the local antipoverty agency,
could sharply juxtapose Atlantic City's reputation of "playground of the world" with the grim fact that "not a single,
well-equipped playground exists in the disadvantaged areas."
Davis described "the inadequacy and fragmentation of social
and health services" and "the woefully understaffed welfare
system," noting that although summer tourist season "is a

happy time," "for almost nine months of the year, when the unemployment rate swings from 4 to 15 percent, living conditions are harsh and grinding." The report called Atlantic City, with a poverty rate of 33.5 percent and a 36 percent black population, "the poorest city in New Jersey," adding that Atlantic County was "one of the poorest counties" as well.[2]

Less than 10 percent of the parents of Coastal 1966 graduates were born and bred in the offshore communities of Wilbur, Channing, or South Bay. More than half were raised in Atlantic County, with approximately 30 percent from Atlantic City and Pleasantville. Roughly one-half came from urban environments, especially Philadelphia(8).[3]

In 1940, half of the county's population was in Atlantic City; by 1970, the portion was down to one-quarter, with a quarter of that declining citizenry over sixty years old. Within a population decreasing from 64,094 in 1940 to 47,859 by 1970, Atlantic City lost much of its tax base. Between 1960 and 1970, of 10,580 leaving the city, 8,258(78 percent) were whites.[4] While there is no statistical measure available, impressionistic evidence suggests that a significant minority of those whites migrated to the three Coast towns.

The offshore communities of Wilbur, Channing, and South Bay were being transformed from relatively sleepy, semirural towns to booming suburbs. Wilbur, for example, with approximately 3,000 people before World War II, doubled by 1960 and peaked at close to 9,000 by 1970. Channing grew from about 1,500 in 1940 to over 4,000 by 1965. And the sea-shanty town of South Bay, with its strip of bars and restaurants, grew from 2,500 in 1956 to 8,500 by 1968.[5]

In addition to the migratory pressure out of Atlantic City and Pleasantville—several parents had come over in two stages, first to Pleasantville, then to one of the Coast towns—there was the stimulation generated by the establishment of the National Aviation Facilities Experimental Center, popularly called NAFEC, in 1958, with its 1800 jobs. Many Coasters recall the tract housing in Wilbur at The Meadow and in South Bay's Greeneville as responses to NAFEC's arrival. Jimmy O'Brien remembers many of his neighbors being NAFEC people, "a lot of them fighter pilots." The presence of a military facility bolstered the red-white-and-blue conservatism already characteristic of the area.[6]

Nevertheless, despite NAFEC and the population explosion, Atlantic City's painful decline weighed down any hopeful economic indicators. Many Coast baby boomers recall that the opportunities in the area were scarce and that many considered leaving for more reliable, if not lucrative, work. The leading nonresort employers at that time included NAFEC, Lenox China, Wheaton Plastics, Spencer Gifts, and Prudential Insurance.[7] Some 1966 graduates hoped to find niches in the security of the local utilities. The general feeling was that the more ambitious were likely to move on to greener pastures.

And yet graduates' parents poured into the Coast towns, first, because it was a step up from Atlantic City and, second, because postwar GI Bill benefits made such migrations financially attractive, with small down payments and low interest rates.[8] And their migrations did stimulate construction and services—for example, the opening of Coastal High School in 1961, expansion of the local hospital, the opening of a new mall, the ground-breaking on a new county community college.[9]

It was a conservative area, dominated by Frank "Hap" Farley's county Republican machine, which controlled patronage and the graft and corruption endemic to Atlantic City since the permanent boardwalks had gone up in the 1890s.[10] The Democrats were barely in evidence, and Main Street values—God, country, family—shaped at least the public discourse. During World War II, over fifteen thousand county residents answered the call; 236 didn't return.[11] The region which resonated with flag-waving rhetoric on Memorial Day and the Fourth of July. Veterans organizations flourished.

In fact, five of the marriages producing 1966 graduates resulted from World War II encounters. Atlantic City had become Camp Boardwalk, with troubled resort hotels contracting to house Air Corps trainees and to serve as hospital, rest, and rehabilitation facilities.[12] Bill and Bobby Green's Southern-born dad met their mom, a native, in Atlantic City during the war. Linda Duncan Gent's father, also from the Deep South, had been a GI; her mother, a nurse. Such marriages gave the region a Dixie flavor, though touched by Atlantic City's carnie sophistication and Philadelphia's ethnic tones and mass media market.

Of forty-seven Coastal 1966 graduates interviewed, fifteen were born in either Wilbur, Channing, or South Bay; thirteen came over from either Atlantic City or Pleasantville; and another five had some urban childhood experiences. Four migrated from local towns or farm areas; one graduate was from a western Jersey suburb; and three were foreign-born. On the average, the twenty-six not born to the offshore towns arrived at age eight or nine. Their parents, often reconstructing their lives and then establishing families as the American economy began to flourish in the late 1940s and early 1950s, typically had two or three children.

The parents, many of them marked by the disruptions of the Great Depression and the war, were not highly educated.

It seems that few were willing or able to take advantage of the educational benefits of the GI Bill. Only six fathers were college graduates; the two Ph.D.'s were earned abroad by foreign-born who had emigrated to the United States. Only a handful hadn't completed high school. A few mothers had college degrees or nursing training, but for the most part, they had been limited to secondary educations.

These Coast families scattered throughout the bungalows and new ranches of the three towns. The wealthiest were in Channing's posh Seaview section, emerging out of the back-bay marshes. Almost all, from factory workers to physicians, were home owners. They were part of the white suburban middle classes, perhaps more distinguishable by family background, reputation, and lifestyle than simply by income.[13] Of forty-four families, six could be called blue-collar, working class; two fathers died on the job in industrial accidents. Another fifteen families were lower middle class, with occupations ranging from milk and mail carriers to delicatessen and sub-shop owners. The middle class, numbering twelve, included bank employees, a principal, and some insurance agents. Among the eleven upper-middle-class fathers were a restaurateur, a technical writer, an engineer, and several owners of successful businesses.[14] Given their high level of social mobility, Coast parents are best characterized as members of the variegated middle classes. Despite the impression many county residents have that the Coast communities feeding into Coastal High School are upper middle class, even rich, the three towns are, except for small pockets in places like the Gold Coast, decidedly what sociologists call middle-middle.[15]

I was interested in finding out about family life, child rearing, parental values, and lifestyles. Within these small towns evolving into suburbs were a diversity of families: military people, tourist trade businesspeople, transplanted Southerners, Italian and Irish Catholic urbanites, Piney rustics, and devout fundamentalists. There was significant upward and downward mobility; some families, sharing in the general prosperity of the postwar years, rose from near poverty to middle- and upper-middle-class comforts.

I was surprised by the relatively small amount of ethnic or religious bigotry. Most baby boomers report that conflicts between Protestant and Catholic, or between Northern Europeans and Italians, were minimal to nonexistent; in fact, there were six Protestant-Catholic marriages in my sample. Suburban experience seems to have flattened out the ethnic rivalries characteristic of city life. There were no "turf" issues in the Coast suburbs. The minor exception was Jewishness, of which there was little within the three communities. To most Coasters, Jewish meant the affluence of nearby Margate and the Channing Country Club where several Coasters caddied. Few gave much thought to the fact that the Channing Country Club existed because of the anti-Semitic restrictions of the other major country clubs in the area. Sally Vincent Rogers recalls being asked for a date by Sam Gordon, a recent arrival from New York—"heavy accent, real nice smile, smooth talker"—only to be told by her father, "He must be Jewish," and not allowed to accept. Gordon turned out to be Protestant. And Ronnie Glueck, whose mother was Jewish, recalls subtle slights and occasional insults. The president of the school board, however, was Jewish.[16] The norm seems to have been a low-grade, social anti-Semitism, kept latent by minimal contact.

Of forty-two families responding, twenty-nine were Protestant, thirteen Catholic. The largest and most prestigious denomination was Methodism, with Channing's Methodist Church serving as an important social center for not only most of the Methodists but also for other Protestants wanting to go to Sunday school or wanting to belong to a youth group with their school friends.[17]

Virtually all of the baby boomers speak of regular church attendance during their formative years. As many as half went to Sunday school and belonged to church-sponsored youth organizations. But by adolescence, church attendance began to diminish as peer-group activities subverted family togetherness. At one end of the continuum, Rachel Barnes's life was integrated with a fundamentalist church; at the other, several graduates reported only nominal church involvement. Perhaps most characteristic is Carol Smith Rizzo's experience, growing up in a devout Baptist home with Southern roots, but drifting away during high school. She recalls, "In the South we used to go there every summer for a couple of weeks—a beautiful church—it was nothing to go to church four times a week, sing and the whole bit. Sunday was the Sabbath; you wouldn't do anything." She notes, however, that such devotion eroded in the North—"you were in Jersey—the Sunday wasn't the Sabbath, the Sunday was the day you rode your bike."

The area had its share of conformist and repressive pressures, manifest particularly in the clash between small-town morality and resort-business modernity. Sally Vincent Rogers, one of several South Bay "bar brats" in the 1966 class, angrily recalls a sixth-grade teacher making remarks about "a saloon keeper's daughter" and remembers her mother talking about a local church that denied the Vincents membership because of their "notoriety." Although the Vincents were not a religious family, they went to church regularly to counter such charges. This wasn't convenient, as Sally recalls, "because my parents owned a restaurant and worked very late hours—and when you work in the restaurant everyone works—[but] even if it meant a taxi ride to church, the children went to church."

A minority of 1966 graduates faced restrictions regarding dances—or, as Al Judson recalls, no smoking or drinking during his Methodist boyhood—but for the most part the suburban milieu, the high school subculture, tended to relax such strictures. Most baby boomers were allowed to get caught up in the rock 'n' roll spirit of junior high school canteens. The larger variation was between regulated and permissive parental responses to adolescence. In some cases, because parents worked hard and long hours, kids had more leeway to do as they pleased. In other instances, parents varied in how much control they exerted once their children entered the high school or, in some instances, the middle school. One Channing native remembers sixth-grade drinking parties, a rarity perhaps limited to a few Seaview homes. More typical was the fairly rowdy crowd of mostly Wilbur guys like Joey Campion and the Green brothers, who began drinking in early adolescence, were able to stay out later hours, and were free on weekends to carouse at their hideaway, The Nest. The parents of other Coasters, male and female, kept a watchful eye on out-of-school hours. Bette Carter Roszak, for example, had to duck and hide in Campion's dad's soda shop, one of the main hangouts, when her father drove past on his way home. To the more traditionalist parents, temptation still lurked in suspicious places—like those containing pinball machines or jukeboxes—especially for their daughters. Youth culture was ascending, but the eruptions of challenges to authority associated with the Sixties had not reached the Coast by 1966. Adolescent deviance, particularly in matters of style, alcohol, and sex, never challenged adult authority. Kids were just kids. Some were a little wild; a few were "bad"; but the assumption was that when reality hit—work, marriage, and family—they'd settle down. There was little reason to doubt such comforting projections in the 1950s and early 1960s along the Coast.

Family life appeared to be stable; at least that's how most, in the context of their own more tumultuous marriages, remember things. I've only been able to discover four cases of divorce among the parents of those I interviewed and perhaps an additional dozen families discussed. Most baby boomers can't remember knowing of any divorces within their parents' generation. Certainly divorce was not as commonplace as it has become to Coast's baby boomers. And one respondent whose mother was twice divorced recalls that "it was very difficult for us children because there were boys and girls who weren't allowed to associate with us. That was like the scarlet letter at that time; it was something terribly wrong; and, of course, there was something wrong with us because we were in that situation."

Fully half of the mothers were full-time housewives, at least until baby boomers left the home. Many others didn't work until the kids were either in elementary or high school, or worked only part-time to supplement family income. Among the exceptional cases were Dave Ford's mother, who took over the family business upon the death of her father, and George Evanson's, who started a successful rental business. Several mothers were nurses, librarians, and secretaries; in four cases, they worked alongside their husbands in family stores, typically twelve to fourteen hours a day, seven days a week. Many baby-boomers shared few leisure activities with their parents; often the parents, after working long hours or a second job, collapsed in front of the television after dinner, too weary to play catch or discuss college plans with their sons and daughters. Christian Olsen remembers his father sleeping when he wasn't putting in eighteen hours in his store: "There wasn't a whole lot left for the kids."

On the other hand, there were a number of parents who became community leaders and activists in creating and sustaining sports activities, church clubs, and scouts. Several parents, for example, actually laid out the baseball fields and built the dugouts and scoreboards for the community-based leagues created during the 1950s. Nora Reilly Bennett's mother was "a pillar of the church", heading important committees and taking a lead in insuring a family-centered congregation. And when parents weren't available, there were other adults to meet children's needs. For example, Tom Rogers, whose dad, a blue-collar worker, died when he was very young, had "a few men in the neighborhood who organized sports" and kept him "on the right track."

Whether mothers worked or not, the family structure and tone were decidedly patriarchal. Husbands assumed, even demanded, that their working wives remain responsible for the children, the cooking, and the housework. The kids, if anything, knew the moms. Matt Blake reflects, "When I grew up, most of the men worked, and most of the women stayed home. If Bob was over to my house all the time, or Rick or Johnny, my mom was their adopted mom; that's how it was; and when I got out of grammar achool, that's when the women started making the break of getting part-time or full-time jobs." Polly Bain Smythe remembers that "when dinner was over, the men got up and went into the living room; the women got up and did the dishes." Changes were occurring; the very fact that more wives were taking jobs as their children became more independent, that they were both insuring a more middle-class living and getting out of the house—finally—suggests a subversion of housewifery few Coasters noticed.

These were mostly old-fashioned people, conservative Republicans in an all-white, mostly Protestant area. Almost 75 percent of the parents were Republicans, and among the 16.9 percent who were Democrats, many, of Southern origins, were quite conservative, possibly more so than the GOPers, who seemed to prefer Henry Cabot Lodge over Barry Goldwater in 1964.[18] All of the baby boomers recall where they were when President Kennedy was shot, and most seem to believe that their parents, despite conservative Republicanism, liked him. But few grew up in households that paid much attention to public affairs outside of the immediate local area.

Politics was not a typical topic at the dinner table, or anywhere else. To most baby boomers, the history-making events of the 1960s, from the Cuban Missile Crisis to the Civil Rights Movement, were distant, marginal. Jack Claire jokingly characterizes Coast households as "Methodist," meaning that silence and repression were hallmarks of the dinner table. These were not expressive families, for the most part; there was more respect than warmth, more love than touching and hugging. Conversations, including those about politics, that threatened to unleash pent-up emotions were avoided.

Few had open disputes; rare was the kind of struggle Rodney Wayne waged with his parents following his college rebellions. (See profile.) In a few relationships, like that between Joey Campion and his dad, tensions did flare. The father, old-world in his values, could talk sports with his son, but little else. "My father and I never got along that well," Joey tells me, "until ten years ago." He recalls, "We couldn't be in the same room for an hour without an argument. My father was very quick to say no to whatever it was. The way he grew up, you didn't walk out your front door if you didn't have a tie and jacket and hat on; down here we didn't know what a tie and hat was." One Easter Sunday when all the Wilbur guys planned to go to the boardwalk, father and son argued after the elder Campion demanded that Joey dress properly—with a tie: "So I didn't go, and we had a screaming match." However, in most families, seething outranked screaming. And certain topics—politics, religion, anything controversial, and anything personal—were forbidden.

Yet these were children growing up with an exploding mass culture—televisions, cars, movies, pop music, record albums, button-down shirts, Ivy League sportswear, ponytails, *Father Knows Best,* and *Ben Casey.* Their parents had to cope with new realities—suburban lawns, a big regional high school, an exponentially growing community, and confusing national and global issues of which they were ill equipped to deal and over which they had little control. Most of them felt blessed that they were providing their children with more than they had ever had, and worked hard and long to sustain those blessings.

They could be narrow-minded and bigoted, especially regarding black people. Nora Reilly Bennett's mom was dogmatic and righteous: "If she was ever on a jury for a rape case, God help that person; everything was black and white—there was no gray for her." Several graduates refer to their parents' rigidity and intolerance. Judd Dennis had an ancestor who was in the Klan, which met just down the road at a local tavern. Harry Kearns recalls his anti-Catholic grandfather turning off the television when Kennedy was on. At the same time, the Christian upbringing of those like Polly Bain Smythe taught that all—including Catholics, Jews, and blacks—were God's children and should be treated accordingly. But given the high level of racial, religious, and social-class homogeneity of the Coast communities, such Christian universalism suffered few tests. And there is no evidence that a significant percentage of offshore people felt uncomfortable with the institutional bigotries that kept blacks and Jews out of their neighborhoods and schools. For example, no effort was made to eliminate such de facto segregation patterns. Indeed, the very nature of suburban life kept the "other," both racial and religious minorities, out of sight and therefore out of mind.

There was considerable stress, hard to assess secondhand. I have, however, discovered enough instances of alcoholism, especially among fathers, to believe that it was a problem, a signal of suppressed dreams, self-doubt, personal demons, and, always, abuse of those one loves. A number of the children carried problems of alcohol abuse into their own lives.

These were not households that prepared children to deal with racial injustice, poverty, the Vietnam War, feminism, environmentalism, Watergate, stagflation, or sex, drugs and rock 'n' roll. But they wanted the best for their kids; as Sally Vincent Rogers states, "My parents' dream was for everyone to go to college; my father was doing something that he really didn't want to do, but he was doing it because he had a family to support; and my mother always felt that she could have gone to college, but life has its own way of turning out." And Christian Olsen, whose immigrant parents were in their retail store night and day, saw college as a way out of a "labor-intensive" life: "We saw that there was a different way from what our parents had given us; I swore I would never do what he had to do." Even within a relatively depressed area, the postwar economic boom that was climaxing as the class of 1966 approached graduation offered hope to the children of hard-working, old-fashioned, and insular Coast families.

Coasters were part of the extraordinary upward swing that expanded middle-class comforts to previously poor, struggling rural and blue-collar people. The GI Bill, tract housing, what Alan Wolfe calls "the politics of growth," which through federal government intervention spawned the suburban-shopping-mall interstate-highway environment literally and figuratively driven by the automobile, the unique and never-to-be-repeated monopoly the United States possessed as the world's only economic power[19]—all of this helped to give flesh to the dreams built into Coasters' self-image. Wilbur, for example, proudly called itself "the neighborly city." The townspeople had every reason to be proud of what they and their nation had accomplished. But the price paid was a narrowing of vision, an intolerance of dissent, and an invisibility to those left behind in the Inlet ghetto of Atlantic City and in all of the other pockets of poverty Michael Harrington was making visible while Coasters were sending their baby-boom offspring to a brand-new suburban high school. This "most marrying generation on record," according to historian Elaine Tyler May, believed that suburban insulation and family stability would contain threats, real and imagined, but now externalized.[20] Their children grew up ill prepared to come to grips with the kinds of challenges, often perceived as threats, associated with the social movements of the 1960s.

Profile: Bill Green, Team Player

A medium-sized, moon-faced man, with a vigorous, youthful presence in tension with his bald-headed plainness, Bill Green is a top executive with a large national firm headquartered in New England, where he and his family live. I had been looking forward to interviewing him because of his central role in the building of "The Nest," a two-room, two-story fort where many of the Wilbur crowd of rowdy guys had hung out during their schoolboy years.

"We had one smaller," he tells me, "probably not as sophisticated, fort, during our time in Pinetree School [K–8]; in fact, there was one right back here." Green points to what was now a cul-de-sac of manicured, suburban homes. "Atkins Field; Atkins was a farmer who lived right on the corner, at the junction of Pinetree and Birch, and he had an old house there, and all of this was his field—there was a woods back there, and we had built a kids' fort, and it was up in the trees. We decided to build catwalks."

"The Nest" was off Airdale and Shockley Avenues. Bill's younger brother Bobby recalls, "The Nest started when I was a freshman in high school [Bill, two years older, but having stayed back in school, was also a freshman] and met a kid named Willie James and I used to tell him about the forts we had and he started to tell me about the forts he had. We all got along and we started to say, 'hey, let's build a fort,' so we built a fort in Wilbur, off Airdale Avenue."

Bill Green designed it: "When we did The Nest, that was all planned out; we knew the perimeters; we knew how far we were going to go; we knew what we were going to do, how we were going to do it, the size it was going to be, the floor sizes. We sat down; we talked about the good things, what we wanted to do, what we wanted it for, why we were going to have it; and then we did it. It was two rooms, but down below, it was a lower level which was a twelve by twelve room, and an upper one which was ten by ten, and the upper was just a sleeping one. We used to sleep out a lot; that was one of the things we did—Davy Hunter, Dan Vitale, Richie Davis, Jim Fuller, twenty or more, it was mostly guys—it was really a guys' club. . . . We used to sit there and drink, drink and talk and tell stories, sit up around the burning fire, and just talk. We'd go out there and just camp and be on our own." Girls could become "buddies" if they were "inquisitive enough, brave enough," but, Bill notes, "it wasn't something that we really wanted, girls; it was our space." Adolescent tomfoolery, like urinating from trees on unsuspecting visitors, was enough to deter most girls.

Green takes particular pride in its construction: "It was very weatherproof; I wouldn't let it leak. It had a roof and it had a heater in there. We had an old ice box, sawdust-full ice box, lots of wood in there. It had special locks with bars that fell down; you had to know what to do in order to get it up. Davy Hunter manufactured it in metal shop, we made it and put it in—you could beat the thing to death, and you couldn't get in. We had a lock on the outside, and if you broke the lock off, you still couldn't get in, because you had to know the inside mechanisms."

He laughingly recalls the purchase of the tongue-and-groove lumber: "It was funny to call the lumberyard and say, 'Have the truck driver go to the end of Airdale Avenue and blow his horn,' and a guy would pull up and blow his horn, and out of the woods would come twenty to thirty guys, pick up all the wood—it was like a bunch of ants. It was swampy; you couldn't walk through it; in order to get back there, we had to build these catwalks. What we did was drilled the pilings down into the mud and then made the catwalks just a couple of inches off the water so they couldn't be seen from the outside but just above the waterline, and at some point we even had to drain the swamp in order to get in there—we'd dam it up and let it fill again."

Bill Green, designer of The Nest, has been described by friends as someone who couldn't spell three words straight. When he moved over from Atlantic City to Wilbur in early elementary school, he brought with him a hearing problem: "I was literally deaf; my parents, my mother would say, 'Billy can hear'; the truth of the matter is that I could not hear her, but I heard her tone. I knew my brother's tone, my sister's tone; I would hear a sound, that sound was not necessarily a word." Finally, at age seven or eight, Bill had an operation on his eardrums and "at that point . . . began to hear." But he adds, "I think I lost a lot of the very basics of sounding out words and understanding words, and as much as I would like to now, I can't seem to pick up those very basic . . . I know they're there. They're very meaningful years, those young years; you don't do it then, you begin to lose things."

Green's folks had met during World War II in Atlantic City. His dad, at that time in the service, was a farmer, oldest of eleven children, with no more than a fourth- or fifth-grade education; his mother, then seventeen, was born and bred in Atlantic City, strictly Roman Catholic. They fell in love and got married just before Green senior was sent overseas. After the war, they settled in Atlantic City. As brother Bobby recalls, they "grew up with [their mom's] relatives, very Catholic, very strict," although the dad rarely went to church, in part because his tobacco addiction made it impossible for him to sit through services without innumerable cigarette breaks. In 1955, they moved over to the offshore town of Wilbur, then less than three thousand residents, just in the process of becoming a suburb.

The Greens were working class in a middle-class milieu. The father worked in Atlantic City as a clerk, loading and unloading incoming trucks, stocking shelves. In the summertime, he worked the boardwalk to supplement his income. Bobby notes, "He would work all night long . . . and leave there, come home for a couple of hours and go back to work on the beach," seven days a week. The mom started working as a waitress at the local hangout when Bill and Bobby entered high school and her youngest, Benjy, was an infant.

Bill Green, unlike many of his buddies, took the college prep program at Coastal High School. "As I look back on it, I didn't put the energy into it; if I had, I would have been a very successful student. It was just that I could get by with Cs and Bs and be fine." He chose not to focus on the industrial arts classes, because "I didn't see anything that they could teach me." Like several of his classmates, he expresses some resentment at the inadequacies of the school's guidance department: "I was just left alone." He received no encouragement to think about college; no one connected his gift for design with career possibilities such as architecture. He did love mechanical drawing class: "I couldn't get enough of Lou Adamo and the drawings, and I wanted to take more of it." His advisor allowed him to drop his Spanish course to take more drawing. He now regrets that "they didn't say, No, you got to stay," and didn't push him to his fullest academic potential.

Bill didn't inherit his mechanical aptitude from his dad, who couldn't "use a hammer"; but perhaps because of the compensations learning disabilities can generate, Bill could "just look at it and know just what to do; I had that ability, always did." He was "constantly doing things, making things, figuring out how to fix things." Bill Green's essential nature comes through in his vision of craft: "The thing that I used to enjoy—and it goes right through my work now—is putting together a program [so] that other people can put it together as easy as I can. I always found it was fine to say, 'Oh, I can do this—I can put up this wall or this paneling'; but to put the pieces together so that other people could do it as quickly as I could, pre-engineered, filling out, I always used to enjoy that."

One of the highlights of high school for Bill, as well as for dozens of his collaborators, was the construction of the prom sets. "Our idea was, we wanted to look down on the prom rather than look up, given the ceiling in the gym," he recalls. "So the idea that came out about the prom was to look down on it and to have a balcony the full length of the gym, and to have sunken pools in the cafeteria—to do all these fancy, big columns." The faculty advisors were more than skeptical, "but the group just didn't let go of it; we said, 'We know we can do it, if you just let us,' and we did. We built a balcony that went the full length, that had curves, stairs; everything was built in pieces, in modules, in my backyard, and brought in Friday morning, and ready that night for the prom. We had some columns that were twenty feet high that we wrapped in corrugated cardboard to look like Grecian columns. In order to get those columns, we went to Pacemaker Boat Company out in Mays Landing, and they cut the round portions out of their boats—it was long, straight mahogany; we got all of that and brought it back to woodshop, cut it into square strips so you could make the long column."

Bill was the organizer, the architect without whom the project could not have taken shape: "It was just a matter of thinking of these things and getting this big group of guys, all this energy, together to make the material, to hold the material—it didn't take a whole lot to hammer and nail, and most of it was clamped together because we knew we wouldn't have time to nail. We used a lot of clamps, a lot of predrilled holes. They had enough faith in us to know we were going to have water in pools with goldfish in the cafeteria. It worked!" Bill throws back his head, delighted still with the triumph that seemed to be right out of an old Mickey Rooney–Judy Garland film.

"One of the biggest concerns," he explains, "was that we could build a balcony that was structurally safe enough to walk kids across. That was one of the first objections: 'You can't build a balcony that won't slip or move,' but I said, 'I know I can,' and I sat down in mechanical drawing and drew it out. Adamo looked at it and said, 'It's going to hold.' I couldn't build a skyscraper at the time, but I knew enough that this was going to be safe."

Time and again, Bill Green emphasizes the central values of planning, efficiency, cooperation, and teamwork. He is thoughtful and honorable, bursting with enthusiasm about people working together, in striking contrast to the highly individualistic portraits filling so many recent examinations of American character.[21] This is no narcissistic personality, obsessed with self-fulfillment; a singular "me" doesn't seem part of Bill Green's emotional baggage. The tongue-and-groove lumber used to build The Nest could stand as a metaphor for Bill's sense of workmanship.

He begins a soliloquy on his high school football experiences that extends the metaphor: "I loved the game; I loved the philosophy of the game: everybody goes out there and everybody knows the play, a person calls the play, the play happens the way it's meant to happen, you score or you do good, and if one person messes up, the whole effort of the other ten people can be for naught. So you have to play together; it's a very team sport. If I couldn't block the guy in front of me, I owed it to the quarterback or whoever was the captain of the team to say, 'Hey, I'm having trouble with the guys in front of me; I'm not able to keep this guy out for more than two seconds, so that he's killing me.' I owe it to the team so that they would play the other way or we could double-team the guy, but we didn't hold secrets back from each other when we played football, and I liked that. It was a plan, we executed the plan, we weren't afraid to play hard, we weren't afraid to play rough—I don't say dirty—we played hard and the scores constantly show that, that we were good and that there was a wide realm of people involved."

Bill Green takes me one by one through the distinctive qualities of his teammates, how they meshed together, the blocking-back ability of Roy Smiley, the lineplay of Mac Schmidt: "Fourth down, three to go, and we didn't care. And the coaches would let us play the game because it was our game. His thing was, 'Next year you guys are going to be gone, and I'll have a new team; then it's their game.' I still use a lot of the philosophy right now."

Sports metaphors, at least since Teddy Roosevelt, have been critical to an understanding of American culture.[22] Like many American men, Bill Green turns to a vision of sports as a collaborative act—designed, then implemented—and of sports as life itself.

Like most of his fellow graduates, Bill grew up in a family that "didn't dwell on what's happening" in the larger, public world, although he is among the minority in claiming that he was aware of what was going on in Southeast Asia. In September 1966, shortly after graduation, he joined the regular army, believing that he would thereby expand his schooling and training options. "I had faith enough to say that if I worked hard and did well, I could do something; and if my time was up, I could come out and have enough money to go to school—so that was my aim."

Once in the army, trained at Fort Belvoir in the army engineers, Bill began "to question" our Vietnam policies, "not why we were there so much—the country had had a record of defending democracy throughout world—it was kind of like taking it back to football. You had a first and goal, and to run something that was totally stupid. I felt that the government was not letting the American soldier do what he was sent over there to do; to sort of go there and play a game that was designed for him to lose—and that would aggravate me—that we couldn't use weapons that we knew. And I'm not talking about the chemical munitions, which I got very, very involved in later. We weren't allowed to cross here; our planes weren't able to chase them here. You started saying, 'Wait a minute; if you want me to do this thing, I'll do it; but if you're going to go out there where it's real life and people are shooting bullets, are you going to be playing the game? Play to win!' That's the way we grew up! I didn't want to go out and shoot somebody, and I had no desire to drop a bomb on them or kill them, but hey, if this was what I was doing and this was what I had to do—this was what I was told to do—then do it the best you can and get out of it; don't let the game go into overtime."

Green reflects on the lessons of Vietnam: "We're a country of winners; we want to win; we can take losing, but we want to win." He concludes that we have learned "to be tough fans, to follow our team and cheer them on, more so when they're down," but that we need to "ask more questions of what's going on." He still believes that we could have won with greater application of force, but admits that if that turned out not to be the case, "then get out of there." He applauded our intervention in Grenada because "we went in there, we did our job, and bang, you're out." On Nicaragua, he asks if the people wanted us there, but defends Oliver North as "a team player . . . told to run a pattern; he ran the pattern, and he ran it with all he had. Whoever threw the ball, okay, he doesn't want to admit, and as I said earlier, if you can't handle your man, you got to say it: you owe the team that. Whether he approved of it or liked it, it doesn't matter; he did what he was told, by the person who told him to do it. Was it the quarterback, or was it the coach? Was it the person who threw him the ball, or was it the person from the sidelines?"

Bill Green is not a frivolous or foolish man; he is serious, thoughtful, and honorable. But something seems to be missing, not in his moral character, but rather in the scope of his attention, in the extent and depth of his knowledge and understanding of the larger world, the world that extends outside of the redneck South, ethnic Atlantic City, and mainstream, middle American Wilbur. His moral parameters are circumscribed by a unquestioning faith that "the country had had a record of defending democracy throughout the world."

Green decided not to make a career of the army, despite significant career opportunities, because he found too much disorganization and inefficiency when he returned stateside from Germany. He came back to a United States, which by 1969 looked quite different. He says that he was tolerant of the lifestyle changes, except that he "couldn't understand why anyone would think to use drugs." But at the same time, he was getting more angry about the war and about how the politicians weren't doing their jobs. For the most part, he dealt with such feelings by pushing them away and getting on with establishing a career and family. He recalls that "the person who at the time made the most sense to me was George Wallace; he wasn't saying what everyone wanted to hear, but I think he was telling the truth." Bill admits that his Dixie-based upbringing was "a little racist," but believes that his experiences in the service and after, when he first got to know blacks, "wiped out almost all of the racism that I had." He is emphatic in denying that it was Wallace's racism that attracted him.

After he achieved considerable success as a construction executive, becoming the kind of cosmopolitan man who thinks nothing of flying down to Manhattan to see a play, he came to admire Martin Luther King Jr. for "trying to form a group, to get them to move forward out of poverty." King became, to Bill Green, "a master for putting together large groups of people for one sole purpose; they all knew what they were headed for. If they were going to march on something, they marched on it, and, by God, you couldn't stop them; it was just too massive—and that was impressive." So over time, the civil rights revolution was subsumed, at least to some extent, under Bill Green's worldview of team effort, effectiveness, and competence, although one might question his assertion that "whatever prejudice I had, they were easily thrown out."

Bill's life history of collaborative can-do effort shapes his views of the poor: "We have to take care of these people; we have to come up with some programs that will make them help themselves. We've got to give them the hope to see again and to know, if they don't do something for themselves, that this is someplace they're going to stay forever—to give them a way out, to show them a way out—not just give them the food and say, 'Here's the food; here's your foodstamps; here's your welfare check."

Bill Green is looking for a political leader "who can put together a good team to play, not the player himself; I'm not concerned with the quarterback." He can imagine being on such teams; in fact, he sees his whole life as built on such definitions: "What was in me in high school—organizing, putting it together, building it, liking to see a team play together—a lot of that is still the very same." As a boss, "I can still have a beer with the guys, I can get on a job site and relate to the carpenters, and I can relate to the top management of the corporation; I can get them to both understand both sides—those are traits I learned here" in Wilbur. It's a compelling mainstream American vision and story, but about one too often unwilling to come to grips with fundamental inequalities based on race, gender, and class; with the realities of power and money; and with the ways in which the rules of the game are rigged. But Bill's integrity—the ways in which I see Bill Green as an authentic American, part Thorstein Veblen, part John Dewey—continues to have a powerful hold on me.

Profile: Frank Feller, Rebel

Frank Feller was more affected than Bill Green by the cultural earthquakes associated with the 1960s. As he told me in the waiting room of his retail business, "I'm a late-sixties child." Frank is a large, garrulous, and shaggy guy who mixes comfortably with both customers and employees. He's the boss, but his style is informal and filled with banter and anecdote. Frank is an immediately likable man with an infectious laugh and is one of the few Coast graduates to identify enthusiastically with the hippie counterculture.

Frank's parents met during World War II; his dad was stationed in Atlantic City and met the future Mrs. Feller on a visit to Philadelphia. They married in 1942 and settled in Atlantic City, where she held a municipal job. Frank was born there, but the family moved to Wilbur when he was only six months old. After leaving the service, the elder Feller worked in retail sales before setting up, in the late Fifties, a successful business in a nearby town.

Frank grew up with the Green boys and The Nest, but his closest Wilbur buddies were guys like Matt Blake, a bit less rowdy and more on the margins of the informal leadership of the high school. In school, Frank says, "I figured out what I had to do to get by, and that's exactly what I did; I only did what I had to do to make sufficient grades so that my parents didn't beat my brains in. I got out with no problem, and I got accepted to college." His primary enthusiasm was a lifelong interest in local history: "I used to go out in my little boat, and I'd find these things in the marshes nobody had the answers to. So I'd find out what it was." Frank tells me that "this

South Jersey area around Wilbur used to be called Hayville and was a great shippingport. There's bulkheads . . . where the sailing ships used to sail in and unload all the stuff. I found the bulkheads one time in the little boat." Unfortunately, Frank's historical passions were not encouraged in what he found to be pedestrian high school history courses. As with so many graduates I interviewed, Frank Feller's imagination and intelligence were rarely stimulated in school.

Between his junior and senior years, Frank cracked up his motorcycle, fracturing his hip in seven pieces and tearing his pelvis; on the operating table his heart stopped twice. He says that he was a quiet, shy guy until then: "I was the guy who stood in the back and watched everything go by." After his six-week hospitalization, he declares, "I decided that from this point on I was going to take each day as it came along and raise hell each day I have to live," adding, "I don't know how much longer I'm going to be allowed to live; at seventeen that's a terrible thing to find out; because now I'm forty and I'm still living the same way. I just have a good time, that's all; I don't see any reason not to."

His good times began at the sectarian college in the Midwest that he entered after graduating from Coast; there he "partied real hard," played some football, and earned only fourteen credits before transferring to the local community college the following year. During the Tet Offensive in early 1968 he received his draft notice. But Frank "wasn't concerned about it"; he exclaims, "I knew that if I was drafted I'd go to Canada; no way, I wasn't going to Vietnam. I didn't give a shit; nobody was going to shoot at this kid." Of course, he adds, "I had another ace in the hole"; in additional to his full-time student status, he knew his motorcycle injuries would guarantee him a 4-F deferment. He was safe.

Frank's parents were "typical of the area, registered Republicans and conservative," or so he inferred, even though such matters were never discussed at home. He recalls coming home—after having finally gone for a physical and failed it—to hear his mom remind him of his dad's World War II service. She wanted him to feel a sense of duty even if he wasn't drafted. He replied, "If they had taken me, I'd have been a Canadian citizen; I'm not going to Vietnam; no little gook's shooting at this kid." So, given the Coast tendency to avoid disagreeable subjects, discussion stopped: "I had my point of view; they had their point of view. They accepted my point of view because it was mine, and I had reasons why, and I think they believed in the same reasons that I had, but in 1968 parents didn't discuss that with kids." Their differences simply became part of a tolerated, because ignored, reality.

In his post–high school years, Frank identified with the hippie movement. About most of his peers, he comments, "A lot of those guys never went to school, were never exposed to other aspects of life." He speaks of those who went into the service or immediately married, "which I thought was crazy." It was at his first college, "one of the top ten partying schools in the nation," that he discovered marijuana and hung around with lots of affluent, more sophisticated guys from the New York metropolitan area; he remembers getting stoned at a friend's home out on Long Island. Concerning marijuana, he stresses, "I kind of liked it, and I still like it." He soon had ponytail-length hair; much later, in 1981, after quitting his white-collar job with a major local company, he had his ear pierced, a symbolic gesture reaffirming his deviant, countercultural self-image.

Frank's partying took a turn when he married: "It was the first serious thing I ever did with my life, and a mistake." She was straight, and Frank was stubbornly rebellious. "After five years, we just realized that we were fighting a losing battle. She wants to have kids, and she wants to have a house and a dog and a fence, and all I want is to have a good time and don't want to be bothered with all that other stuff." Frank also entered the straight world, working nine to five, in white shirt and tie. He continued work on an associate degree at the local community college, then decided to drop out—a decision he blames on his wife's jealousy about his intellectual growth ("I couldn't get her to do anything but just go home and clean the house"), but finally, as the marriage drifted toward dissolution and he realized he was falling behind, returned to complete the degree: "I had figured out that I'm at the outside edge of the baby boom, and if I have something that I can offer, it's better than what the rest of them behind have, then I'll be able to be successful. If I don't, I'm going to be the guy behind the counter at the parts department for the rest of my life." After earning his associate degree, he started on his bachelor's at Stockton State, a public four-year liberal arts college, but his advance took a detour when, after his father's death, he took over the family business. He hopes to return, at some point, to get his degree. I suspect he will.

Frank's shift from hedonistic hippie to ambitious and measured baby boomer seems consistent with the media-disseminated images of the shift from Sixties ideals to Seventies materialism. Was he merely a weekend hippie, romanticizing detours from the mainstream? Possibly, but more persuasive is the thought that Frank's life indicates considerable continuity. He speaks of his sister, who "on the outside appeared to be the hippie type," but unlike him, "inside she was straight." Frank explains that "she wasn't strong enough to figure out how to make things bend her way." Frank's determination to do things his way, his expressive and his utilitarian individualism, informs both his hippie and entrepreneurial sides.[23]

Frank Feller's initiatives included another failed marriage, this one lasting fourteen months. He exclaims, "When I met her, I told her, what you see is what you get; if you see something you don't like now, you won't like it later—and if there's something you want to change about me, forget it." He continues, "I woke up in the Bahamas and said, 'Who's this broad sitting next to me? You got about three weeks to straighten out or you're out of here.' " And so it went.

Meanwhile, Frank maneuvered within the corporate system: "It was the only way you could do it; it had to be a game, and I played their game with my rules." "When I put on the tie," Frank recalls, "I became a different person; as soon as I walked out of the building, I unconsciously took my tie off, then I plugged Pink Floyd in the tape player, turned it up, and just went off."

Frank Feller discusses his corporate years with a deadly precision: "I went to work there in 1970, October 13; I worked there until May 1, 1981—eleven years, six months, and seventeen days." Soon after his dad died, he resigned to take over the family business, a change that excited little remorse but much relief: "I proved what I wanted to prove," he asserts, "I got as far up the ladder as I figured I could make it without really having to change my own values—and I said, 'I'm out of here.' These guys wanted to know who I was sleeping with, that I didn't dress right. And that's enough; I had enough."

This lover of the Doors, Eric Clapton, Led Zeppelin, and Iron Butterfly is now his own boss and lives on a ten-acre farm in an outlying town, with a woman he has been with since the early Eighties. He has no desire for children. He speaks of his simple pleasures: "I build things that I can enjoy; I'll come home tonight, hit the showers, hit the deck [he built], and that will be it." Frank still has an active and restless mind; he tells me, "I read incessantly; I read everything Robert Ludlum ever wrote—I just read a Spenser. I enjoy reading much more than I enjoy watching TV or going to the movies." This twice-divorced free spirit devoured "The Art of the Deal." "Trump, he's my hero. I think there's nothing wrong with being rich; he had a good head start, but he made it work for him. He's arrogant, he's brash, he does what the hell he wants, and if people don't like it, they can kiss his ass." Frank concludes with what seems to be his philosophy of life: "I think that's the way life ought to be; I think you should be able to do anything you want to do, as long as you don't really piss anybody off—nobody gets hurt, I think you can do pretty much as you want to."

As opposed to many of his classmates who remain deeply ambivalent about the effect of casino gambling, especially as it touches family life, Frank, admitting that "the old values are gone," defends the changes: "Casinos have benefited everybody; the guy next door, if he was smart enough, made himself a kazillion dollars, and he's living pretty good—he's driving a Porsche; and if the guys I grew up with didn't work hard, and just waited for it to come, got the secure jobs at the electric company and New Jersey Bell, and they go along and get their regular salary increases on a day-to-day basis, and are afraid to take a chance, then there's a little bit of jealousy there—not jealousy but 'That guy's doing better than I am.'"

Frank's sudden embrace of competition is jarring. It seems to conflict with his Sixties values and lifestyle, his admirable rebelliousness, his singularity (not the least part of which is his six-foot-seven, two-hundred-fifty-odd pound frame). In many ways, Tom Wolfe's "me generation" could be personified by Frank Feller, an auto racing fan, but never merely a spectator, who rewards himself with a sporty car: "The car's my toy; I don't have kids, so I just have toys."

Bill Green constructs his life and its meaning through the metaphor of team sports, which informs his central commitments to family, community, and work. Frank Feller is more focused on work and play; work hard, play hard. He chooses to live at a distance, with his ten acres separating himself from those who might intrude into his space. At one level gregarious, his singularity remains striking; here in GOP country, in 1980, he voted for John Anderson: "I couldn't vote for Reagan; I couldn't vote for Carter. Reagan himself is a zip as a president, but somebody was smart enough, maybe it was Nancy, to hire the right guys to pull the right strings to make it work. Carter went and got all the losers to work for him. Who the hell ever heard of Carter? Jackson? I'd go to Canada. Bush has been elected because the CIA has decided that he's in." And so Frank Feller, who likes "to be aware of what is in the world, not just in our little hole," expresses his fiercely independent political views, averse to conformity and yet buying into the quintessential American entrepreneurial dream.

Parts of both Bill Green and Frank Feller express the best and the worst of white, male, middle-class culture and behavior. They are representative of sharply divergent cultural and ideological extremities: Green in his commitment to modern technology and with his instrumental sense of interdependence, of teamwork; Feller in his antinomian individualism, his fierce sense of an imperial selfhood, a Protestant doing of his own thing. Green is more the yea-sayer, the believer in the standard shibboleths; Feller is the skeptic, the critic, the iconoclast. Green is a square, a straight; Feller is a hip postmodernist.

Bill Green's translations of his sports images into parallel political ones presuppose the integrity and fairness of our polity. His eloquently expressed belief in well-run, efficient, and humane business enterprises also shapes his assumptions about American democracy. Though it is possible to imagine Bill resonating to Ralph Nader's spartan efficiency, one could also hear him imploring, "Ralph, get on the team; we can work together on this; why are you always carping out there?" But the kind of dissonance that might have jolted Bill Green toward rebellion would have required, at the least, an alternative design of the public interest based on craft, technics, and cooperation.

Frank Feller has always been willing and able to rebel; rebellion is at the center of his love of life, his robustness, his boyishness. But his tendency to define the world in terms of winners and losers, those who take risks versus those who play it safe, and his juxtaposing of self-expression and social responsibilities suggest the limits and the cost of his form of rebellion.

I study politics and war, that my sons may have
liberty to study mathematics and philosophy. My
sons ought to study mathematics and philosophy,
geography, natural history and naval architecture,
navigation, commerce, and agriculture in order
to give their children a right to study painting,
poetry, music, architecture, statuary, tapestry,
and porcelain.
   —John Adams, 1780

School Days

The week the class of 1966 graduated from Coastal High
School, Ronald Reagan won the Republican gubernatorial
primary in California; James Meredith was shot walking to
Jackson, Mississippi; the Gemini 9 astronauts walked in
space; Secretary of Defense Robert McNamara announced
that more troops would be sent to Vietnam; and Robert
Kennedy attacked apartheid before students in Capetown,
South Africa: "It is your job, the task of the young people of
this world to strip the last remnants of that ancient, cruel
belief from the civilization of man." Locally, it was the year
that conservative Republican Charles Sandman became the
second congregational district's representative; Searstown
opened in what was to be the area's first shopping mall; and
St. Catherine's, the largest Roman Catholic Church on the
Coast, was completed.[1]

Coastal graduated 246 students that June. The high school, which first opened its doors as John Fitzgerald Kennedy took office, had been brought forth by baby-boom pressures that forced two neighboring High Schools to inform the Coast towns of Wilbur, Channing, and South Bay that the schools would no longer be able to accept their children. The new high school was considered from the start to be the most affluent and prestigious within the county, although, with the exception of those from Channing's Seaview section, its student body was less upper-class than firmly middle-middle-class.[2] In some ways it was Atlantic County's first truly suburban high school.

Those growing up in the Coast communities during the 1950s and early 1960s experienced fundamental transformation as suburbanization began to penetrate what had been small-town life. Most 1966 graduates retain positive memories of the still semirural qualities of growing up, of adventures in the woods, of hikes and bike rides without concerns about vehicular traffic, but also of the wonders of new housing construction, new neighbors, indeed, a new high school.

Wilbur seemed to be the most homogeneous, a town whose residents ranged from working-class to upper-middle-class white homeowners. South Bay was a town stuck with a reputation for its strip of bars but was fast becoming more conventionally suburban; kids growing up there felt they were on the outskirts of the Coast, traveling longer to get to the new high school, stigmatized at times for coming from the least prestigious areas, somehow branded by their poorer, more disreputable elements. Channing, on the other hand, was known for its stately homes east of Coast Road, the envied Seaview section just then emerging; yet it had poorer, rural families at its westernmost borders. In all three towns, suburbanization was homogenizing toward the middle. In fact, since so few of their parents and most of them were not born on the Coast, the families of the class of 1966 participated in creating the character of their new suburban communities.

The Lynds' seminal account of the transformation at Middletown High School between 1890 and the 1920s, when the Latin class motto "Deo Duce" was replaced by the sports cheer "To the Bearcats," points toward the increasingly social and sociable nature of the comprehensive, suburban high schools of the postwar period. The new suburban communities sought and found a sense of identity through their school sports teams.[3] At Coastal, the Bronco football and basketball teams quickly became the focus of school spirit. As at most American high schools since the 1920s, social life predominated over scholarship.

The student body can be divided into clearly identifiable groups and smaller friendship circles. The larger groups sometimes overlapped, but the overall pattern remained distinct. The elite groups were the rowdies and the preppies. Cutting across these categories were jocks and brains, with a characteristic but not essential pairing of jocks with rowdies, and brains with preppies. In addition, the rowdies/jocks were mostly guys, with a disproportionate centering in Wilbur; the preppies/brains, on the other hand, were more of a mix of males and females, with a Channing coloring. South Bay students either gravitated to one of these two poles or, like the majority of students, stayed within their own smaller friendship circles and, typically, outside of school leadership.

The Rowdies

Judd Dennis's folks moved from Pleasantville to Wilbur when he was eight. The move was a measure of the remarkable rise of his dad from unskilled service jobs to successful store owner. Such social-class mobility blurred in significant ways some of the distinctions between working- and middle-class families. Since few became truly wealthy and most hadn't gone past high school educations, the similarities among most Coast families counterbalanced, if not outweighed, any income differences. Only Channing's Seaview section stood out from the region's homogeneity of experience.

Judd believes that "Wilbur kids stuck together," but he is really talking about the rowdy guys he grew up with in his neighborhood: "I lived here, Richie Davis was across the street, and right around the corner was Billy and Bobby Green—Jim Fuller, Eddie Sharpe—we all lived right there; that's who you associated with; I can't remember any of us really being interested in girls until after we got into high school."

Bobby Green talks of Wilbur as "a great place to grow up—it wasn't the coolest town, but you were close to the beaches. Everybody in Wilbur knew everybody; even if you didn't hang out with the person, you knew him, and you knew two or three years ahead of you and two or three years below you." Bobby offers an example: "My girlfriend's five years younger than me, and she grew up around the block, and I knew who she was, and here we are together now. I knew her brother and sister a little better, and I knew her father."

The Wilbur crew, many who had been born in Atlantic City or Pleasantville, jelled during grade school. When they started at Coastal, they were already tight. Joey Campion describes himself as "strictly one of the clowns" and as a leader of the rowdies, along with Bill Green. As they mixed with guys from the other two towns during ninth grade, they brought others into their informal group. Bobby Green recalls boasting to Willie James, a South Bay kid, about the forts he and his Wilbur buddies had built in the rural stretches west of County Road. So, under the leadership of Bobby's brother Bill, they built The Nest (see Profile: Bill Green). Joey Campion claims that they chose the name "in the basement of my father's store [a central rowdy hangout], where we had the first meeting and said, 'Well, what do we want to call it?' and I said . . . 'Let's call it The Nest.' " The 1966 yearbook is filled wih allusions to adolescent adventures at The Nest. It became central to the identity of several dozen or more teenage boys.

Joey Campion recalls, "We used to sleep out; this would start in our freshman year. I would come home from school at 4:30, five o'clock, grab my pillow, my sleeping bag, tell my mother I'd see her Sunday. I'd go to Bobby Green's house— usually that was the congregating point on that side of Wilbur; him and Billy, they were extremely popular guys, plus that was the hub of where all the other guys lived; within a six-block area of Bobby's house lived maybe fifteen of our members." He continues, "We would always meet there on a Friday night, usually go to one of the local dances, like a canteen, or watch television, and at 10:30 make our way back to our fort, and we'd stay there all night. Next morning, get up, some of us would play basketball, some guys might work, some guys would fish, back again on Saturday night—that was usually when we had our party."

Judd Dennis laughs: "You'd think we were a bunch of aborigines that did this; we'd spend hours and hours, we'd camp out there, we'd go down to Davis's [farm], and they'd set out the tomatoes they couldn't sell, and we carried all the baskets back, and we'd strip down to our underwear, and we'd have tomato fights—and then, of course, you had to go to County Road and throw one at the cars." Sometimes more than a dozen guys slept over, often sleeping off beer-induced hangovers. They had access to a few local bars, and several brag about supplying beer to upperclassmen. The core came from Wilbur, but Channing guys like Dave Ford, South Bay roustabouts like Willie James, and even some kids from neighboring towns entered The Nest.

Many Coast graduates, however, never even knew about The Nest. Some girls ventured out, but it was essentially an adolescent-male preserve. There's some disagreement whether girls risked their reputations by spending any time at The Nest. Joey Campion says that sexual experimenting was "normal": "The two biggest things that we had in our four years of high school—we had the drinking, which was way out front, and I'll say that sex was a close second." He quickly adds that there were no drugs and no serious delinquency within his circle of rowdies. Interviewed in the late 1980s, former rowdies emphasize that the experimentation associated with the 1960s hadn't hit the Coast town during the years of their adolescence.

Dave Ford, who grew up in more affluent Channing but "spent a lot of [his] time with Wilbur kids," admits that "nobody really knew what Channing people were all about." Yet he speaks warmly of his carefree childhood, living "like Mark Twain": "We were hunters and fishermen; we had army fights; I went crabbin'; we went clammin'; we did all the stuff the bay rats [from South Bay] did. When I grew up in Channing, Seaview was just becoming Seaview; my mother

had corn fields back there and watermelons." Dave describes
high school life hanging around with his "crazy" Wilbur
buddies: "We hung the asssistant principal in effigy the first
week he was at school; they went around to drive this guy
crazy—we liked the guy!" He adds, "He was a real nice guy,
Mr. Turner; it was just that we disliked the idea of having an
assistant principal. About two weeks after he arrived, we
passed the word that we were packing guns, and within two
or three days, they did a complete search of the whole school
building—we didn't have any guns." Dave, roaring with
laughter, tells of boyish pranks: "We did a mock shooting on
the steps of the local diner. Davy Hunter had a '57 Chevy; he
pulled up in front of the diner and got out, and we had these
cap guns, but they were real loud; [Davy] pulled it out, pulled
up in front of the diner, shot this guy on the steps, ketchup
packets all over, picked him up off the steps—this was
Saturday night, busiest night of the week," he interjects,
"threw him in the trunk of this car, and sped off. The cops
were all over The Nest—we drove 'em crazy."

Indeed, the rowdies, finding little stimulation in their
classes, found ways to drive the adult world crazy without
crossing the line into full-fledged delinquency. School was
simply a place to see one's friends, survive, and occasionally
have some fun with the authorities. With pranks, mock
shoot-outs, and classroom high jinks the rowdies were mostly
trying to keep from being bored. Davy Hunter describes
himself as "a motorhead," who, with many of the rowdies,
rebuilt cars, raced on rural roads, played sports, and partied.
He was bartending at seventeen. There was lots of teenage
drinking, including during the week. Joey Campion says,
"We drank everyday, after school, never before school; you
get done school, quarter after three, the guys chip in and buy

six quarts of beer, and we'd ride around in a car for two hours to five o'clock." "Just beer," he emphasizes. "We never really touched the booze until we got to our senior year, and that's when a couple of guys decided they were whiskey drinkers. They thought they were big shots: go to a dance, have a little bottle—that was probably one of the reasons they switched, because they'd get into a dance with a little flask—the guys would get themselves wiped out drunk. The beer drinkers had the most fun, and I would say 95 percent of our group was the beer drinkers." Dave Ford recalls being picked up on Friday afternoons by his Channing buddy Mac Schmidt (see profile): "We'd fill his car with beer, fill it to the top—beer was only three dollars a case—you could buy as much as you wanted, kegs of beer. I'd drive around, pick up people, get nuts; nobody really cared." For most of the guys, it would be a passing phase, a sowing of wild oats before settling down. But for some, serious problems came later, considerable alcoholism and several alcohol-related deaths.

Bobby Green admits, "I wasn't a good student; I was a little bit rebellious about school, about English—they just kept trying to throw these diagram sentences at me, and adverbs and pronouns and adjectives, and I just . . . I didn't like that stuff. It bored me." Bobby had to go to summer school after failing English "and that bothered me, made me a little bit bitter." About the future, he recalls, "I didn't think about it at all." In his yearbook, his ambition is listed as "bartender," an ambition he would fulfill and a job at which he would continue for many years before working for the casinos. Few of the Rowdies took school very seriously; if they had interests, they tended to be in vocational and technical areas. But there were lots of resentments. Dave Ford, who was good at mathematics, hated his math courses at Coastal. His guidance counselor offered little direction or assistance. According to Ford, he'd ask, " 'What do you want to take?' He didn't say, 'Do you want to go to college? What would you like to prepare for?' They never did anything like that, the guy just sat there and that was it." Guys got some encouragement and training from shop teachers like Lou Adamo, but for the most part their creative energies—to make things, to build, to design, to tinker, to work with their hands—only found an outlet outside of school. It was a tremendous waste of talent and time. Too often the best one could hope for was the kind of history class described by Joey Campion: "The teacher doubled as a gym teacher, and after ten minutes, you knew if you started talking basketball that was the other forty minutes, and you walked out of there with nothin'." Campion, who notes a few stimulating classes, still reflects, "I look at it now and I wonder, Did I impair my education by letting that happen, or how much more would I really have learned?"

The rowdies overlapped with the jocks, several of whom were non-Wilbur guys with more serious academic ambitions and often from more affluent families. They mostly played football, and well enough to win their conference championship. They were natural leaders—imaginative, funny, often obnoxious, occasionally bullying—but mostly, they were working- and middle-class white boys who assumed that schooling was inversely related to curiosity and who consequently created their lives around, but not within, the institution called high school.

The Preppies

Everyone I talked with agreed that the other elite student group was the preppies. The preppies were most likely to come from the most affluent homes, especially in Channing, to dress stylishly along Ivy League lines, to be popular and comfortable, to do well in school, and to go on to college. Rodney Wayne, son of a prominent local professional man, was often mentioned as a preppie leader (see profile); Mary Perle Ives (see profile), daughter of an affluent Channing family, and Pam Baird Lane (see profile), like Wayne, from Wilbur, were also perceived as preppies.

Preppies were less likely to drink, especially on a daily basis. They weren't, however, straitlaced; in fact, one Channingite speaks of drinking parties in sixth grade. Preppies were more likely to restrict drinking to weekend social life; in addition, they were often alienated by the grosser aspects of the rowdies' boozing. Preppies were into being collegiate, which meant being almost, but not quite, grown up, with value placed on formalities like student government and clubs, dating, and proper dress. They were also under a tighter leash; their parents were less likely to tolerate the kinds of carousing, including weekend sprees at The Nest, available to many of the rowdies. More of their energies were focused on school proper. Rowdies were strictly male, their leadership preponderantly working-class; the Preppies, engaged in more adult-approved and regulated activities, were more affluent, more college-bound, and decidedly more coed.

Sally Vincent Rogers, daughter of South Bay merchants, recalls, "I wanted to be a part of the 'in' group, the Channing group, the girls who dressed nice and were running the school; they were preppy and intellectual." Carol Smith Rizzo remembers her initial experiences in shifting over from middle-middle-class South Bay to Coastal: "I hung around with a group of kids in Channing, and I went through a period where I thought, 'Why don't I look like that?' At fourteen, I thought that it [Seaview] was just the ultimate." She was enamored with the sense of style, the fashionable tone, the air of superiority, of her Seaview classmates. Eventually Carol stepped away from such friendships and longings: "I found out that I'm better off where I am. They were self-centered and selfish people." She was affected by how some of the Channing preppies abused one of her girlfriends: "They were very mean to, totally, and crushed this poor girl." The sharp edges of social-class distinctions make their presence most felt in such angry recollections.

The 1966 yearbook indicates that preppies, more than the rowdies, dominated class offices, prestigious clubs, and academic honors. They were on a clearly delineated road to college: guys, toward careers; girls, toward marriage to college-educated men.

At the same time, the preppies were not identical to the brains, the most accomplished academic achievers. The brains, often ridiculed for a lack of social graces, athletic ability, or good looks, were not part of the school's social elite. Again and again, graduates described the brainiest students—often stereotypically presented as what today would be called nerds—as wearing glasses, carrying slide-rules, always doing homework, and never having fun. One of the brainiest, Elliot Carter, admired but always with a shade of contempt, was the son of a local minister. This subgroup shared academic honors with the most academically ambitious and capable of the preppies. From a high school that sent less than 50 percent of its graduates off to college, little more than 20 percent graduated with bachelor's degrees. The brains and academically oriented preppies went off to elite colleges like MIT, Columbia, and Harvard; most of the preppies, both by choice and competitive realities, went to less prestigious but expensive private colleges, often wellknown for their social life.

It's important to emphasize that the two groupings of rowdies and preppies, as well as those identified as brains, had informal and fluid identities that were never structured and rarely even noted. A few graduates deny that such groups existed, insisting that there were no cliques at Coastal and that everyone got along with everyone else. But a class of 246 inevitably subdivided in ways reflecting status and prestige, and most Coasters readily affirm the primacy of the two elite groups. Those outside of the elite groups remained, as usual, most sensitive to the subtleties of adolescent pecking orders.

Certainly, most of the class of 1966 falls outside of or at the margins of the elite groups. Some resentment was directed at the rowdies and the preppies, especially at the latter; given the social priorities of the high school culture, the rowdies and jocks were more envied. But most students, tolerating or accepting the pecking order, simply existed within smaller circles of intimacy and friendship based on shared lives and common interests.

Harry Kearns

Harry Kearns grew up in Wilbur, the oldest of four; his dad worked for the city; his mother was a housewife. The Kearns were a deeply religious Methodist family. Harry remembers church activity being central to his youth: "There were quite a few of us who attended Wilbur Methodist Church because it had an extremely strong youth group. Probably our social life, more so than the school, was built around the church, in junior high and into high school, probably into our third year in high school more so than our senior year, because you tend to get ready to break away." Harry's family and church life distinguish him and his circle of friends from both rowdies and preppies. He declares, "Religion was probably the backbone of our family." His dad, who worked on Sundays to supplement the family income, "was very concerned that we would attend Sunday school every Sunday and that my mother ran the church nursery and that mom took us every Sunday morning, and it was very important." Harry recalls that even when the family was off on summer vacations, they would search for the nearest Methodist church for Sunday services.

He was ambitious, but unsure of himself: "I remember the biggest fear I think I had all through high school was of getting into college—'Can we get into college? or will we get into college?'—because at the time, college was probably the most important thing in our lives, who was going to go where and who was going to do what." Harry's parents supported his collegiate ambitions: "When I brought home my first report card, my first set of midterms, I failed Latin, I failed English, I failed . . . I can't remember, but my parents weren't too pleased with that, and we set down and had a long talk. If I was going to go to college, I was going to have to do more than play basketball and be out every night. I think that's what opened my eyes to education. I realized I had to buckle down if I wanted to go anywhere."

Harry wasn't involved with the rowdies, who were drinking, smoking, and generally raising hell, although he admits to an occasional beer. His friends were mostly college prep, although not the most academically accomplished. He was only a C+ student: "I was involved in sports, in the band, in choir, in the youth group—I just spread myself too thin."

Most of all, Harry had a goal he feels the high school frustrated, and he remains bitter about the ways in which the school limited his options and denigrated his potential. As far back as sixth grade, he wanted a career as an industrial arts teacher, but the guidance department at Coastal told him that because he was college prep and already had band activity filling an elective, he couldn't take the shop courses he sought. At the same time, "they told me I'd never get accepted in college, that I didn't have the grades, that if I did get to college, chances are I wouldn't last there, because I just didn't have what it took."

But Harry persevered. He expanded on his boyhood interests in woodworking: "I really just enjoyed making things with my hands, putting things together." He went on to graduate from a state teachers college and recently was honored for his achievements as an industrial arts teacher. A large number of boys apparently had Harry's interests and abilities (see profile: Bill Green), yet Coastal rarely put such aspirations, such passions, to use.

Carol Smith Rizzo

Carol, born in Atlantic City, lived in Pleasantville before her family moved over to South Bay when she was in second grade. She describes her adolescence as normal. Her father was a small businessman, and her mother stayed home to raise the kids. They were religious and strict. Carol was the baby of the family. She feels that her parents' involvement in her childhood—they were Little League coaches and active in Baptist youth activities—ensured stability, but adds, "I regret the fact that school wasn't pushed more with me. It's okay; I was this cute little thing that ran around the school and knew all the teachers; I passed, but I just passed." By high school, the church had become less central, and social life began to consume Carol's free time. She had academic abilities but saw no connection between her own future and doing well in school. She recalls, "I was a good, clean-cut person; I was just [there] to have fun. School was very important to me; it wasn't important to be an all-A student. My father used to say my brother would go to school—and he did, and I was going to be a housewife, I guess, like my mother."

Carol loved to dance and speaks enthusiastically about the canteens and parties of her high school years. It was a period when a rock 'n' roll youth culture was moving into a new, more rebellious phase marked by the British Invasion. In her sophomore year, the board of education had initiated a new, more restrictive dress code, which mandated trousers no higher than two inches above the ankle, "no excessively tight pants," no jeans, shirts buttoned to within two of the top, no tee-shirts, skirts at mid-knee caps, no bee-hive hair-dos or "excessively teased hair" or black stockings.[4] The school's literary magazine of fall 1964 featured the Beatles. In an informal poll, the girls favored the Fab Four eighty to thirty-two, while the guys, leaning toward the Beach Boys, voted sixty-three to fifty-three against. But Carol suggests, "Nobody ever really got really wrapped up in the music; we were just your typical little school; we were all proud to be there; I don't remember anybody getting carried away; I think we were too much of a small town." She tells me that she never paid attention to the lyrics. As late as the spring of 1966, most Coaster teens kept their musical tastes within boundaries only superficially uncomfortable for both their families and for those marketing adolescent tastes. As their parents had jitter-bugged to Benny Goodman's swing sound, so they learned the new American Bandstand dances. Parents in both eras bemoaned the collapse of musical taste and warned of the decline of Western civilization, but rarely meant it.

Carol Smith was friendly with the rowdies; her high school boyfriend and eventual husband, Vinnie, although attending nearby Atlantic City High School, had become one of them. She was gregarious and extremely popular and seems to have thoroughly enjoyed her high school years. Her regrets seem afterthoughts. But there is an interesting wrinkle to her essentially homogeneous world as she describes Stan Albright and Allie Rowe, who were "real" musicians, interested in jazz. Stan was her "best friend; my parents knew his parents; we grew up together. And I just thought he was the neatest thing because, yes, he had different views, he looked different, the only one I can tell you got wrapped up, but it was all music—he was a jazz musician, and he used to write poetry. And he'd write me this poetry, and I used to say, 'This is wonderful,' but I didn't understand it." Carol stresses that Stan was "very much a part of our group—we all liked him," but adds, also of Allie Rowe, "they were more worldly, like they should have been in New York or North Jersey, you know what I mean?"

Stan Albright was able to sustain difference without sacrificing popularity; some of the rowdies approvingly describe him as "a tough guy." But as in most high school subcultures, difference most often was costly. Guys who seemed to be effeminate were taunted cruelly as "faggots." The environment wasn't unusually harsh, but its social class and racial homogeneity reenforced patterns of conformity and intolerance. There was little baiting of Catholics, but there was some baiting of the very few Jews in the area. And the blacks, who did domestic work for the more affluent families and lived off of the Coast, were always "the other." One teacher remembers when the school finally hired its first black, a matron on the janitorial staff. He says that the students harassed her to such an extent that she quit. Coasters openly defending civil rights or other deviant views risked ridicule or ostracism. There were no bohemian students at Coastal; the only student described as a "beatnik" was actually a flamboyant class clown more renowned for his singular pursuit of wealth. The mainstream flowed homogeneously and tolerated little deviation from its middle-brow paths. Indeed, Coastal's very homogeneity allowed greater community delusion about its tolerance and openness; it offered little testing.

Susan O'Hara Dennis

Susan describes herself as "an army brat," living on bases abroad until her family moved to the Coast. Her mother, an Atlantic City native, would exclaim, "Why would anybody want to live here?" And Susan, arriving during her sophomore year, found it difficult to break into the social life of the school. There is still some resentment in her voice as she speaks of "the two years it takes to be accepted no matter where you live: the first year you're the newcomer, and the second year they kind of think you look familiar—they don't know where from, but you start to get accepted." Her acceptance was helped when she began to date Judd Dennis, one of the rowdies: "Then his group accepted me, to a point; the guys accepted me as an extension of Judd, but [without him] they would never have even seen me."

Susan's sense of being an outsider wasn't helped by the strictness of her religious upbringing; for example, she wasn't allowed to wear slacks or shorts. Because of her mother's alcoholism, she was responsible for the household, cooking meals and cleaning. Her dad came to depend on her, even to the point of discouraging her from getting a job or planning a career. The situation didn't allow her much of a social life.

Al Judson

Al Judson had a different experience, moving to South Bay from Philadelphia when he was in eighth grade. His parents, who moved to take over a family-owned store, were "pretty straitlaced Methodists" but eased up partly because their business took so much of their time. Al, whose three older siblings all graduated college and became teachers, found Coast schooling so easy that he took a year off: "It was kind of backwards here; I felt that I was in clam-digger territory." Al now loves the shore area but recalls that, at the time, "I couldn't believe that we were moving from Philadelphia to here; South Bay was nothing, it really wasn't . . . I was not happy about the move at all."

Al, however, quickly found friends and more than adjusted: "I felt a little sophisticated when we came down, because I was one of the few boys who knew how to dance; for example, we would have dances, and I knew how to do the twist and whatever the new dances were because we knew them in Philadelphia." Al fondly recalls dancing during lunch breaks, noting, "They were all shocked because all the other boys were playing basketball and 'Who's this kid dancing?'—*and* I could play basketball too!" That didn't hurt.

Al met his future wife, Meg, when he was a junior and she was a year behind him. He tells me that he "didn't hang around with the really wild guys." But Meg intercedes, "He calmed down a lot after he met me." Al counters, "I didn't drink; like drinking was big in high school, and I really didn't drink." He describes some of his teammates on the football squad, rowdies, who did some "heavy drinking."

Like so many Coastal students, Al admits, "I never did as well as I could have; I never applied myself. I probably could have gotten mostly As; I never studied" except "when the pressure was on." He loved sports but also had to work at his parents' store after school. He considered joining the Coast Guard after graduating, but instead, without much of a sense of direction, decided to go to one of the state teachers colleges.

The social structure of the class of 1966 rests on a solidly middle-class foundation. There were poor kids, some of whom never made it through high school. There were lots of working-class and lower-middle-class students, with parents either delivering the mail or the milk or operating the ma-and-pa stores that provided the cakes, the sandwiches, and the pizzas. The communities were built on a small-town, Protestant base, but were significantly changed by the influx of families, often of immigrant Catholic stock, from cities in crisis, like Atlantic City or Philadelphia.

The kids paid little attention to events occurring outside of their immediate environment. They often felt that the cities, like Atlantic City, were being taken over by blacks, a social phenomenon they neither understood nor empathized with. They knew of international events, the seemingly endless crises between the Free World and the Communist world in

Berlin, Cuba, Laos, the Congo, and Vietnam. Their villains included the bearded Fidel Castro and the shoe-thumping Nikita Khrushchev. They recall admiring the dashing young Irish Catholic Jack Kennedy and all can describe what they were doing when they heard the news of his assassination. But their knowledge of politics and world affairs was sketchy. For the most part, such historical events were very much in the background; the foreground was occupied by the diverse growing-up experiences only partly shaped by Coastal High School.

The high school itself was large, more than one thousand students, spread over a campus built on the farmland of one of Channing's most prominent families. Edward Jones, who describes himself as "one of those stuffy old principals," was an experienced administrator who "ran things by the book." Students were expected to be properly dressed and respectful; their job was to learn. The first faculty created what one veteran calls "a comfy-cozy" atmosphere, with faculty bowling, faculty parties, faculty basketball team," and good rapport with the student body. Bill James, longtime teacher and counselor, speaks of a "laid-back" environment, basically conservative and patriotic; but "when you watched television, you were astounded by what was going on, because it didn't seem real to us; [it] didn't occur around here at all."

James remembers very little awareness about Vietnam, for example, in the years when the class of 1966 was moving toward graduation. He recalls the general feeling at that time: "How can anybody be against . . . what our country's doing?" He reflects, "I can't think of anybody [on the faculty] who was that liberal," and agrees that any kind of active opposition to the war "would have been frowned upon." In fact, the history and civics faculty included "some veteran teachers who had been in the war—Korea—and felt very strong about, 'Hey, there's no place for that'; so as much from an instructional viewpoint you try to be as objective as possible; it's going to show a little bit, I think." Students were unlikely to hear viewpoints or opinions from their teachers that challenged the basically mainstream, Cold War conservatism upon which they had been raised. We were the "good guys," defending the Free World from the atheistic Communism being generated from its epicenter in the Kremlin. The beginnings of the Vietnam conflict seemed to flow undifferentiated from the same stream as Korea, Lebanon, Quemoy and Matsu, Berlin, and Cuba.

The school literature reflects such values. In one instance, a science teacher warned that "the greatest threat to our national defense is the possibility that an enemy nation might beat the United States to scientific discoveries that could upset the balance of world power." One student, wondering, "Isn't it possible that a lax policy could be just as detrimental to the causes of peace and freedom as a strict one," proclaimed that the United States "can never turn its back on any war, however small, when that war is fought in the cause of freedom." Yet in the same issue of the school magazine, politics is defined as "having a flashy smile and a dry hand," as "the art of being glib." Most Coast baby boomers eschewed any version of idealism, right or left. In this laid-back community, the only fanaticisms tolerated were sports related. Coastal students were more comfortable with the moderate Republicanism of Henry Cabot Lodge than with either Barry Goldwater or Lyndon Johnson in 1964.[5] I found no one caught up in the emerging conservative youth movement, no one joining Young Americans for Freedom, no one idolizing William F. Buckley Jr. and subscribing to *National Review,* no one reading the never-ending novels of Ayn Rand.

The yearbook contains no indications that the class of 1966 was aware of living through extraordinary times, from the military escalation in Vietnam to the War on Poverty, from the sit-ins of the Student Nonviolent Coordinating Committee (SNCC) in Greensboro to the Watts ghetto uprising in 1965. Coastal students of the mid-1960s, taking for granted the relative prosperity of the times and the suburban insulation of their growing-up years, were rarely challenged by their formal schooling. There were a few inspirational teachers; a math instructor was lauded by many graduates, but for the most part, life was experienced outside of the classroom. The rowdies put most of their energies and imaginations into having a good time with buddies; the preppies prepared themselves for the kinds of upper-middle- and middle-class roles the adult world would offer them; and others sought to find friends and lovers in an environmental matrix of church, family, neighborhood, and school, over which they laid their dreams about the future.

Within their midst were jazz musicians who wrote poetry, troubled alcoholics, adolescents who would carry into their adult lives resentments about being left out, and teen sweethearts who would still be married twenty years later. One of their classmates, Maria Haratzi, had fled with her parents from Soviet tyranny. She stood apart, intimidating many of her classmates with her combination of brains, beauty, and sophistication. And her parents, seeking to maintain Central European culture in suburban South Jersey, protected her from much of the social life that filled the days and nights of most of her classmates. In fact, there were newly arrived families, often affiliated with NAFEC, who found the scholastic environment so deficient that they moved to the more westward, Philadelphia-oriented suburbs.

Chris Olsen

In the battles for class offices, the sophomore class president had been Lydia Kovacs, described by several Coasters as "dominating and aggressive" and "just very different." Several graduates add that she was heavy and not especially attractive. The junior class president, Dickie Turette, on the other hand, was a star athlete and a rowdie; he defeated one of the brains. For vice-president, another jock bested several preppie female leaders.

As the class approached its senior year, Chris Olsen from South Bay pondered running for sergeant at arms. He was a capable student from a hardworking immigrant family who owned a local store. He was placed in most of the more advanced, college preparatory classes, wasn't an athlete, and had to help out after school at the store. He states, "There were two groups that ran the dances, sports, the yearbook, everything else; they did all of that stuff; everybody else was just a little outside of them," including Chris. He recalls the difficulties in penetrating the elite groups: "It's very difficult to get to know those people, or to get very close with them, because they had their own friends, they didn't seem to want any more." But by his senior year, Chris felt a bit more accepted and, on the advice of a teacher, ran for senior-class president instead of sergeant at arms. His opposition included the incumbent, a jock/rowdie, and a leading preppie, Rodney Wayne. But Turette "had a chip on his shoulder," and

Wayne, to Chris, "was even worse." He reflects, "I think I represented the people who were not in the cliques, not the jock type or the Wilbur type; I knew everyone in the school." Chris was the upset winner.

Chris Olsen, while content with the education he received at Coastal, is among those who resent treatment by a guidance counselor: "He made a comment to me that I should stick . . . I don't even remember the name of the school, and I threw his list away and applied to all the schools I wanted to—and got accepted in all of them. And when he found that out, he told me that I wouldn't last a semester. This was not the kind of guidance I needed." Chris's resentments are matched by several others among those I interviewed. Coastal was not a particular bad school in the mid-1960s. It provided a decent education to many of those who went on to college, including high achievers at some of our finest institutions. But there are too many tales of students finding themselves unprepared for even the most accessible colleges, of students uninspired by their high school classes, of students with imagination and talent and personality undetected by their teachers and consequently untapped by Coastal High School. The significant number of complaints against the guidance office suggests some displaced anger at an institution too complacent with its local status to work at uncovering and nurturing students' dreams: Bill Green's remarkable design skills, Frank Feller's historical passions, Jack Claire's and Rodney Wayne's dreams of writing, Polly Bain Smythe's engineering ambitions, Melanie Combs's rebellious identifications with Brigitte Bardot—all undeveloped, if not frustrated. The school nurtured future secretaries and future business leaders of America, but it didn't reach down and then lift students' imaginations, their visions.

And, as we shall see, Coastal did not prepare the class of 1966 for a more global world, where ten thousand miles away young American and Indo-Chinese men and women were being slaughtered, and where just beyond the suburban cocoon, and then stretching across continents, nonwhite non-middle-class people, caught up in the dislocations of market forces beyond their control, were trapped in ghettos and barrios. As such, the class of 1966 faced the world after high school ill equipped to come to grips with its political and ethical challenges, but nevertheless likely, as white children of the middle class, to survive and even flourish in the more recognizable arenas of work and family.

Profile: Jack Claire, Writer

Jack Claire is a finely featured man, almost delicate in appearance, with a quiet, shy quality about him. He describes his youth as "invisible," intentionally so because of his concern with being compared to his older brother Tom, "the golden boy," a star athlete only two years older. Whereas Tom loved team sports, Jack "liked tennis, singles; I liked pool, anything that I could play myself." He wasn't interested in school, avoided homework, and had no desire to go to college. But he had dreams of something special: "I thought I was going to be a writer." Then, after a pause, he adds, "Someday, I may still be a writer."

By middle school years, Jack was writing "crazy poems, radical things, funny stuff, a war story." He and some of his closest friends played war games, and Jack began writing a book about their imaginary ventures. He recalls with amusement, "If you were my friend, then you didn't get killed in the book, and if you gave me a hassle, you were wiped out." Jack's ambitions and dreams were invisible to Coastal High School: "There wasn't anybody . . . a teacher that said, 'Well, this is what you should do, or you should pursue that'; there was nobody who ever came along and took Jack Claire aside and said, 'I think you should go in this direction.' " Since he was a mediocre student, he concludes, "I don't really think I caught any of their eyes that they said that he's got potential to really break out of his mold. I don't know if I ever showed them any potential." As in the cases of Bill Green, Harry Kearns, and Chris Olsen, the high school left untapped the dreams and, indeed, fantasies of many of its lackluster students.

Jack notes that his community college experience, "completely different than what high school was," showed that school could be "interesting and motivating." "Had high school been like that," he wistfully adds, "instead of being so structured maybe, and just loosened up a bit, not had so many rules and regulations," maybe he would have flourished there. Yet, at the same time, he is ambivalent about the consequences of too little structure, bemoaning, for example, the erosion of school spirit that he sees as one result of the greater permissiveness he ascribes to the era following his graduation. "Our graduating class," he brags, "still had school spirit."

In describing his Channing boyhood, Jack begins with his religious background: "I guess everyone I knew was Methodist; it was just a Methodist, Republican town." As a boy, he attended the prestigious Channing Methodist Church, where he met boys who would become high school friends. His father worked for one of the local utility companies for thirty-five years. Jack talks about his dad, who "should have gone to college" and who seemed frustrated with being "always under somebody's thumb," adding, "He wasn't happy with the company; as he got older in the business and younger people were in charge of him, that disturbed him, and he hated to hear the phone ring."

Mr. Claire, who, like Jack, loved to work with his hands, built their home and got extensively involved with the local Little League. "He was one of the pioneers, built the ball field, built dugouts, offering a lot of his time and skills in building things for people," Jack proudly states. The dad also was extensively involved with the phone company's charitable club, "helping crippled children, repairing wheelchairs, collecting things, building things, always building things."

Jack's mother remained a housewife until he began high school. She then rather quickly moved up to a position within the municipal government. He describes her as "strictly Republican," whereas his father was more independent. But there were virtually no political conversations at the Claire table. Jack, emphasizing the muted aspects of a Methodist upbringing, notes, "It was hard to talk to my father." He loved and admired his mom and dad, but no more than the school system did they nourish Jack's aspirations, his love of writing.

Jack loved the Beach Boys, identifying with the blond-surfer subculture, although still within his loner preferences. More characteristically, as somewhat of a pool shark, he ranked Willie Mosconi as a personal hero. He can't recall intense feelings about any of the political events associated with the early 1960s. "I didn't have deep feelings," he says about civil rights. "We never felt we were bigots; it was they just didn't happen to live in Channing, so it wasn't something you had to deal with on a day-to-day basis." He says that he always has believed that "everyone deserves a fair shake," and "is now finding out what a great person" Martin Luther King Jr. was. As with most Coast kids, the universe seemed to stop at the suburban parameters of television and popular music.

Jack's dad was a major in the National Guard with thirty-five years of service. Jack says Mr. Claire joined right out of high school "because they would take them up in the Poconos and they would ride horses, and the story he tells is, the year he joined, they got rid of the horses." Mr. Claire, like many Coast fathers, served in World War II. Jack recalls, "I always grew up thinking, I'm going to join the army, since I was in love with the army. He always had me over at the armory, climbing on cannons, him being an officer; we were always over there, and it was prestigious to be with somebody who was somebody." The family took their vacations near Fort Drum in Canada during Mr. Claire's two-week summer maneuvers. But when Jack talked army, his dad, referring to Vietnam, told him "that the war wasn't like it was when he was over there and you could shoot at the other guy and see who you were shooting at. All the rules were changed now—now they were digging pits and sticking stakes, and the enemy may be days away and still killing you." So Jack, knowing that, and given Vietnam, and with the draft beckoning, joined the Navy Reserve, even before finishing high school—one year inactive, two years active, and then three more inactive. He adds, "I never pictured myself getting on a boat and heading out to Vietnam"; he didn't think the navy was involved over there. He was active for eighteen months, a boatswain's mate on a guided missile destroyer with the Sixth Fleet, and did two tours of the Mediterranean. He recalls, "I was innocent, but I fought the navy the whole time I was in it; I was very negative. I didn't like the idea that I was in there." "But," he characteristically counters, "finally, they say everyone should join the service because they make a man out of you."

Jack began dating his wife in high school; the relationship continued when he served in the navy, but broke up after he returned. He felt that he should go out and sow his wild oats before settling down. He traveled to visit old friends at college, just bumming around, working as a garbage collector in Channing. "I guess I was right in there with them," he says of his forays into the countercultural rebellions of the time, but adds, "Not a full-blown hippie; I wasn't a radical, going to meetings or being out at any groups but just going against the grain. If it could bother someone from the older generation that was still saying we should be in Vietnam, then I was there to . . ." He pauses, then continues, "I was against the war." Jack, however, never went to any demonstrations, although he "was for them." Mostly, he recalls, "I had long hair, in ragged jeans, sewing patches on my legs with radical sayings"; he continued to live at home until his mother's persistent demands that he get a haircut led him to say, "That's enough." He then moved out.

Like most of his friends, he smoked marijuana but "wasn't into LSD or any of those things." Several of his closest friends, already married and building careers, remained totally straight, still beer drinkers. "I guess it made me feel radical that I was on the other side, rebelling," he reflects, but quickly qualifies, "But we weren't really rebelling; we were just here safe on the East Coast, and the war was so far away—we didn't feel threatened." Jack's wife, Ann, a product of a Catholic school, worked in local offices; she shared in Jack's muted rebellions. "Even now," Jack notes, "occasionally I'll smoke a joint," and he seems to take some pleasure in still being kidded by some friends about being a hippie. "I think there's still a group of us out here," he adds, "that if we could get hold of it on occasion . . . I call it being on different planes, and if you get everybody in the group and they all do the same thing, you're all on that plane. But when this group is doing that and the other [straighter] one isn't, the conversation doesn't make sense." The Sixties came rather late to the Coast communities, and in muted form, but nevertheless, dichotomies between the hip and the straight linger. Jack, with a writer's dreams, highly individualistic and yet low-key, laid-back, resonated with the hippie lifestyle but not at all with that of any kind of activism.

After drifting for several years, Jack found a job as a bellhop at one of the prestigious country clubs in the area. He recalls, "They said, 'You're going to have to get your hair cut, and you're going to wear a uniform; you're going to be expected to be respectable.' " "And," he admits, "basically, I was that type of person, and I was playing this hippie character." So he learned how to cater to a wealthy clientele over the next three years and became "a completely different person." He and Ann finally decided to marry, and for a while he got involved with Amway. "It gave me a taste that you can really make your own business," he tells me, "if you put a lot of energy into it." Finally, he began working with a fellow bellhop who did windows and doors on the side. They quit the country club to start a home supplies business. Over the years, the partnership fell apart, but Jack remains in the business, mostly working for himself.

Jack Claire, husband, father of two, independent business-man making out modestly well, voted for George McGovern in 1972. He doesn't know any Vietnam veterans, but has been interested in recent television treatments of their plight: "I'm glad that I didn't have to go through that . . . right now, everything that I've been through—and I've been through some pretty heavy things in life other than wars—it's just one less thing that I'm glad that I don't have to deal with. Life's tough enough as is." He believes that we've learned from the Vietnam experience, declaring, "America shouldn't rule the world; it's not our job." At the same time, he worries about the loss of respect for authority: "When Eisenhower was going to talk on television, it didn't matter what you were going to do, you'd make sure you were home to see him speak." But, he adds, "when Nixon was on television, it was like, you wouldn't make a point of staying home—and seeing what Nixon had to say. Agnew, all those guys—it was just a whole group that destroyed this image that we grew up of America, and they took that away from us, and they started taking us away and sending us to some place that we didn't belong, without a clear-cut plan, so we just rebelled." He blames Nixon more than Johnson, with unusual ferocity, proclaiming, "He got what he had coming; he was disgraced; he disgraced himself, and he disgraced the country." Yet, Jack adds, "I think he's been humbled by it now, and I think the guy's got something to say, that he's not a total jerk."

Jack is bothered by the materialism within the culture. "Money's a problem in America," he tells me, "it's the basis of everything; that's how it is." He talks of his investment banker brother, of the ways in which the casino industry has accentuated the centrality of money in the area. "I keep thinking," he muses, "that at some point I'll buy a sailboat and sail away, and go where it's not this pace, because the pace is just getting crazier and crazier." He understands how terrifying it would be to live in a rust-belt region, plagued by layoffs. Living in a casino-driven economy, Jack declares, "This is sort of like the center of the universe now; if you're not making money, then something's wrong, 'cause there's work everywhere."

But Jack doesn't dwell on the implications of such conclusions; he returns to thoughts of writing. One of his oldest high school classmates, now a playwright and screenwriter, has been encouraging him to write. He did very little reading until reaching his mid-thirties: "I picked up a book about sailing and now I just read books about sailing. I think once you go to sea, you do fall in love in some aspect with the ocean and in reading these books, it does bring back a lot of nights that I was out in the middle of the ocean." Jack reflects, "I wish I had had a different attitude when I was in the Navy, so that I could have experienced it different, and maybe taken some pictures."

The torch has been passed to a new generation
of Americans
   —John F. Kennedy, 1961

The greatest legacy of the war in Viet Nam is
that I will never believe my government again.
   —William Ehrhart, Vietnam veteran

3

Vietnam

In James Fallows's influential "What Did You Do in the Class War, Daddy?" Harvard antiwar activists are juxtaposed with the sons of Cambridge blue-collar workers.[1] The collegians, mostly exempt from the war through anything from student deferments to psychiatric rationalizations submitted by friendly shrinks, look on as the less privileged march off to boot camp. The imagery is powerful and, as I shall suggest in this chapter, deceptive. In our images of the generation who lived through the Vietnam era, we tend toward a dualism of doves and vets, the soon-to-be yuppie twentysomethings and the victimized "salt of the earth" GIs of Oliver Stone's *Platoon*.[2] In brief, the Sixties generation is divided into those who served their country and those who opposed its policies.[3] And it follows that those who opposed the war from the safety of the class-privileged deferments and evasions lose the moral high ground, in fact, face the charge of hypocrisy and cowardice.

The responses of baby boomers to the Vietnam War are not captured by such a dove-vet polarity. There is a sizable group among the Sixties generation whose experience fits neither that of activist doves nor that of blue-collar vets. Lawrence M. Baskir and William A. Strauss describe, in their *Chance and Circumstance: The Draft, the War, and the Vietnam Generation*[3-5], the demographic characteristics of baby-boom males. Twenty-seven million men became eligible for the draft in the period between the Gulf of Tonkin Resolution of August 1964 and the withdrawal of the last military forces from Indochina in March of 1973. Of these men, 8.6 million served in the military during the Vietnam period, 2,850,000 in Southeast Asia, 2,150,000 actually within Vietnam.[4] This leaves more than 18 million draft-age men who did not serve in the military, and 26 million women. Given even the largest of the estimated sizes of the antiwar movement, the number of active protesters could have formed no more than 20 percent (10.6 million) of the total population of the generation.[4] Indeed, a 1973 study by John Mueller shows that "those *under* thirty consistently supported the war in larger percentages than those over thirty."[5]

One may reasonably conclude that of the fifty-three million members of the baby-boom generation who did not serve in Vietnam, a majority of them were neither activists nor in possession of any strong sentiments against the war. I wish to argue that in addition to those who protested and those who served (and in significant proportions also protested), a third contingent must be highlighted: those who were part of the silent majority of baby boomers. Such people, whatever their feelings about the war, rarely engaged in any organized opposition and, at the same time, made conscious efforts to minimize the possibility of finding themselves on the battlefield. In sum, most of those who benefited from their social-class privileges were not antiwar protesters. Most, in fact, stood on the sidelines as some went off to fight and others marched in opposition. The Coastal class of 1966 reflects this third possibility and stands as such a silent majority.

The three Coast towns were among the most affluent within a then economically struggling and still semirural county. For example, in 1969, Channing ranked second, Wilbur fourth, and South Bay thirteenth in median family income within Atlantic County; Channing's income was virtually double that of the most impoverished, Atlantic City, ranked twenty-fourth.[6] Coasters were solidly middle-class Americans.

The graduating class of 1966 includes 129 males. I have been able to track 102 of them. No one from the class of 1966 died in Vietnam, and I have found only five who served there, including one actually at a Thai air base and another off the coast on an aircraft carrier. In fact, there were no graduates from any class at Coastal who died in Vietnam; one Channing resident died there in 1962, but he was born in 1930 and consequently went to high school before the new school existed.

It's of some value to compare Coast's Vietnam experience with those of less affluent, more minority-based communities. Atlantic City, for example, with approximately twice the population, lost sixteen young men; next-door Pleasantville, with two-thirds the population, lost seven. The large ghettoized city of Newark contributed 111 of New Jersey's total of 1,480 Vietnam War deaths. Edison High School, a mostly

Latino and African-American institution located in the North Philadelphia ghetto, lost fifty-four students to the war.[7] Indeed, the inequities of the draft guaranteed that the Vietnam War would have most impact on working-class, poor, and minority communities.

How did Coasters respond to the developing involvement of the United States in Vietnam and the rest of Indochina? The area was decidedly hawkish and conventionally anti-Communist. Many Coast baby boomers had dads who had served in World War II or Korea. Pro-military feelings were reinforced by the families' working at NAFEC, particularly those associated with the 177th Tactical Fighter Group, stationed there. Coast families valued patriotism, flying the flag on appropriate holidays and coming out to commemorate service and sacrifice during holidays like the Fourth of July. They were disposed to accept the words of Channing Mayor George K. Francis, spoken at the 1966 Memorial Day services: "We are demonstrating our reverence for those who shed their life's blood defending our nation's freedom." Francis posited that Vietnam was "a critical test of the so-called wars of liberation as instigated by Communism." His declaration that retreat from Vietnam would "be catastrophic to peoples throughout the world who are working to achieve their independence" was well within the ideological framework of most Coast residents.[8]

1966 was the first year in which the Vietnam War was likely to impose itself on graduates of Coastal High School. The class of 1965 received their diplomas before Johnson's "best and brightest" confirmed and put into motion troop commitments of close to two hundred thousand by the end of the year. War was in the air, but graduates still weren't feeling the heat. By June 1966, the war's pressure on the draft was

apparent. It is striking how few Coast 1966 graduates answered the call. At least upon reflection, many speak of
resistance to marching off to war. Something seemed awry—
this wasn't a declared war; it was off somewhere outside the
students' focus of attention or knowledge. They listened to
their history and civics teachers, often veterans, evoke Cold
War shibboleths, but somehow it all seemed remote, alien, at
least until senior year. Of the twenty-five males I interviewed,
ten were deferred from service because of injury, school, or
lottery number. Twelve men served in the reserve or National
Guard units: six in the Navy Reserve, two in the Air National
Guard, and one in the Coast Guard. Only four went into the
army, two of whom served the standard one-year tour in
Vietnam, although neither in combat situations. One of the
Naval Reservists, while on active duty, served a tour aboard
the USS Ticonderoga, a carrier whose bombers struck enemy
targets from the Gulf of Tonkin. For most 1966 Coasters,
Vietnam remained at some distance; many speak, in the
1980s, of knowing no Vietnam veterans, knowing no one
who was killed or seriously wounded over here.

Bobby Green, describing Vietnam as "a poor man's war,"
tells of several Coast dropouts who served in combat. Bobby
remembers being in high school when Timmy Aker came
back to tell war stories of his marine tour in Vietnam:
"Timmy was a tough kid, every other word he used when he
was young was 'motherfucker,' m.f. this and m.f. that; he had
a real neat style about him, a little bit wild. Well, he quit
school, and he joined the Marines, and all of a sudden
Vietnam is starting to make the news, and Timmy's over
there; all of a sudden, boom!, Timmy's back, Purple Heart;
something happened and a mine got tripped; couple of people
got killed, and he survived it—now he's out. We're out in the

woods drinking, and Timmy would come, and he could take twenty, thirty guys, and we'd all stand around, and he would talk, tell stories, and we'd laugh, listening to him talk about his experiences over there. Now it's starting to come to us." To Bobby and his mostly lower-middle- and working-class buddies, "it was the America kick-ass kind of thing; it was a skirmish still at that time." Bobby recalls when a book on the Green Berets came out: "Joey Campion's wife's brother, whose name was Vic Wills, he read the book, and he was telling us one night [reading from the book], 'And he came running over the hill and grabbed some gook by the neck and ripped it out by his mouth, and the blood and the killing and all that'—wow!"

Bobby and his rowdie buddies were patriotic, even gung ho, but still wanted to enjoy the summer before joining up: "We used to go almost every day down to the Marine recruiter in Atlantic City and sit and talk to him, and he kept saying, 'You got to go for four years,' and we'd say, 'No, that's too long.' Timmy Aker used to say, 'Don't go for four years; go for two. And if you find out you like it, you can always re-up.' That made sense to me, 'cause I know how I am with authority and regimentation; I love to play football, but I hated to practice." So the rowdies kept talking with the recruiters: "We used to ask the stupid questions: 'When we're out in the field, will you bring us cold beer?' 'Oh, yeah, we'll bring you beer.' Then about a month after that our apartment got raided for underage drinking; got our names in the papers, the whole bit." Several of the guys immediately took the four-year marine enlistment, but Bobby resisted. Then in early 1968 he got his draft notice. At the time, Bobby Green knew no one who either opposed or was involved in protesting against the war. "It was still 'Yah, we'll kick ass and we'll win the war and all that." The campus demonstrations "weren't affecting us here." Bobby couldn't have found Vietnam on a map at that point. The network news and newspaper headlines may have been highlighting "the armies of the night," the campus rallies against the draft, the Students for a Democratic Society (SDS), but on the Coast such news was at best distant, and more typically ignored.

Al Judson concurs; like most 1966 graduates, he knew next to nothing about Vietnam, "I don't remember talking about it in high school." College-bound, more middle-class students like Judson had less interest in the war than Bobby Green and his academically bored buddies. They assumed that four years of college would protect them; of course, this war against a backward Third World country couldn't go on for that long. Harry Kearns says that he had vague knowledge of the war, but mostly, "I knew the Communists were trying to take over and we didn't like the idea." But at the same time, Harry thought, "It will never affect me anyway, because I'm going to college." And like others who entered college in the fall of 1966, Harry received the 2-S deferment. Mel Farmer, who joined the army rather than wait for the inevitable draft notice, and who served in Vietnam as a convoy driver, bought the Cold War atmosphere of his high school years: "I remember that missile crisis; it was a scary time; I was glad Kennedy . . . he showed them what was what—you're either going to turn it around or we'll come and get you; that was good." He admits, "Everyone was sort of, not brainwashed, but concerned about communism; you know, they kept taking over smaller countries." Mel didn't seek military service: "I figured if I would enlist, maybe I'd have a chance picking where I want to go, and not getting sent to Vietnam." In September of 1966, he went off to Fort Dix for basic and then intensive training, sixteen weeks in all. Like most of his fellow trainees, he got shipped out at Christmastime, to Vietnam.

Matt Blake says, "I would do anything that I had to do not to go; that was my own feeling," despite growing up the son of a World War II veteran. "Not that I wouldn't fight for my country," he adds, but somehow not in this war. Judd Dennis shared this reluctance to risk being "in the bushes over there"; instead, he joined the Coast Guard for four years. He didn't understand why we were fighting in Vietnam: "I knew no one who could define it, and they're still having trouble defining why we were there, and even at that time, there were some against, people going to Canada." Judd knew this second-hand and quickly qualifies, "I didn't want to disgrace my family nor myself by going to Canada." To Coasters, open resistence or avoidance—for example, protest, conscientious objection, flight—were beyond the pale. Yet at the same time, many sought more socially acceptable means to minimize possible Vietnam service—what I call "respectable" draft evasion.

There were exceptions, like Bobby Green or Dave Ford, an upper-middle-class Linwooder but a rowdie, who received his draft notice while still a high school junior. Dave, influenced by his parents, immediately joined the Navy Reserve, which allowed him to graduate before starting boot camp. He looked forward to active duty: "I felt real good about being in the service because I was a rah-rah American kid, and I still am; I'm an American and proud of it too." But, he adds, most of his fellow reservists didn't share his enthusiasm. And when given the choice of being "a boatswain's mate on a swift boat in the Mekong Delta with a life span of about four days," Dave elected the safer option of more advanced training. Dan Vitale, also patriotic ("I'm the type of guy who salutes the flag," he tells me) admits that "when I had the choice of going there—in the Navy you had to volunteer, unless the whole unit was sent—I turned it down." Thus, even among those Coasters with the most flag-waving propensities, there was little inclination to choose combat in Vietnam.

To many, the confusion about the war centered on its undeclared, seemingly restrained aspects. Jimmy O'Brien, protected by a heart murmur, flat feet, and a host of other disabilities that made his failure at the physical a foregone conclusion, says, "I could never understand it, totally, why we were there. If we were there, let's go all out; what's the sense of going into a fight if you're going to use one hand? All through history, going through high school, always talking history, World War I, World War II, we fought all out and did everything we could to beat the enemy." Such feelings were the rule. Dave Ford believes that "everybody liked Nixon at the time" because he said he would end the war. Nixon supporters like Dave were reenforced while in the service: "I think the reason that they were there was a good reason, but I was taught through the military to believe what they wanted me to believe. The people out on the streets don't know what war's about, unless they've actually been there." So concerns about the war rarely led to protests; instead, most Coasters invested in the Nixon administration's quest for "peace with honor." And most had a rising intolerance for the protesters.

Regarding Vietnam, the class of 1966 divides along gender lines but also between those males going off to college and 2-S deferments and those immediately facing the draft. Social-class background was significant in distinguishing the two paths, but enough exceptions exist in both categories to mandate caution in making any claims of a strict class determinism. In one instance, a college-bound Coaster, Tom

Rogers, justified privilege rather glibly: "I felt that Vietnam was for the dummies, the losers." Interestingly, Rogers himself was from a lower-income family. Since class lines on the Coast flattened toward the middle, few of "the dummies, the losers," came from the Coast suburbs; most were at a distance, in blue-collar and poor city neighborhoods and in backwater small towns and farms.

For those going off to college, there were few instances of the kinds of experiences conventionally associated with campus antiwar protest. Sally Vincent Rogers has more memories about the space program than of foreign affairs crises. Although her husband, Tom, pooh-poohs it, Sally speaks proudly of her activist period at Glassboro State College: "There were a big group of us that were very active politically, marching against Vietnam, creating a huge banner," traveling to Trenton for a demonstration. Sally was involved in student government; she recalls working on a huge Christmas card and an "I Love You" banner for GIs in Vietnam. Interestingly, Sally, already married, never spoke about her antiwar views or activities with her conservative parents. "I didn't bring that home; I wasn't an organizer," she admits. "I was more or less a follower." She was delighted when Tom's lottery number was high enough to minimize his chances of being drafted. "He would have gone in; I disagreed with the war, and I wanted it over because I thought it was unfounded, that we had no business being there; I'm sure Tom felt the same way, but you don't have a choice in these matters." Sally and Tom were among those mainstream Americans shifting against the war by the time of the moratorium in the fall of 1969; they were political moderates, uncomfortable with activism, but, at least regarding Sally, willing to join the more respectable antiwar opposition.

There were a few other antiwar voices, Rodney and Melanie Combs Wayne, for example, also in New Jersey colleges (see profiles). But like Sally Rogers, Rodney Wayne kept at the margins and, with Melanie, was more comfortable with the cultural aspects of campus rebellion. Countercultural experimentation did cut across antiwar feelings, as with Frank Feller (see profile), but I haven't found any example of significant involvement in antiwar activism among any Coasters from the class of 1966. Most characteristic perhaps are the feelings and experiences of Polly Bain Smythe, who also attended Glassboro State College, preparing to become a teacher. Coming from a fairly protected, religious home, she found college to be an eye-opener and was attracted to almost all of the dissent and protest she encountered. She says, "In college, I began to challenge everything that I had been taught, politically." She "wanted to be seen as a hippie, absolutely, but didn't have the guts to go out and join the marches." There was something in Polly's background, her strict Methodist upbringing, her self-consciousness, her lack of contact with anybody who had ever rebelled against authority, that constrained her. Protest was simply out of character. Polly Bain Smythe rejected Nixon's call for a silent-majority answer to campus rebellions, but she found it impossible to break through her inhibitions. Like many on campus, probably the majority, at least away from the elite institutions, she remained silent. She rooted for the protesters, envied them their courage, but held back.

Most Coastal graduates who went on to college did not experience even such milder, muted forms of protest and activism. They went to fairly conservative private or public colleges and universities, often located in the South. A significant number were members of fraternities and sororities;

many focused on preparing for their postcollegiate careers. There were marriage plans, some, as with the Rogers, consummated while still in school. Those who were more lower- to middle-middle income, worked to pay for college expenses. They had little sympathy for those students with the time to protest government policies. And they often knew no one serving in Vietnam. As such, for the more collegiate of Coastal's class of 1966, Vietnam, the war itself and the controversy surrounding it, remained distant and marginal to their lives.

For those serving in Vietnam, there was a different reality. By the time Bobby Green arrived in Vietnam in early 1968, "the word's out; guys are coming back and saying, 'Hey, you can't do this, you can't do that,' finding out the war was not the old 'win 'em' thing." Bobby's first night at Kontum "there was a racial fight which scared the hell out of me." He had been assigned to work on generators but didn't like the work, so he volunteered for the convoys that went back and forth between Kontum and Pleiku in the central highlands, a thirty-five-mile run. It was risky, mostly because of Vietcong sniping, but Bobby adds, "The whole time I was over there nobody got hurt bad, some wounded; I wasn't in the bush too much." But his frustration built: "The war was starting to change in my mind; what's going on, you know, we could be winning this? Okay, you hear, they're bombing certain military installations in North Vietnam. I'm not a warmonger, but sometimes total war is the only way you could win a war." However, his anger focused on the brass: "Hamburger Hill happened when I was there. I'm blaming the military officers; it seems like they enjoyed the war. They're in Saigon at night and fly around the battlefield during the day, kind of like what happened in World War I, where they sent those millions of boys into those machine guns—'Send us more bodies.' " Bobby jokes about his ignorance concerning the peace movement: "Soldiers are coming from other military installations; they're going like this to me [he makes a V peace sign]; I thought it meant victory; that's the honest truth." By the time he returned to the States, Bobby Green was "swaying to the protester's side." Yet he never considered joining antiwar vet groups like the Vietnam Veterans Against the War. He now had long hair, experimented with drugs, and felt rebellious, but had no thoughts of activism—and neither did any of his friends.

Mel Farmer, who also drove trucks in Vietnam, considers himself lucky to have escaped the infantry. He remembers the suffocating heat and the poverty of the Vietnamese, many of whom, he feels, "didn't care for us." He came to see the war as senseless; he asks, "Weren't we getting near a recession at that time?" But his conclusion that we shouldn't ever have gone there never tempted him to act, "I wouldn't protest against it or run to Canada or nothing like that." In fact, he got mad at the protesters, especially Jane Fonda: "I still hold that against those people. It's America; you can voice your opinion, but it doesn't help the people who's over there fighting; you're against those people." He believes that protesters have the right not to fight, but "at least do your time; you can type; you can do something." Mel adds, "Basically I came back the way I left." When he landed in Philadelphia, he decided to take a limo home: "I didn't have my uniform on, and the guy in the limo said, 'Where were you?' And I said, 'I just come back from Vietnam.' And everyone's asking how it is and all that, and I tell them, 'Atlantic City.' And he says, 'Hey soldier, no charge.' " But, Mel adds, after this pleasant welcome, "nobody really seemed to care; in fact, when I got back, you'd hit a couple of parties; I felt like an outcast." "The ones that didn't go," he suggests, made him feel unwanted. They weren't antiwar, he continues, but they saw him as a sucker: " 'Why did you go?' type thing; I really didn't have a choice, that's why. I just felt down; nobody really wanted to talk about it then; if you don't talk about it, nobody's going to say anything." So Mel Farmer stored away his experiences and feelings and began to get on with his life.

Not all had easy adjustments; Bobby Green fell into a partying life that verged on the self-destructive. Joey Campion speaks of one marine veteran who went berserk at a local tavern when an army guy bad-mouthed the corps's efforts in the war: "You weren't in Vietnam; you don't know." Military life itself could be difficult; in at least three instances, Coasters went AWOL from the service for considerable lengths of time, hiding in shore-area motels from the MPs.

Those who married and started families right out of high school, like Mac Schmidt (see profile), probably had the smoothest transitions to adulthood and those least troubled by the Vietnam War. Their deferments rested on fatherhood. They focused on building careers, saving for a house, and paying the bills. For such high school sweetheart couples, the Sixties, as a decade of rebellion, did not exist, except from afar. And they often had no contact with either Vietnam GIs or peaceniks. The war was, at best, little more than a few minutes on the nightly news.

The experiences of those who chose what remains the characteristic Coast baby-boom option, the reserves or National Guard, were most varied. Such an option was the preferred and respectable way to resolve the dilemma of both upholding one's patriotic duty and avoiding Vietnam service. It was what Lawrence M. Baskir calls "one of the routes especially designed for the thinking man."[9] Approximately one million draft-eligible baby boomers entered reserve or guard units during the Vietnam War years.

Stan Burke grew up hard-nosed about foreign policy: "I knew that Castro was a son of a bitch, and we should have thrown him out of Cuba; I thought the Bay of Pigs was a good try, but they botched it." While attending a technical college, he avoided any involvement in campus rebellion, little of which was occurring at his institution: "I had no interest in demonstrating against the war or anything else for that matter, really; I was interested in doing what I wanted to do." In fact, he was interested in getting a security clearance to apply for work in intelligence. But he ended up at the phone company, still having to decide how to handle his military service. Stan states emphatically, "I wasn't particularly thrilled with the idea of crawling around in a rice paddy, shooting people—not that I wouldn't have if that's the way it would have worked out." But he made an effort to ensure that that wouldn't be his destiny, letting the Navy Reserve, where he had contacts, know that he was a ham operator: "He [the recruiter] almost jumped over the desk, grabbed me; I signed the papers, and they jumped me over a six-month waiting list." Stan adds, "So I guess you could say I pulled a 'Dan Quayle.' " The interview occurred when the controversy over the selection of George Bush's running mate was at its height.

Stan continues, without prompting, "I did exactly the same thing he did; his parents may or may not have exerted some influence, but the man did serve; it wasn't as if he didn't. This whole thing has been blown out of proportion. It's ridiculous; find me a congressman or find me a senator who hasn't used his pull for some purpose."

Harry Kearns was sitting in his college fraternity, "with pizza and beer and having a grand old time," when the lottery drawing occurred in late 1969. After the first fifty numbers were called, "the phone rang; it was my mother. She said, 'We made it to fifty, we won't have any problems now. My little boy's not going to war." And while on the phone, his number was called: "Fifty-two, fifty-three, or fifty-six, I can't remember, and she started crying; she just burst into tears and after a few minutes we settled her down and I said, 'Mom, I'll take care of it.' " But he was thinking, "Holy shit, now what do I do?" Harry was looking forward to student teaching, a career, graduate school; but in April he received his draft notice. He went home to go for his physical, but "in the meantime, I didn't know this, my father—it's ironic that we're talking about this now, because this is what's going through Quayle—my father had made a few phone calls and talked to friends of his in the National Guard." Harry indicated to the guard that his education could meet their need for instructors. He is highly agitated as he tells this story: "Half of us were going to Vietnam; half of us were being sent back to our units; it really upsets me to hear them talking about the National Guard the way it was, because we could have been called at any time."

In basic training, Harry felt like "the National Guard were treated like dirt, until they realized that we were all college graduates, that we all had something to offer and that they might as well use our talents, while we were there, to train these other people, make it a little easier for them, who probably were going to go to Vietnam." Harry's platoon included a Harvard Law School graduate, an engineer, and two other teachers; they became the squad leaders: "They used us in the training roles, as models, because most of the other boys were black or poor Southern boys who had enlisted, and their whole life was to enlist in the army." Harry's training was rigorous, but it left him with mixed emotions about Vietnam: "I didn't think we should have been there; I personally didn't want to go there. I didn't want to go to war for the sake of going to war; it wouldn't have mattered if it was Vietnam or Korea, Europe or anywhere; as a young person, twenty, twenty-one years old, I didn't really understand like I do today what was going on in Vietnam. It would seem to me at the time that it was a very senseless war, that we were sending people over there to be killed for absolutely no reason whatsoever." But Harry Kearns has changed his mind over the years: "I now see a reason why we had to be there," although he qualifies, "I'm still not sure I agree with it. I can now see why we have to do what we have been doing in Nicaragua; I can see why we have to be careful in Panama. I can see the same types of things happening, and I can think back—I was probably thinking very selfish back in the Sixties and I was thinking of I instead of the country." Harry now follows current events religiously in the daily newspaper. He isn't convinced that the United States has learned any lessons from the Vietnam War. He doesn't watch any of the commercially popular Vietnam War movies: "Subconsciously I think I avoided them; consciously I just haven't gone out of my way to . . . they're not types of things I want to remember. I see it was 'Jeez, I could have been there'; that bothers me still to a point."

Whatever is bothering Harry Kearns, he admires Dan Quayle because "he reminds me so much of myself and he's got to stand up and fight for something he really shouldn't have to stand up and fight for, as far as I'm concerned. It just kind of ticks me off, to see a guy go through what he's going through." Harry concludes, "He didn't do anything illegal. Bush said, 'He didn't burn an American flag; he didn't flee to Canada.' That's true." Harry Kearns has been an active member of the American Legion now for twenty years.

Others voice some mixed feelings about the choices they made. Judd Dennis's wife Susan recalls, "We ate dinner to the death marches; we ate dinner to the death toll in Vietnam, what was going on, who, how many of our boys were killed, the blood bath." She interjects, "I had brothers in Vietnam." Judd admits, "Sometimes I would feel a little guilty because I was able to get into the Coast Guard and get out of it and knowing that 90 percent of those guys didn't really want to be there." Then he adds, expressing what I think is the predominant sentiment, "But they were like me—if you were drafted, you went, and if I had been drafted, I would have went. I wouldn't have wanted to . . ." Susan, one of whose brothers suffers from problems caused by Agent Orange, bitterly concludes, "What did Vietnam teach me? It taught me that the government doesn't tell you the truth."

Susan Dennis's responses are not unique but are more decisive than what most graduates feel. There is still a lot of queasiness and confusion about the war and about those who fought it. Many of the white middle-class Coasters could use connections to beat the draft, but essentially their midde-class environment created the possibilities "behind their backs."[10] Life in mainstream Middle America comes with built-in privileges; such benefits acquired through the use of family and community networks are part of the informal system that gives an edge to their children. And they are available even to many of those from the least privileged, working-class families who derive advantage from their whiteness and from their community membership. This invisibility of social-class, gender, and racial advantages, particularly in a nonelite environment like the Coast towns, is critical to any effort to understand Middle American life and culture. Middle-class baby boomers could feel unease, but rarely chose to act in ways that put themselves at risk.

And the offshore cocoon is often sustained by an abysmal ignorance of history. Coastal High School rarely inspired or encouraged curiosity or knowledge about the world. And in the years since graduation, few have paid much attention to history, politics, or international affairs. Matt Blake credits Gerald Ford with pulling us out of Vietnam and would still vote for Nixon, "even though he was the one who committed" troops to Vietnam. "Wasn't it Nixon?" he asks, and then concludes, "But I don't hold him responsible for it; I blame whoever was in office to begin with, which was Johnson?" Aggie Jones Rizzuto, whose husband served in the navy, feels the war as remote, in part because no one seems willing to talk about it: "Nobody got killed, and to my knowledge I haven't met anybody who didn't come home and pick up their life; you know they show you the things where they have hallucinations, they can't get themselves back together. Fortunately, I don't know anybody that that happened to."

Some Coasters do watch the movies and television shows about Vietnam which, for a while, flooded the airwaves. George Evanson, a 4-F, after watching the acclaimed HBO documentary "Dear America," felt embarrassed about how little he knew. "I was asking my wife, 'Did you ever know anybody . . . what did you think about this?' And she said, 'It never bothered me.' And I said, 'Did you know anybody that died?' And she said, 'No.' And I said, 'Neither did I.' I don't know anybody; it was very removed; the war always continued to be of some distance; I never really knew what was going on except that we were fighting for a cause." George had a colleague who had served in Vietnam: "He would tell stories about stuff he used to do, and I used to call him a liar and say, 'You're crazy.' He would say, 'We used to get them up in a helicopter and throw them out of the helicopter.' 'We wouldn't do that stuff!' He said, 'We sure as Hell did.' And I said, 'We wouldn't do that!' And he said, 'We're just as bad as everybody else,' and he was really . . . I said, 'John, why are you telling me this?' He said, 'It's the truth, we used to go up, asking questions, and if the first one wouldn't answer, we'd push him out of the helicopter.' I said, 'Nah' . . . I was absolutely shocked." George Evanson, who still avoids foreign affairs news, represents a significant segment of silent majority baby boomers. Because of his circumstances—for example, his lack of combat experience, his lack of significant contact with Vietnam veterans, his avoidance of mass media presentations touching on the war's pain, his lack of any contact with antiwar activists—George is able to sidestep coming to grips with the realities of Vietnam and is shocked when occasionally forced to face such realities. Al Judson, college graduate and teacher, found the film *Platoon* interesting "because I don't know a whole lot of people who were there. If it's a honest portrayal, which I don't know, it felt uncomfortable, it felt kind of scary, the things the war caused people to do." On the other hand, vet Mel Farmer went with his father to see *Platoon* and concludes, "That's what it was like."

For Coastal baby boomers the antiwar activism that often is portrayed as characteristic of college students, even faddish, was at best marginal, and most typically nonexistent. To actively oppose the Vietnam War seemed alien, odd, out of character. Most 1966 graduates find it almost unimaginable to protest openly, demonstrate, or engage in more conventionally defined electoral political activity regarding United States foreign policy. It runs against the grain of their upbringing. These behaviors are not reducible to selfishness or narcissism, as suggested by some cultural critics. Coasters are, for the most part, people who care about others; however, their caring tends to stop at the borders of the family, the neighborhood, and the local community. They have built walls to protect themselves from those aspects of modernity they mistrust and fear. Ultimately, their justification rests on their ignorance. If they have derived lessons from Vietnam, they have been muted. They don't rally round the flag as easily as their World War II parents did; at least they didn't until the Persian Gulf War. They aren't as willing to risk American lives; they have more skepticism about the rhetoric of their government. But at the same time, they tend to vote for conservative, defense-oriented Republicans who seek to overcome what Ronald Reagan called Vietnam syndrome. And some either don't vote or have few expectations when they do. So long as such essentially decent but parochial people remain a silent majority, the lessons of Vietnam will be limited to the view that American military interventions will be supported or, at the least, tolerated as long as there are minimal risks to American lives.

Profiles: Melanie Combs Wayne and Rodney Wayne

Few Coast baby boomers were touched in any major way by the eruptions associated with the 1960s. A remarkable percentage have managed forty years of life without intimate contact with black people, political activists of any type, or cultural rebels, hippie or otherwise. At some point in many interviews, I ask people who they most admire. The question often yields a pause, even a long silence, somewhat uncomfortable, even embarrassing, during which the interviewee struggles to bring forth a hero. In such situations, students often name entertainment celebrities; 1966 graduates, after a pause, often name someone like Lee Iacocca or Donald Trump. Melanie Combs Wayne, a tall, blonde, and athletic woman, quickly, mischievously replies, "Jackson Pollack and Brigitte Bardot."

Melanie describes her father, affectionately, as "a slob; he wore a black leather jacket" and worked at "anything he could do for a while, and then he would flash his money, and then he wouldn't work till September." Her husband, Rodney, bearded, casually dressed, adds, "He gambled all the time; he played pinball, he played pool, and bet on anything. He was always playing cards. He was just . . . you know . . . he was what you could have been and raised a family back in those days. He had a nice house that he built himself; he always drove a pretty good car; [he was] an ex-pro baseball player." Melanie notes that her more conventional mom tried to get him to settle down, "but she always let him have his way; she was totally submissive, a good-hearted person who tried [unsuccessfully] to be very strict."

As a young girl, Melanie went to church and kept up with appearances, but regarding her mother's attempt to control her, she confesses, "I lied to her; I did what I wanted to do and told her the things she wanted to hear, and then I did what I wanted. I lied to her all the time." As a young teenager, Melanie hated school, and she emphasizes, "I always wanted to rebel against being shy and totally restricted by my mother; so I wanted to be bad, wild." As she approached graduation, her shyness began to yield to a developing, one might say latent, assertiveness, perhaps encouraged by her romance with Rodney, who she began dating in their junior year.

Rodney Wayne's background was more privileged; his ancestors on his father's side were Southern slaveholders "wiped out by the war": "But my grandmother carried on a kind of Tennessee Williams sense of loss," and "although they moved north to Philadelphia, they tried to maintain that kind of old Southern values and saw themselves in a very real kind of sense as superior to a lot of people that were around them." Rodney was raised with a sense of aristocratic special-ness. His father, a prominent physician, taught him to resist imitating what other kids did and to resist coveting what other kids had. The elder Wayne would lecture: "It has nothing to do with your life, because we're different, because when you grow up you're not going to be round these people at all—so you can associate with them, but you don't need to be too concerned about how they feel about you." Both parents were conservative Republicans, Southern on racial matters, but whereas his mother was conventionally religious, his dad raised him to be an atheist: "I'd get Friday night discussions of Darwinism" and once was kicked out of Sunday school for bringing evolution into class discussion.

Whereas Melanie was shy, but athletic and attractive, Rodney became outgoing, a leader of the preppy group. In the 1966 yearbook, he was voted "best dancer," "best conversa-tionalist," and "wittiest" among the guys. He tells me, "I wasn't much of an athlete, and I couldn't fight or anything; my thing [was] I could dance; I made jokes and I could dance." He adds that he dressed well. So as others saw Rodney, he was a somewhat cocky preppie leader; yet within his private world, he found stimulation reading Steinbeck and Hemingway. Rodney was a closet intellectual: "We never talked about that stuff, that was too queer. I never, never— maybe to Melanie—but I never told any of my pals; that was loss of dignity." So, to all appearances, Rodney and Melanie were dancing partners, one part of the pairing off so characteristic of high school culture.

Coast was not an environment conducive to interests or behaviors deviant from the mainstream of sports, pop music, clothes, dating, conventional ambitions. The most striking note of rebellion appears under Melanie's graduation photo, where her ambition was "not to be a housewife." Rodney's dream of becoming a writer remained private.

Certainly the ways these kinds of students grew up made them more inclined to break ranks, although one could hardly predict such deviance from high school behaviors. But identification with her high-spirited, undomesticated dad, in Melanie's case, and encouragement to be a freethinker, if at the same time a snob, in Rodney's experience, played some part in bringing these two iconoclasts together. After all, as Rodney adds, "they grew up together," attending the same schools from fifth grade; their mothers used to take them to the beach together. Melanie's dad had been Rodney's peewee football coach.

Melanie hadn't thought very much about college until she noticed so many of her friends preparing their applications, "and I thought, heck, I want to go to college too," so she scrambled to get into a new college located in sparsely populated Nebraska. She confesses, "I had no grades, they

were terrible. They took me just because they needed students." She lasted one semester: "It was a real shock. I gained
thirty pounds because I didn't have my mother. I was loose;
you could do what you wanted, and it was a little frightening.
I wasn't able to handle it." She returned to Atlantic Community College and then transferred to Glassboro State in art
education. Once she adjusted to college rhythms, Melanie
flourished with scarcely an effort: "I had no trouble with
college; I would get As; in fact, I only went to college about
half the time—I just skipped my classes and didn't treat it
seriously. It was very easy." Melanie tended to take things in
stride, whereas Rodney, always self-conscious, hard on himself and others, struggled.

Rodney—wanting to be "an artist, a writer, an actor, or
something" and resenting but yielding to his strong-willed
father's desires that he choose a more respectable direction—
had gone off to a prestigious state university in the South. But
his resistance stymied academic success. Rodney flunked out,
returned home, and joined the Navy Reserve. He recalls, "At
that time you couldn't do what the hell you wanted—this is
1967—I didn't care much for Vietnam; you were either in
college or married or ran off to Canada or went into the
service; you got drafted." The two-year reserve obligation
seemed attractive; however, an asthmatic condition led to his
being sent home, and as Rodney sardonically notes, "I had to
go to college again, because of my dad." He explored becoming a journalist, but the local paper told him he needed a
degree, so off to Monmouth College he went.

College was a liberating experience for both Melanie and
Rodney; it offered an environment much more supportive and
encouraging of their desire to be different, to break away

from conventional roles. Melanie describes herself then as a hippie: "I physically looked it; my hair was down to my waist. It was fun, to do all that stuff—I mean, everybody was virtually in a costume." She laughs, recalling the wonderful foolishness of the times. Yet other 1966 graduates at Glassboro were seemingly untouched by such countercultural moments. Her memories, however, center on what seemed to be a renaissance of creativity: "Every day you'd get through, and the night clubs were so neat; it was a very artistic time, which is what both Rodney and I enjoy most about people— their artistic abilities. This overabundance of artists in every corner, in every little bar and cafe—it was great fun doing that!"

In his senior year, Rodney did a sociological study of student protesters on campus: "My conclusion was, really, it was highly unusual to find anybody who knew what the hell they were doing, and most of them were there simply because someone had said, 'Oh, we can cop some dope there,' or, 'Hey, we'll pick up some girls.' " He admits there were some dedicated people among the leadership, but the study reenforced his tendency to maintain some distance from the activists, despite sharing most of their values. Whereas Melanie exclaims, "We wanted to be there, we wanted to enjoy the excitement," Rodney muses, "I came to think of myself as some kind of intellectual." In college—he continues directing his comments to me—"I met all of these guys like you, these guys who had read all this stuff—Marx, Malatesta, Frantz Fanon, and all this stuff—giving me all this stuff to read; I read it, and unfortunately, I believed a lot of it, these outrageous ideas and these marvelous thinkers. I just was devouring this." He maintained his distance from activism, however, at least until his last year, and even then approached it reluctantly, cautiously. Melanie was less cerebral, less intellectual, more of a free spirit.

At home, Rodney's college years were traumatic. He remembers his mother discreetly putting his copy of Eldridge Cleaver's *Soul on Ice* out on the porch. She never said a word. More difficult, however, were confrontations over his refusal to study medicine, a refusal that by this point was merely the tip of an iceberg of rebelliousness: "I was against the war, and I was riding a motorcycle, and I had a beard, and I had hair, and I was wearing a leather jacket and openly defying them on everything and telling them that I was smoking dope and I didn't give a damn what they thought, and if they didn't like it, I'd just quit school and go my own way." Conflicts with his dad escalated: "I went right up against him, nose to nose. I punched him out once—he had me by the collar, screaming in my face, and I told him what I was going to do if he didn't let go of me, and I did it." Rodney Wayne's family had to deal with what seemed to be rebellions against sacred values, against a way of life. They had difficulty understanding their son's behavior. Rodney now looks back with more understanding—and remorse: "That is to my everlasting shame, and I think to his too, because he was the adult. My dad was an extremely hardworking man." Rodney speaks of the long hours his father worked and of his dedication to his patients. "We didn't really know each other, and suddenly all these things in society are changing, and he's telling me to trust him and I [respond], 'How can I trust you? I don't know you.' "

Rodney and Melanie got married when they were both twenty-five; their first of two daughters followed three years later. Melanie believes that they were always "extremely idealistic," emphasizing, "I was never interested in money;

cars didn't impress me; nothing like that impresses me; he and I wanted to lead the romantic, the ideal [life]." Rodney, who clearly admires his wife's more visceral rebelliousness, reflects, "Melanie was never a political-type person; Melanie just did absolutely whatever she wanted. She never thought about it; she just went and did it. Whether it was clothes . . . she was wearing bell-bottoms, pants, before any of these other women. She was a teacher in school; she came in pants suits, and they told her she couldn't, and she told them, 'The heck with you; I'm going to anyhow,' and within a couple of weeks they were all doing it. She started this business just because—a women's weight-lifting gym? Where's that coming from? Well, Melanie had the first one that I know of, certainly the first one around here." Melanie left teaching to work as a commercial artist, turned down modeling offers from the Wilhemina agency, and eventually established her gym operations, at one point running three branches. She shows me a videocassette on workouts that she is trying to market.

Rodney has had a more difficult time finding his own way. He has worked as a newspaperman, substitute teacher, social worker, ditch digger, and construction worker before settling, uncomfortably, into his present job as a probation officer. He calls himself a "Mother-Earther": "The Sixties counterculture, I bought into it, and I've stayed in it to the extent that I've been able to without hurting my children." He gave up the self-destructive, drug-related aspects of rebellion years ago. For a time, he made himself into a self-sufficient person, rebuilding a house, living in a cabin without modern conveniences, once canoeing from Pittsburgh to New Orleans. He adds, "I was a real dropout; but I decided, 'I'm a writer and I'm going to do this thing, and I did it up until . . .'" He pauses.

"I'm a failed novelist; I write novellas, short stories; I used to write novels when I wasn't full-time working."

There's something sad and compelling about Rodney Wayne. He is energetic, animated, still in love. But the offshore Coast communities have not been supportive of sensitive, sometimes difficult intellects such as Rodney's. Melanie, inheriting her dad's individualism, simply is a rebel; she doesn't need to think about it or theorize. In examining her feelings about feminism, she asserts, "I never felt any of the pressures on women, like the movements do now; nothing ever bothered me. I always felt like I could do exactly like I wanted to do. I always knew I was good at athletics, and when you're good at that, you always feel like you're good at anything. So I never once ever felt like a woman couldn't do something—never. I was afraid of water; I passed my lifeguard test, and that was just to prove to myself that I could do this. Even in high school, even though I was shy, I still knew that I could do lots of things." And she has.

Melanie emphasizes that one of their primary goals is to be mortgage free: "People always say play the mortgage game, make money off of this; people look at us like we're strange, but our goal is to have total financial freedom. He's considered weird at work. I'm definitely strange; we're both strange—we're not compatible with the people that I have around me." Melanie finds it boring to talk with most women: "I played with boys; I liked boys to play with; you can say that I'd rather talk to a man than a woman. I just don't find them interesting." About her relationship with Rodney she reflects, "He and I wanted to be free spirits; we didn't want to get married, and we didn't want chidren, and we ended up doing both." Melanie doesn't seem unhappy with those choices, but thinks about relocating southward.

She'd prefer raising her kids further away from both suburban blandness and casino glitter. She is still attracted to a vision of hippie simplicity.

Rodney describes how his job, as well as some construction work on the side and helping out in Melanie's business, keeps him busy: "Just to talk to you right now, I don't do this sort of thing—I'm enjoying it; I don't know why, but there's really no one to talk to. I don't know people who read." He adds, "I probably didn't belong here; I haven't met people with similar interests in all the years that I've lived here. If you don't know the ball scores, there's nothing to talk about to anybody about." He jokes, self-consciously, that he isn't "too ingratiating."

Rodney no longer finds aesthetic interests to be "the embarrassment" they were to him as a young boy. He reads "a lot of Gandhi," Hemingway's short stories, Turgenev, Tolstoy—"I was almost a Tolstoyan for years," he interjects—Joseph Conrad, Isaac Babel (a "certifiable genius too dangerous to be allowed to live"), and Kafka, who "had a drudge job like me—a frail guy, the sheer force of his will he did these things." But Melanie adds, "He gets too devastated" by both an unsympathetic environment and publisher rejections. Rodney, who tried to squeeze short-story writing into his busy life, responds, "I always feel like I'm cheating on my family; to really do it, you have to lock yourself away."

At the time of our interview, Rodney wasn't writing; he had come to the conclusion that even the best stories were only appearing within esoteric magazines read by academics but by nobody else: "So for somebody like me who's a writer and wants to live off it, it's an absolute self-delusion. I got so disgusted with myself for having flushed fifteen years of my life down the toilet that I haven't picked up a pencil since."

Rodney is hard on himself and on others. Even in his more activist days, he never really was a joiner: "I protested, but I didn't go crazy on it. I never went and marched on Washington—I always thought there were a lot of people who didn't know what they were doing, this was like joining the Boy Scouts, another kind of conformity, to be a nonconformist. Everybody was trying to be hippy-dippy, and there were a lot of pressures to conform into this." But Rodney, shedding the sociable masks he wore at Coastal, resisted: "I tried with my limited resources to figure out my way through this. I used to spend parts of my summers down in the rural South with my mother's people, and then I'd come up here, and I always saw the times I spent with my grandfather back in the woods as really some of the best times of my life—back in the marshes, catching fish, turtles, and I felt, I still feel, very strongly about the destruction of natural habitat, the oceans—it causes me a lot of pain." He admires Ralph Nader and Harrison Brown of World Watch, and he voted for Barry Commoner in 1984. But making ends meet limits his ability to be active: "I'm just trying," he explains, "to keep my head above water." Since the interview, Rodney Wayne has started writing a nature column for the local newspaper.

Men reject their prophets and slay them, but
they love their martyrs and honor those whom
they have slain.
  —Fyodor Dostoevski

We are people of this generation, bred in at
least modest comfort, housed now in universities,
looking uncomfortably to the world we inherit.
  —SDS's Port Huron Statement, 1962

The Sixties

Only occasionally does reality break through the stereotype
concerning the Sixties, or baby-boom, generation. A 1989
Gallup Poll concluded, "Although we tend to characterize the
youth of the '60s as being politically and socially rebellious,
large majorities of those now up to 49 years old say they did
not get involved in anti-war or civil rights movements, did not
smoke marijuana on a regular basis or experiment with
psychedelic drugs, and did not 'dress like a hippie' twenty
years ago."[1] More typical, unfortunately, is the gushing prose
of *Time*'s "Pictorial History of 1968: The Year That Shaped a
Generation," which highlights "a struggle of generations"
peaking in a year best defined as "the original myth of that
tribe" known as baby boomers.[2]

Coast baby boomers, as indicated in Chapter 3, were
characteristically neither protesters nor Vietnam grunts, but
rather tended to be able to sidestep a war most either passively

supported or silently opposed. Such behaviors are typical of the reactions of the class of 1966 to the entirety of the 1960s volcanoes relating to race, poverty, equality, war, patriotism, values, and lifestyles. As Susan O'Hara Dennis suggests, her class was "a kind of in-between group," caught between the postwar Eisenhower era and the tumult of the late Sixties. Susan, perhaps melodramatically, adds, "We were the end of the whole era" of father's knowing best. Such reflections exaggerate the traditionalism of the pre-Sixties decades but, at the same time, capture the fact that the challenges of the 1960s, most particularly those of the trinity of "sex, drugs, and rock 'n' roll," arrived later in Atlantic County than they had in more sophisticated urban and suburban areas and elite college campuses.

Only a few Coast baby boomers, such as Frank Feller, Jack Claire, and Rodney and Melanie Wayne, flirted with the hippie counterculture after graduation. Yet even in these instances, the predominant pattern was compromise, either in terms of employment or marriage. Feller lived a double life: daytime with Prudential, evenings and weekends partying. Jack Claire's rebellion seems muted, ironic; he took secret pleasure at being in the know, but was always ready to throw off the garb when reality impinged. The Waynes are the most countercultural in substance and over time, but their isolation in the area is perhaps most revealing of the area's cultural traditionalism. (See profiles on Feller, Claire, and the Waynes.)

Carol Smith Rizzo, although a lover of rock 'n' roll, felt no hippie influence. She only began to blend drinking and partying in 1969. Carol explains her naïveté: "The first time I saw the movie *Hair* I didn't know what was going on, and then I went to Philly and saw the show, and I was like, wow!

I can tell you that the first time I ever even . . . we went to Bay Shores. This was a bar that was happening; everybody went there, '70–'71. We're walking from the parking lot and it's packed, and I smell grass—not meaning grass, marijuana—I'm talking about grass; something's on fire. He [her husband] says, 'Hush!' 'What's wrong?' So we get in there, and he says, 'Don't you know what that is?' I said, 'I have no idea.' He said, 'That's marijuana.' " Carol adds that some of the guys were more involved with experimental drugs, "but the girls weren't; we were not aware of it." Some of the guys at parties would slip into another room, and Carol's husband would let her know what they were doing.

Even among those attending college, only a few experimented; almost all concentrated on alcohol, mostly beer. As late as 1968, Diane Ruth Halsey hesitated going to "a drinking party" at college in fear of getting caught. And some, like Al Judson, "walked out of a lot of parties because it was just like a drunken brawl." Al, planning on a teaching career and marriage, "looked at [hippies] with disgust: 'Look at the hair on him!' " Although his friends soon began to grow their hair a bit longer, they remained "hostile toward the hippies." Several, like Mary Perle Ives, viewed hippies as society's losers, the scruffy, disorganized, and disgruntled. Many Coasters, though not the rowdier crowd, in college entered the fraternity and sorority worlds where drinking predominated. Harry Kearns didn't even hear about marijuana until 1969 or 1970, "and that was on such a low key; it wasn't around. I just heard people say they tried it. It never really affected me because I couldn't stand the smoke."

Like a number of 1966 graduates, Al Judson had younger siblings who got more caught up in the counterculture, although not at all in any form of political protest or activism.

By 1969, certainly by the early 1970s, the drug culture had reached the Coast towns. Some 1966 grads speak critically of the effects of hippie lifestyle on their younger brothers and sisters. Al Judson feels that his brothers and their friends are still messed up: "Like we would go, 'What the heck is wrong with you guys? Why can't you get your act together?' Getting married, having a good job, eventually having a family, buying. a house—all those things were important to us, whereas they didn't figure in their long-range plans. And they'll say, 'What's the big deal? Lay back, relax,' still, right?" he asks his wife, Meg. She, a Coastal graduate in 1967, agrees, "I wouldn't want my kids growing up in that period." To Al and Meg Judson, other than a commitment to environmental protection, the Sixties mean childish, self-destructive behaviors still haunting those seduced by the counterculture. On at least five occasions 1966 graduates describe younger siblings as caught up in what they perceive as self-destructive drug dependency. Many Coasters, consequently, find little to admire in the hippie counterculture; they perceive it as an actual, experienced danger, responsible for harming people near and dear to them. Within this silent majority of baby boomers, there is little nostalgic longing for the Sixties, especially its psychedelic aspects. Their younger baby-boom sibs may have different reflections, having grown up in the midst of what 1966 graduates experienced rather late in their youth.

Much rarer among the straighter people is the kind of tolerance Nora Reilly Bennett expresses: "I didn't see anything wrong with smoking pot." She "didn't do it," but she equates it with drinking. Excess, on the other hand, is not acceptable: "Anybody who would do LSD was mental." The most religiously orthodox and culturally conservative baby boomers were predictably the least tolerant. Bette Carter Roszak grew up in a strict household that she has replicated in partnership with her husband, Mel. He was in a rock 'n' roll band, but she, speaking for both, asserts, "I love the music of the '50s, Elvis, good old hard rock 'n' roll, country rock, not acid rock, Led Zeppelin." Bette resisted the San Francisco sound: "I always associated it with drugs. I have to be in control. I have a fear; I have to be in control." She recalls throwing one of Mel's younger sisters out of the house when the sister offered the Roszaks drugs: "I'm judgmental in a lot of ways."

Most 1966 graduates were less judgmental; in fact, the Sixties contributed to the ongoing erosion of a more inhibited, moralistic culture. Sixties Coasters clearly differ from their parents as a result of a sexually and morally permissive and challenging era. The rowdy element and many of the preppies were already, by 1966, part of an adolescent subculture committed to weekend, in some cases even weekday, drinking and partying; and premarital sex, if not the norm, was at least not unusual. But the shift was more in areas of discretion. While in high school, Coasters still adhered to the code of appearance, double standards, lies of convenience. They concealed their behaviors from the adult world, for the most part, and with their parents conspired in not openly talking about obvious violations of sexual and social norms. In fact, it is likely that many of their parents engaged in similar behaviors in the 1920s and 1930s, when they were adolescents. After graduation, class of 1966 Coasters became less discrete, more open, although it is still striking how many of them continued to hide even the mildest countercultural behaviors from their families. But there were certain unmistakable challenges—hair got longer and mangier, clothing styles shifted toward informality and display, and musical tastes were more subversive of old-fashioned values—something was happening, and the Mr. and Mrs. Jones of the Coast towns didn't really know what it was and, certainly, didn't like it one bit. But one must add that a sizable minority of baby boomers, like Al Judson, Harry Kearns, the Roszaks, didn't either.

Less than a fifth were significantly, deeply touched by the cultural rebellions of the period. Even in musical tastes, there were few, like Frank Feller, attracted to the more subversive sounds of Jefferson Airplane. Many, like George Evanson, hold to early adolescent passions—"My favorite group is still the Rascals, and the Beach Boys"—or agree with Jimmy O'Brien: "I didn't get into hard-core Janis Joplin; I always liked Marvin Gaye, Aretha Franklin." Most characteristic is Linda Duncan Gent's refrain—"I liked the music, but I didn't necessarily listen to the words"—or Nora Bennett's: "I never looked for deep meaning." Coasters were most attracted to the brilliantly arranged, danceable, lyrically adolescent sounds of Motown.

Within the Coast culture apparently nested a middle-class desire to both lose control and yet remain safe, a fear of anarchic disorder, which shaped many musical tastes. The hardest, raunchiest, most countercultural sounds did turn on some Coasters, especially the less respectable guys, but strictly for the sake of partying. On the other hand, most class of 1966 graduates were made uncomfortable by the cultural subversions and seeming chaos of artists like Janis Joplin and Joe Cocker. Pam Baird Lane, reversing what many baby boomers experienced, captures this feeling: "Music was very important to me in high school, but it was not important to me in college; I didn't like acid rock! I hated it!" Pam, who preferred Motown to both Elvis and the Rolling Stones, explains, "I don't like ugly; I cannot tolerate ugly, so the music was ugly."

For those Coasters who married right out of high school, like Mac Schmidt and Vicki Lewis(see profiles), the Sixties never existed. They began scrimping and saving for a house, starting a family; they were not in the slightest tempted to tune in, turn on, or drop out. One's youth—and the Sixties—tended to end when one entered the adult world of marriage and kids and bills. The Coast dividing line is less between squares and hippies than between those entering adulthood and those prolonging their youth.[3] In the former category are many, but not all, of those attending college, planning college-based careers, and/or planning early marriages. But some who neither went off to college nor married early entered the adult world, by disposition and choice, quickly. To them life was too serious to waste on a faddish hedonism; or, in some instances, they were simply too timid, too repressed, to risk displeasing their parents. In the latter, extended-youth category, which is certainly more male, but at the same time less exclusively so than in high school, are those sowing their wild oats. Several married couples, for example, held off having children, recognizing that such responsibilities would limit, if not close off, their ability to party. The times encouraged young people to "love the one you're with," but it seems likely that a protracted, hedonistic youth would have occurred without the additional countercultural seductions. The hippie ideology simply added an extra impetus for what was already the norm. Many stretched the fun morality of adolescence as far as it would stretch, which usually meant into the late twenties. After that, eyebrows would begin to rise at those who seemed perpetual adolescents, unable to grow up.

The guys who went off to military service were often in the forefront of a partying youth subculture. Davy Hunter's initial encounters with drugs were in the army. Dave Ford, returning from the navy, rebelled against parental restrictions: "I want to party; I want to raise Hell." The South Bay bar scene, especially Tony's, and old reliables like the Hurley Inn in Wilbur became places where the old crowd reassembled, some returning from the service, others from college. Bobby Green remains nostalgic for those hell-raising days: "We used to go in, and on a certain night we'd take up all the way around the bar, playing darts, pool, good times; that was when we were twenty, twenty-one, when we all started getting back together again." He describes Chris Olsen: "Like me, he was not caring, and he was partying a lot; for a four- or five-year period, we were drinking, had some good times." Bobby, who like several other rowdies became a bartender, saw things changing rapidly by the late 1960s, early 70s, "when the guys started coming out of the closet, the women started doing their own thing, and the blacks started doing their own thing." But such changes, while occasionally topics for barroom conversation, remained at a distance for most Coasters.

Bobby talks of guys who "loved to drink." Even with some drug use—mostly marijuana, some pills, rarely LSD—the overwhelming choice remained alcohol, especially beer. The high school rowdy crowd, now in their twenties, with some drifting away, others recruited, became "the pigs," embracing the epithet tossed their way: "You're nothing but a bunch of pigs." This crew hit the bars regularly. Several of them were married but without children; some of the husbands still lived the bachelor life. They didn't want to settle down as so many of their classmates were already doing; children, insurance, and mortgage payments would come soon enough.

Hair was longer, clothing was hippyish, but the tone was of more "good old boys, and some girls, partying. The more rebellious Rodney Wayne discovered that sports were still the common medium for male bonding in the Coast bar scene. Aside from appearances, little had changed. It is at least as appropriate to place the late 1960s, early 1970s scene at the shore in the context of a youth culture with roots in the 1920s, if not earlier, as to link it with the rebellions of the Sixties. A consumer culture had long been eroding Victorian standards; having a good time before settling down was only in part shaped by hippie hedonism.

At least three-quarters of the Coasters I interviewed were married by 1973. Several young married couples chose to delay having children so that they could enjoy their youth. Two-income families, even in precasino Atlantic County, could sustain a lively social life. The price paid, at least by some, would be significant alcoholism and divorce when the party was over. I haven't encountered a single instance of drug abuse within the 1966 class; on the other hand, the tales of alcohol abuse, including several deaths, suggest an strong undercurrent of stress beneath the hedonistic surface.

The counterculture of sex, drugs, and rock 'n' roll brought some excitement to the shore area in 1969 when Philadelphia promoters put on the Atlantic City Pop Festival just weeks before what was to become the emblem of a generation— Woodstock. On the weekend of August 1–3, such acts as Janis Joplin, Jefferson Airplane, Little Richard, Joni Mitchell, Santana, Frank Zappa, Chicago, and Creedence Clearwater Re-

vival entertained an estimated 110,000 at the local race track.
Local authorities were less than ecstatic about the conver-
gence of slovenly tribes of freaks along the roadsides of Route
40, the Black Horse Pike: "The possibility that 'hippie types'
will attempt to camp out on our private property is disturbing
several nearby businessmen and at least one municipality."
George Hamid, owner of the famed Steel Pier, warned that the
concert would "destroy Atlantic City's image in the eyes of
tourists." This at a time of the city's virtually total decline. He
continued, "These kids, who are repulsive to 95 percent of the
respectable people, will be coming in without leaving 20 cents
behind unless, of course, they buy a hot dog and some pot."[4]
Indeed, few concertgoers would bring much business to the
boardwalks located miles from the offshore track. This "International Youth Explosion" shocked many locals, but not
their participating children: "One young man danced in the
nude to the driving bass of Iron Butterfly. No one seemed to
mind." The crowds, even with some rain, were enthusiastic;
there was one unfortunate auto death, eighteen drug arrests.
Only Frank Zappa, with the Mothers of Invention, seemed
"irked" by the crowd's demand for "the hardest rock and the
heaviest blues" and "snarled," " 'We didn't want to take too
much of your time.' "[5] At the opposite end of the ideological
spectrum, Hamilton Township mayor William Davies
stressed that there would be no more such concerts in the
foreseeable future.[6] And there weren't.

Several Coasters attended the concert; it was the big event
of the period. Many still regret missing it. But finally, it was a
visit, even an invasion, not a located, rooted domestic uprising. The countercultural train of liberation and self-expression arrived late to Atlantic County and took on lots of

passengers, but most were simply along for the ride. Hedonism wasn't new to the area; the accoutrements of a Woodstock Nation were. But most class of 1966 Coasters, certainly
more so than their younger siblings, were children of the
complexities of the Eisenhower era, engaged in subterranean
deviations from the ideology of family and community, in
what Barbara Ehrenreich calls "the flight from commitment."
Coasters, for the most part, didn't perceive themselves as
"growing up absurd," but they did recognize and seek out
greater zones of choice and longer periods of youthful cavort-
ing before inevitably settling down to adult responsibilities.
Few became hippies; more were what one partier calls weekend warriors, those who tried to balance conventional aspirations with libidinous dreams.[7]

Part of the difficulty in assessing how much the Sixties
affected baby boomers lies in defining such a decades-driven
category of historical meaning. In brief, what do we mean
when we refer to "the Sixties"? Indeed, there are many
meanings, sometimes contradictory, certainly confused. I
would contend that the Sixties refers to that historical period
roughly beginning with the election of John Fitzgerald Kennedy and ending with the collapse of South Vietnam in 1975.
The distinctive quality of this period is its belief in what
Richard Flacks calls "making history," the emergence of
an optimism, a hopefulness that people can and will trans-
form the body politic.[8] In more conservative periods, like
the years between the end of World War II and the comple-
tion of Eisenhower's second term, the hope that one can
change the world collapses, and "making a life"—that is,
attending to one's personal, familial, and community business—is all.

What produces such moments of public, historical hope? Perhaps most significant is the existence of an agent of social, historical change, a group within the body politic, that achieves legitimacy as representing important civic values and goals. In the Thirties, it was the workers, the CIO unionists, Steinbeck's "people";[9] in the 1960s, it began with the heroism of the Southern-based civil rights movement. From there it expanded, at times exponentially, but for the most part building on the struggles begun in Montgomery, Little Rock, and Greensboro.

The dilemma at this point is that the Sixties forked: one path focused on issues of social justice, poverty, and peace; the other on liberation, self-expression, and experiment. And, to confuse matters, the paths wound like a DNA molecule, with many Sixties travelers pursuing both strands. Those on the freedom road were usually identified as part of what they called the Movement; they were members of the New Left, identified with, if not formally members of, Students for a Democratic Society (SDS), often just called radicals. Those on the liberation road were heirs of anti-middle-class bohemian rebellions, like the Beats, identified with a counterculture, and were called hippies or freaks.[10]

From another point of view, the Sixties raised fundamental questions that became central to the political discourse: What is patriotism? (Can it include refusing to fight for your country when you feel your country is wrong?) Can we be a racially just society? (Is integration possible, desirable?) How do we decide what is right and wrong in personal behavior? (Premarital sex? Doing your own thing? Drug experimentation? Nudity? Profanity?) Are there any authorities outside of onself? How are men and women to live together in a postindustrial society? How can we reconcile economic growth with the well-being of the environment? I would emphasize that we are still struggling with these issues: nation, race, human nature, gender, nature; in that sense the Sixties are still with us as the questions over which we argue and disagree and on which we sometimes compromise.

Many Coast baby boomers were affected, at the margins, by the countercultural aspects of the Sixties. They "loosened up," although one must emphasize that the counterculture was only a stage in a long-term trend toward sexual permissiveness. They were touched less, on the other hand, by the political radicalism. Coasters interviewed did not know any activists and, for the most part, were hostile to the kinds of history making in which they believed activists were engaged. There were no New Leftists on the Coast. In fact, there was considerable controversy when, in 1969, an SDS activist from NYU was invited to speak at Coastal High School's Political Science Club forum, along with representatives from the NAACP and the John Birch Society.[11] Such a rare event was never repeated.

Rodney Wayne (see profile) came close to being an activist while in college, but as he notes, he held off and kept some distance, believing most campus radicals to be posturing. Tom Rogers kids his wife, Sally, about exaggerating her involvement in one fairly moderate peace vigil. Pam Lane pokes fun at her flirtations with being antiauthority. Rodney fought pitched battles with his parents; the more countercultural Frank Feller had an uneasy truce with his; but it is striking that most Coasters even marginally involved with either activism or the counterculture lived two lives: one at school, the other at home. Their explorations away from the mainstream did not include what was perhaps characteristic of dissident youth—the direct, even perversely pleasurable challenge to one's parents, the freaking out of the straights, the bourgeoisie.

In some instances, this timidity was deep. Polly Smythe longed to join the rebels but felt constrained, unable to act. In other cases, a distancing irony allowed some intellectual joining but only through deflating the professed motives of the activists. But very few even felt the urge to rebel; the vast majority felt either obliviousness or disdain.

The majority of those who attended college state that their campuses had either very small protest movements or none at all. These were often Southern schools, some very preppy in reputation, others sectarian and very conservative. As Mary Ives describes her "yuppie heaven" campus, "I think I remember protesters once; it was no great shakes. I was insulated from it." Mel Roszak can't recall any antiwar protests on his Southern campus.

Diane Halsey went to Glassboro, which had some activist presence. With a future husband soon to join the Navy, she reacted: "They had me very irate; I got angry at them because here's [my husband] who is not being forced to do it but chooses to do it, so that we have the right to stand up and holler and scream. I didn't necessarily agree with every single thing [about the war], but we can't pick and choose in something like that, what you're going to go along with and what you're not." Jimmy O'Brien, at a large Southern state university, was friendly with a few of the antiwar activists in his freshman year, especially one coed, but "she then went into the hard core, anti-Vietnam," he explains. They would occasionally talk, but Jimmy, who "didn't have too many feelings one way or the other" about Vietnam, found that his sports involvements led him away from contact with activists:

"It was kind of like you stayed within your own athletic realm." Sports, fraternity and sorority life, and work to support school were all factors in restricting contact with campus dissidents. Too often the literature on Sixties campus activism suggests almost a New Left reign of terror or, at the least, a fashionable conformity.[12] Coaster experience indicates that many campuses remained safely mainstream and, in fact, intolerant of the isolated rebels, cultural and political. The experience of being an activist, someone consciously attempting to produce social change, is deeply alien to the mainstream; it is almost as if the activists were foreigners, even creatures from another planet. To Coasters it is close to impossible to imagine oneself engaged in such visible and deviant behaviors. For the most part, Coaster's view such estrangement more with amazement than with anger; but resentments at what seemed to be privileged and snobbish activists occasionally erupted.

Matt Blake, at culinary school, "right in the center of Yale," feels that "they treated us like we were dirt, Yalies. There was a lot of protesting; I wasn't bothered by it." But he adds with heavy sarcasm, when Yalies deigned to speak to him about some political issue, "I just said, 'Right on,' and I'd go to work." Few Coasters went to the most elite, Ivy institutions. Several mentioned rumors that the few who did go to places like Columbia lost their bearings and got caught up in "all that hippie stuff." Ann Holvi was one of the rare Coasters to live in the midst of Manhattan's adversary culture in those years. When her urban, Jewish boyfriend ridiculed her for not knowing who César Chavez was, she stood revealed within the Coast insulation that had isolated her from the kinds of public issues energizing elite campuses and cosmopolitan cultural centers. And the anticipation of such ridicule lays at the base of some segment of mainstream suspicion of Sixties radicals.

Several female graduates had husbands serving in Vietnam; they tended to view antiwar protesters as putting their loved ones at risk. Conflicts were sometimes brought home; Carol Rizzo's Vietnam-vet husband still will not talk with one of his cousins who ran to Canada to escape the draft.

There was significant sentiment for George Wallace, the candidate most reflecting resentments at the challenges of the Sixties movements.[13] Five male graduates voiced enthusiasm for the Alabama governor during the late Sixties and early Seventies. Several others, including women, while not endorsing Wallace, shared much of his right-wing populism. Racism certainly played a role in such loyalties, since more than a few Coasters expressed resentments about what they perceived as reverse discrimination, for example, affirmative action quotas on the job and special treatment for low-income scholarship students. The "backlash" against African-American gains and demands includes a strong minority of Coasters, although this must be balanced with a comparable segment who became more racially tolerant.

Mel Farmer, who thought Wallace was "a basic guy" saying what others felt, admits that race "may have had a little to do with it." All but one of the pro-Wallace baby boomers did not go on to college. They sought jobs in an economically troubled county where old-boy networking had been the norm. As adults they have felt squeezed by new rules and new players. The civil rights challenges matched up with others, especially those from women, to produce resentments. The entire environment epitomized by the Coast suburbs seemed under seige. And the attackers occasionally were within; for example, several graduates blame Ray Brenner's divorce on his wife's feminist demands, and Davy Hunter views the failure of his several marriages to his difficulties adjusting to the changed expectations of his more egalitarian wives. Life was difficult enough without having to cope with these new marital expectations and threats to job opportunity.

The Sixties movements invested their hopes in particular insurgencies. They looked outward, sometimes romantically, to Third World struggles. They saw the American Dream as illusory, if not carcinogenic. As SDS radicals and McCarthy liberals and yippies and hippies chanted, "The whole world is watching," during the Chicago Democratic Convention in 1968, most Coasters were part of the viewing audience—if they tuned in—that blamed the demonstrators for the "police riot."[14] They were, in some ways, less a part of what is labeled the Sixties generation than a generational extension of the American middle classes going through turbulent times. They were, as Richard Nixon identified them in 1969, part of the silent majority.

More than 70 percent of them voted for Nixon in 1972, their initiation into the electoral process. Interestingly, the silent majority was decidedly male, with men going for Nixon more than four to one and women splitting fifty–fifty between the Republican candidate and George McGovern. Almost 25 percent didn't vote. By 1976, the gender difference lessened, as nearly 80 percent went with Gerald Ford, including a two to one female margin. By the 1980s presidential elections, the gender gap had disappeared.

Many blamed Johnson for the war, but Nixon, at least in retrospect, is not viewed heroically. Most Coasters respect what they perceive as his accomplishments and believe him to be a very smart fellow, but a sizable minority lay the burden of America's crisis of confidence during the 1970s at his feet. Most Coast baby boomers are similar to their parents in preferring moderate, pro-business Republicans; it would be difficult to find someone more of a fit to Coast specifications than George Bush.

Yet during the 1988 campaign, I heard little enthusiasm for Bush's candidacy. Most characteristic was a suspicion of all candidates, a feeling that the campaign was just a manipulative show, the results of which would be without significance. Most voted for Bush, but it was mile-wide and inch-deep support. Coast baby boomers share with their generation a deep skepticism, at times cynicism, about politics and politicians.[15] They do come out to vote, at rates averaging approximately 80 percent, but their hearts are elsewhere. In this sense, they are very much a part of the baby-boom generation.

It would be easy to conclude that Coast baby boomers, like Bush's vice-president, "glided into manhood as if the Sixties never happened."[16] At least the guys. But Coast class of 1966 graduates are, with few exceptions, neither as privileged nor as callow and hypocritical as Dan Quayle. Only a very few approach genuine wealth and privilege; more critically, most eschew the bombast of right-wing rhetoric. Their silence is not golden, but it has the silver lining, at the least, of some modesty.

Only a handful are part of the 18 percent of their "dramatically diverse" generation who joined, at any level, the hippie counterculture. Indeed, more are part of the 30 percent of baby boomers who opposed such rebellions. But the largest proportion fit within what a Hart Associates survey indicates as the 76 percent of baby boomers born between 1947 and

1956 who say they lived through the late 1960s and early 1970s without any involvements in the various movements associated with that era.[17]

According to the Hart survey, the Sixties movements affected 21 percent of baby boomers "only some," and 34 percent "not that much."[18] The life experiences of Coasters essentially occurred within such parameters. And yet one must be cautious and sensitive to the contradictory realities. For example, several of the Wallace supporters also admired Robert Kennedy and his idealism. More strikingly, many members of the class of 1966 have found themselves changed, often unwittingly, by the movements they characteristically ignored or eschewed. Several have become modest supporters of environmental causes, joining organizations like Greenpeace. Most express reservations about foreign adventures, another Vietnam, and like their generational peers have a mistrust of government authority that distinguishes them from their parents. Many, despite the continuing segregated realities of their lives, are genuinely more tolerant racially. True, it is easy for people in the last years of the twentieth century to say complimentary things about Martin Luther King Jr. and the struggle to eliminate legal segregation. But the rights movements of the Sixties signaled an erosion of certain parochialisms regarding race, but also religion, ethnicity, gender, and lifestyle. People are more tolerant because of the 1960s. Certainly some, unfortunately, are part of the regression toward bigotry associated wih the Reagan administration, but most have learned, at several steps removed, important lessons. One feels it when baby boomers talk about their parents' prejudices, when Carol Rizzo chastises her dad for disapproving of the drop-in visit by an African-American neighbor: "Get with it; it's the Eighties!" Gender changes seem to be occurring more slowly (see Chapter 7). Slowest of all are reductions in homophobia; gay bashing seems to be one of the remaining arenas for legitimate and open ethnic humor. It's quite possible that among Coasters there is more homophobia now than thirty years ago.

Finally, Coast baby-boomers, for the most part, avoid coming to grips with the kinds of questions and challenges concerning patriotism, race, values, nature, and gender raised during the 1960s. They are truly silent, if not a majority. They stay within the cocoon of their suburbs, concentrating on what they feel they can control: family, friendships, sometimes local community. Thus they make a life and leave making history to others.

But history already made continues to impinge on their lives. Carol Rizzo's husband doesn't talk to her about his Vietnam experiences. Like many Vietnam vets, he only shares such memories with fellow vets, in this case, Bobby Green. Carol says, "Vinnie lost his best friend that he went in with; my daughter went last week and took his name off the [Vietnam Veterans] Memorial, brought it home for her father." History, like weeds, has a way of finding its way between the cracks that inevitably form in our skillful efforts to cement over the past.

Wealth in itself is innocent. The rich man in himself is innocent. But wealth and rich men surrounded by poverty and poor men are guilty.
   —John Fowles, *The Aristos*

5

White on Black

The Coastal High School 1966 yearbook is lily-white. There were no African-American students, administrators, teachers, maintenance or custodial workers. A black matron was hired on the janitorial staff several years later but "left because the kids were so rough on her." Most 1966 graduates do not recall knowing many blacks while they were growing up. Some admit that their parents, especially their fathers, were "like the Archie Bunker–type guy," with strong prejudice directed toward blacks, but also some aimed at Jews and Catholics. One graduate with deep local roots had a grandfather who belonged to a local Ku Klux Klan klavern, and Melanie Combs Wayne remembers that during a walk with her dad when she was a little girl two black men came "running out of the woods, tarred and feathered." Most racial prejudice, however, took less violent form; housing and job discrimination and racial jokes were all too characteristic of the area.

New residents are sometimes reminded that Atlantic County is south of the Mason-Dixon line, evoking stereotypical images of *Deliverance* rednecks with shotgun racks in their pickup trucks marked by Confederate flags and Smith and Wesson decals, swilling beer and itching to terrorize blacks, Jews, hippies, and anyone else suspected of deviation from the gospel according to George Wallace or the Reverend Carl McIntyre. Indeed, such images reflect some part of local reality, especially among those with Southern roots. Six parents of the forty-seven graduates interviewed were born and bred in the South, mostly fathers who met their wives while in the service at Camp Boardwalk during World War II. As Linda Duncan Gent recalls, "My father's from the deep South; they [my family] hated blacks, so I grew up with a lot of hatred." But such attitudes weren't restricted to the Southern-born; Diane Ruth Halsey remembers her stepfather hassling her over a college girlfriend who he assumed to be black because of her name. Yet others offer less prejudiced upbringings, often shaped by what Nora Reilly Bennett calls her parents' "Christian outlook," the belief that we're all God's children and, therefore, deserving of compassion and respect.

Perhaps most characteristic is the perception among almost all Coast baby boomers that their parents carried contradictory but deep prejudices. Pam Baird Lane recalls, "My parents weren't terrifically tolerant and yet they wouldn't allow us to be prejudiced. But my dad called black people 'spear-chuckers,' you know; he's intolerant of everything—he's intolerant of bad drivers, of me." To Coasters, the bigotry almost softens in its universalism. Her mother, Pam declares, "doesn't like gay people or fundamentalists. She's not anti-black, but it's like blacks better keep their place; they better not start up too much." Coasters often subvert their denials of racism with incriminating caveats.

This sense of keeping one's place and being invisible is central to understanding the Coast racial environment. Few pay attention to the area's recent past. Most prefer to downplay the long history of racism within this part of South Jersey. For example, the Atlantic City public schools were segregated until 1947; as late as the 1930s, African-American nurses could not train at Atlantic City Hospital, nor could African-American physicians use the facilities for their patients. As historian Herbert James Foster describes the environment up to the Great Depression, "Blacks were barred from restaurants, amusement piers and booths; they were denied various privileges by stores; were admitted to hotels only as servants; were segregated in clinics and hospitals; and could only bathe in one section of the beach at Missouri Avenue."[1] To most Coasters, this is, at best, merely the past and without much relevance to what they claim to be a more racially neutral contemporary environment.

For the most part, members of the class of 1966 do not recall much about race, racism, or civil rights during their childhood and adolescent years. "I didn't have deep feelings, I was removed from it," Jack Claire explains. "We had no black people in Channing. We never felt that we were bigots; it was, they just didn't happen to live in Channing; they lived in Pleasantville. We weren't in contact with them, so it wasn't something you had to deal with on a day-to-day basis." But many others agree that racial epithets were quite common. Rodney Wayne admits, "There were no feelings that blacks were equal; they weren't even called blacks; they were Negroes and niggers and spooks and jigs and all this stuff."

Many Coasters had moved out of Atlantic City or Pleasantville as urban decay and black migration into formerly
white neighborhoods generated flight. Only 37.5 percent of
1966 graduates were born in the offshore towns; 32.5 percent
were born in either Atlantic City or Pleasantville; and 42.5
percent spent some of their infancy in urban environments
experiencing rising black populations. Despite the nostalgia
many Coast baby boomers evoke for the tranquil, small-town
stability they identify with their growing up, their lives were
significantly shaped by geographical mobility and, consequently, by what they had left behind. Fewer than 10 percent
of their parents grew up in the offshore towns of Wilbur,
Channing, or South Bay. As such, Coasters were part of the
postwar transformation of our landscape through the twin
processes of suburbanization and ghettoization. To Coasters,
the issue of race translates as the tragic story of what happened to Atlantic City and Pleasantville, that is, how those
towns were ruined by the influx of African-Americans. The
names of towns become the code words for complex racial
resentments.

Nora Reilly Bennett, who grew up in Pleasantville, denies
having any racial problems: "one of my best friends was
black." But she notes, without a sense of contradiction, that
things "just steadily got worse; they started moving on our
street." Carol Smith Rizzo, born in Atlantic City, moved out
of Pleasantville to South Bay when she was in second grade.
"We moved," she admits, "because colored were moving into
Pleasantville, and that was the only reason that we moved."
Marilyn Hager recalls that when the new Coastal High School
opened, the families of at least two girlhood friends whose
families moved over from Margate to Channing to escape the

increasing minority enrollment at Atlantic City High School.

Rodney Wayne remembers an incident at the Mill Road School in Wilbur: "An all-white school in an all-white town, and a black kid came walking down the road, and every kid on that school ground, a couple of hundred of us, ran up to the chain-link fence and stood there and watched that black kid walk by as though he had walked off a spaceship. He looked scared to death—he didn't look to the right or the left; he just looked down and kept going." Rodney also recalls a black family coming in for breakfast when he was working as a busboy at an Atlantic City restaurant: "I remember standing there staring at them in the doorway to make sure that they could know and see my contempt before I would condescend to bring them their coffee, and I did everything except spill it in their laps to make them feel they weren't wanted."

"If they were black," Matt Blake recalls thinking as a youth, "let them go to Pleasantville High School or Atlantic City, but stay away from here." But many, like Mel Farmer, minimize the racism, claiming that "we never really thought about it," concluding, "Nobody would burn a cross in front of their house, or anything like that; it didn't happen." As Mac Schmidt asserts, "We called a black person a nigger, [but] it wasn't necessarily a bad thing to be calling him a nigger—it was the way it was." "The way it was" limited contact, at least among guys, to sports competition, during which there were tensions but also some breakthroughs of respect based on performance on the field. But off the field, white Coasters, other than shopping or movie trips into Pleasantville, saw few blacks. Actual knowledge, albeit of a special sort, was limited to those whose affluent families had black servants. Margaret Jensen Ricci fondly remembers her parents' housecleaner Clara: "I loved her dearly; she was in her seventies or eighties, and she used to get the bus and come over from Atlantic City. She was fabulous; she waxed the floors, and she made great fried chicken. I really liked her a lot, and she told me about her father that was a slave, and picking cotton in Georgia." Dave Ford says that he "was raised by a black lady, and she's more my mother than my mother is. And because of that," he concludes, "I think I understand black people more."

Margaret Ricci remembers one of her public school teachers telling the class that sometime in the future there would be a black child in their school: "and I just remember thinking, 'Oh, my God, that would be awful.' " Yet when she had attended a Catholic grammar school, she had had black girlfriends who were allowed to visit her home. She remembers thinking that Martin Luther King Jr. was "a bad person." Her father had told her, "That nigger's really stirring up trouble." And, she adds, "I saw them all gathering together and I thought, 'Oh, my God, there's going to be riots and everything.' I was really afraid." In reconstructing her sense of black life back then, Margaret concedes, "I had no idea what their problem was at that time because I thought, 'Well, they're allowed to vote and they have jobs and everything.' I really couldn't understand it."

Such confusions are typical of Coast baby-boomers. They show little curiosity about the history of African-Americans, though they are aware that slavery was evil and that as a result the South was different. Many bolster their sense of their own racial tolerances by comparing their environment with that of the South. Within this framework, the Klan represents racism, next to which less venal prejudice appears insignificant. Several of the rowdies used to go to the South to hunt with the Green boys and their dad. They felt reenforced, as Joey Campion asserts, in their belief that "racial problems all centered in the South." But he adds that "kids our age, we kind of took pride in saying, 'I don't give a shit about politics, I don't care about the blacks.' " And given their ignorance, Campion admits, "it was easy for us to say, 'It's the nigger's fault.' "

A few Coasters still hold to their parents' prejudices, agreeing with Bette Carter Roszak that blacks move up to the area from the South "to get onto welfare. The mothers would send the kids to Woolworth's," and they would hit the bars, where they "were getting pregnant from every Tom, Dick, and Harry." Bette, who admired Robert Kennedy, declares, "I detest Martin Luther King because of how he was going about it, pitting the blacks against the whites," encouraging "minority screaming minority."

On the other hand, such reflections need to be contrasted with a growing racial tolerance and understanding on the part of many Coast baby boomers. Jack Claire, who remembers blacks required by custom to sit in the back of the buses that took him to Ocean City, doesn't recall any discussion of Martin Luther King Jr. in his classes. As he has aged and come to a greater knowledge about the racial past, mostly from television and the newspaper, he has found out "what a great person this guy was." Carol Rizzo recalls being oblivious to the civil rights movement. Many, like Mel Farmer, viewed King as "a troublemaker." Judd Dennis, who now sees him as a "great man," reflects, "Hindsight's a wonderful thing, but you must remember, when all this was going on we said, 'Why don't he go home? Why's he stirring up the pot?' And that was my feeling at the time. I can see now, or at least I think I can, 'Thank goodness he did or it would be a worse world.' ''

When I asked about their political heroes, many recalled John Fitzgerald Kennedy, but none associated him with civil rights. Indeed several admired George Wallace, whose political star as a national candidate was rising in 1966. Most look back on that admiration as an error, but in most cases only reluctantly admit that racism was a factor. They prefer to recall pro-Wallace sentiment as an attraction to the Alabama governor's honesty—"He was telling it like it is"—skirting the issue of what was the nature and tone of the telling. And more than occasionally, Coasters take comfort by reminding themselves that South Jersey is different from, less racially prejudiced than the South, that, in brief, they are not Klansmen.

It is difficult to get beneath the surface rationalizations about race and racism. Most perceive that they are at the least less racially prejudiced than their parents, if not color-blind. They seem to believe that racial prejudice can be tossed off like a worn-out coat, that the past is, simply, the past. Nevertheless, within that past, Coasters paid little attention to the 1964 Democratic Party Convention held in Atlantic City, at which the Mississippi Freedom Democrats vied for seats following the exhilarating and gruesome Freedom Summer of voter registration, freedom schools, and the murders of Goodman, Chaney, and Schwerner. They did not hear Fannie Lou Hamer, from Ruleville, Mississippi—fired, harassed, threatened, beaten, whipped for her courageous voter registration efforts—stir the convention and a packed assembly at the nearby Union Baptist Church.[2] This was a nonevent for most Coasters; what could they have made of Fannie Hamer other than a poorly educated agitator or, at best, someone living in a radically different universe from themselves? Was it possible easily to throw off one's racial prejudices without coming to grips with the history, with the biographies, of the civil rights martyrs and heroes, with the day-to-day humiliations intertwined with acts of human dignity and courage that together made up our racial heritage?

The Atlantic City area of the 1950s and 1960s wasn't as different from the South as Coasters like to recall. The problems, however, until the civil rights revolution began to reach the lives of white middle-income people, were invisible. In fact, they weren't perceived as problems but merely as the way things were. In discussing the absence of blacks in the South Bay bar scene, Sally Vincent Rogers muses, "Isn't it awful; I don't remember having any problems with it. They just didn't [patronize]; in fact, then everybody had their own place; I mean, Atlantic City, Pleasantville, they were all in their own communities—everyone was happy to have their own community. I never thought about them having to come in; I really don't remember too much about that." The majority Northern culture, able to compare itself favorably with the stigmatized, Jim Crow South, accepted patterns of de facto segregation, assuming in its ignorance that such arrangements were the natural order of things.

Life after high school—in the service, at college, and at work—helped to shake up such illusions, but didn't characteristically stimulate new understanding. In some ways, it established new wrinkles on older biases.

Most of those who were in the service minimize racial tensions, suggesting, as Dave Ford does, that "we had to live with these people; we all had a job to do, and we knew what we had to do." Several vets refer to problems they heard about but didn't directly experience, although Bobby Green saw an ugly racial brawl his first day in a combat area. Mostly the service added to the growing awareness during the later 1960s that blacks were deeply aggrieved about racial injustices and that many whites were resistant to accepting such challenges. Most of all, Coaster service experiences reflect the unstated realities, the invisible truths, of racial and social-class advantages. Harry Kearns, who, in a striking example, used pull to get into a guard unit, easily accepted himself as a "role model" for "black or poor Southern boys" destined for Vietnam (see Chapter 3).

For several, college was the first place they had any experience with black people. A few recall such experiences, supplemented by course work, as critical to their shedding of stereotypes. Pam Baird Lane did her student teaching at an all-black school in a town in Virginia: "Maybe my soc. courses made me [more tolerant]; I just never had a problem with black anything. They were people; they deserved everything that anybody ever deserved; so, I mean, what's the big deal? But I was repulsed by whatever authority was being used to put them down." Harry Kearns joined an integrated fraternity at Montclair State: "I'll never forget one of the first times I brought one of my fraternity brothers home; he was a Puerto Rican, Bobby Castro. I said, 'Mom, I'm bringing home one of my buddies; his name's Bob.' She said, 'Great, bring him home,' so I brought him home. This guy's a great big 210-pound Puerto Rican; funny—my parents, he had them rolling on the floor."

Yet while education and actual experience seem to have softened, if not eliminated, much racial stereotyping, there remain notable caveats. Among those Coasters who attended Glassboro, there was deep resentment, still smoldering after

nearly twenty years, over what they perceived as racial favor-
itism. As Al Judson describes, "The [Martin Luther] King
scholars were low-income blacks who they were trying to give
an opportunity to go through college, and they were just . . .
they were a bad element—they had guns on them." His wife
Meg adds, "Everything was paid for, plus they were given a
monthly allowance—there were people like Al and I: Al was
working; I had two jobs to try to put myself through college;
but they were given an allowance. They didn't even go to
class; they never even went to class. They were going out
buying stereos and threatening white students; it was a real
fiasco." Diane Ruth Halsey adds, "When I got to Glassboro,
I saw the extreme of the Martin Luther King people, who
were there strictly because they were black and underprivi-
leged . . . they would meet in front of the hall and tell us how
oppressed they were—his dorm is all paid for, his books are
all paid for, his meals all paid for, driving away in a new car,
and my parents didn't give me a penny toward college. I made
myself every cent, put myself through college—with the
exception of my grandmother, two semesters did give me
tuition—but the rest I worked. While I was in school, all
through, at ACC [Atlantic Community College] for three
semesters, at night I was working full-time at the phone
company." Diane's seething resentment was matched by that
of Sally Vincent Rogers, married and pregnant while seeking,
along with her husband Tom, to graduate: "I can remember
feeling angry because we worked so hard to get through
school; we saved every penny we made in the summer; I'm
telling you we spent nothing on anything extraneous. And
here are all these black kids who were going for free, and they
weren't even studying—and that grated on me, that bothered
me. Of course now I think, 'Why didn't I see if they had

something for us?' but we never thought to go to the social system for help. . . . These kids walked across the campus; there was militant groups all across the campus, and I think that the civil rights was really coming to a head there; I was ambivalent about it because I felt, 'Why them and not us?' I didn't really understand everything that was going on."

Coast baby boomers had grown up in a white, relatively affluent cocoon, often hearing grown-ups blame the deterioration of urban areas like Atlantic City on blacks. They knew next to nothing about the legacy of slavery and Jim Crow, or about the mechanization of Southern agriculture, which forced many blacks north in the post–World War II environment. Most clung to the belief that prejudice was declining and that equal opportunity was now the norm. As such, they could not understand or accept what they perceived as reverse discrimination, special privileges. Most have a strong desire to demonstrate that such opposition is not evidence of racial prejudice. Al Judson, for example, tries to provide balance to his criticism of the King scholars program at Glassboro: "I knew [black] guys who were trying to do the best they could, [but] they were in the minority."

Most Coast baby boomers are not wealthy; many come from families closer to the lower middle class: small store owners, bakers, postal clerks. Many have worked hard for what they have achieved. But at the same time, there is often an exaggeration of their hardships, a downplaying of relative privileges. For example, one critic of the King scholars was able to shift, without breaking stride, from stories about his penurious youth to discussions of his season tickets to Philadelphia Eagle games at that very time.

The issue here isn't the abuse of social reform; it is quite likely that significant corruption existed in the Glassboro program at that time. Liberal remedies, often driven by white guilt, have all too often patronized African-Americans in not holding them to appropriate standards. This is, tragically, a part of our present racial agony. And it is not enough to reduce concerns over such corruptions, such violations of fairness and equity, to racism. A hardworking white student from a lower-middle- or working-class household is under-standably angered by liberal policies that reward the unwor-thy. But at the same time, one must explore the highlighting, the zeroing in on such corruptions, the single-minded virtual obsession with black violations. No such resentment seems directed, for example, at the less qualified or lazy white student accepted only because one parent is an alumnus, or at the less qualified or incompetent worker accepted into build-ing-trades unions because of family or friendship networks. One graduate, when asked about her teaching experiences in mostly black Pleasantville schools, immediately started a tirade against the King scholars. What accounted for such a diversion? How could any Coaster really, with accuracy, assess the extent to which black students took advantage of their scholarships? How many black people did they knew, to what extent, with what level of intimacy? It seems that middle-class white baby-boomers were thoroughly unpre-pared to come to grips with any civil rights challenges that went beyond a formal commitment to equal opportunity. None recognized or acknowledged the vast array of govern-ment transfers, from the GI Bill to the 1956 Highway Act, that helped to sustain their own good fortune, or the ways in which the Jim Crow, racist past was inevitably going to distort a present-minded color blindness. The shift to color blindness—at least as stated goal, if not accomplished real-ity—should not be denigrated; it's more than most of their parents were willing to concede. But it rested on a assumption that a light switch had been turned in American racial attitudes and behaviors by, let's say, 1970, that white Americans had finally, reluctantly, under pressure from a belatedly valued civil rights movement, come to accept equal rights and treatment regardless of race. America, within this perspective, was now beyond race and therefore, by definition, racism.

For those who entered the workforce, either directly from Coastal or after service or college, there were similar contradictions. Bobby Green, who returned to the area in the late Sixties looking for employment, says, "Everything changed; we're not crying that now the white man is the underdog, but you watch a lot of things change; I remember coming out of the service and trying to get into the utilities, that was my goal—you worked for the electric company, Bell Telephone, the gas—'Sorry, we can't hire you; we have to hire some of these people.' Kind of made me a little bit bitter." Joey Campion recalls his first experiences with blacks at a local plastics company as "unpleasant," "a bad work experience" of absenteeism, theft, malingering, and complaints. At the same time, he contrasts his moderate views with those of the bigoted white workers who refused even to work with the newly hired blacks.

Dave Ford admits, "I don't say that I don't sometime call someone a dumb nigger or something like that, but I don't think that I'm that prejudiced." At that point in the interview, Dave turns to his wife for confirmation; she replies, "You're not like that, but you talk like that." The key is, perhaps, the caveat "that prejudiced"—an advance, but an unmeasured advance, which therefore leaves lots of room for ambiguity. Dave counters by telling what happened to him while working for Hilton Hotels: "They wanted me to be the executive chef and take the job away from this guy who was a black chef; they didn't want a black man out in front, walking around our hotel—and that's when I left; I said, 'I'm not going to.' He was the one who trained me. 'I understand what you're trying to do, and I don't want to be a part of it. I like this guy a whole lot—you're going to take his title away and give it to me, and he's still going to be a chef, but you don't want to see him out in front?' I said, 'That's prejudice; I'm not interested in being a part of it. I don't care how much money you offer me; I'm not interested.' " Dave perceives his behavior as a measure of his commitment to equal rights, to an American sense of fair play. Would he have acted as nobly if he hadn't personally known and liked the black chef? There is progress; many Coasters, particularly those with broadening life experiences such as college, no longer find crude racial epithets or racial humor acceptable. They want to believe that they have left prejudices behind them, but their contemporary attitudes reveal tensions.

Rodney Wayne, who is among those Coasters most touched by the political currents of the 1960s and now works as a probation officer in Atlantic City, seeing drug problems, broken families, and child abuse, suggests the dilemma: "I became in danger of becoming a racist for a while there because people just didn't give a shit about me or their own children, no respect for lives, their own lives or anything; and I started thinking, 'This is what they're like,' you know? I was fortunate to work with some people who were some of the finest people I've ever known—it's just that there are a whole lot of those others out there, and I don't know what it would take to change them." While Rodney and some others seek, with little expectation, resolutions to our racial and poverty problems, others, like Nora Reilly Bennett, feel squeezed:

"You have to be very rich or you have to be very poor, and the middle class really the very worst end of the deal. Everyone else has a shrewd way of getting tax breaks, or you're on welfare, okay? and we get the brunt of it, and that I get upset with." As one of those closer to middle- and lower-middle-class realities, Nora reflects anxieties about possible misfortunes: "If, God forbid, my husband was out of work and we didn't have the insurance and had to go for foodstamps, we'd probably be denied because we thought enough to save some money—but we can't drain our savings to pay for the food, so we'd be denied foodstamps, and that would really upset me. When you have these poor slobs, these rotten people, out on welfare, having kids, and more kids, by all these different fathers . . . Don't get me started on that!"

In the same vein, Aggie Jones Rizzuto warns, "Don't get me started," and then begins to express her resentment over high auto-insurance costs: "There is no middle—Middle America is breaking down, shrinking down, and there's no way. Everyone wants Middle America to pay for it, and you can't. I'll grant you that there are some of these people who are probably victims, couldn't get insurance because someone else hit them, but I'm paying for them. Who's paying for me? *Meee?*"

This perception of being victimized, squeezed within the middle, needs to be taken seriously and with respect. These, after all, are hardworking people struggling to sustain traditional values about hard work, family, and responsibility in a hedonistic environment. Some are remarkably honest and self-critical, like Matt Blake, who admits that "there are still a lot of prejudices": "I'm not going to say that I'm not a prejudiced man; how would you feel if a black family moved next door to you, even if that black man is working with me, side by side? I would feel uncomfortable, and I don't know how to express that. Working with people, if we have to do a job together and we're both making X amount of dollars, why not? Why is he getting three dollars an hour less than I am? Because I'm white? That's not right. So I do have prejudices, but in some respects I don't." Others, like Stan Burke, while noting his neighbor's discomfort with a black family that moved in, suggests that he doesn't find it to be a problem "as long as they're not disruptive."

One measure of remaining racial sensitivities is the visceral responses to the mention of Jesse Jackson. One of the most iconoclastic Coasters, the still-hippyish Frank Feller, when asked about Jackson as a president, replies, "Jackson? Canada, I'd go to Canada." I am struck not so much by the negative evaluations as by the tone, the intensity, often the rage of the responses. "I'm certainly not thrilled with Jesse Jackson," Carol Smith Rizzo asserts. "I don't think he's president material; I don't like his views. He's on [television], I'll turn him off." The self-described born-again Christian Sue Ellen Bach fiercely proclaims that it's "a lie" to compare Pat Robertson (her favored candidate) with Jackson, whose candidacy "kills" her. Pam Baird Lane, a more moderate and secular voter, has "a great deal of respect for the man," but is alienated by his special interest candidacy: "I don't care if he's black; he just represents a special interest group that will go along with him because they're a special interest group, when it may not be the best for everybody—so it just scares me, and it would be the same if we had twelve billion gay people and they all supported a gay candidate."

Most Coast baby boomers aren't unreconstructed Wallaceites, although some, without prompting, slyly suggest during discussion about the 1988 campaign, "You know who

I *don't* like!" More characteristic is an effort at balance and fairness, as in Diane Halsey's admiration for Jackson's oratory but annoyance at his ghetto style when speaking before black audiences: "Why are you coming down to a lower level? Isn't your thought to bring that level up?" Diane, an elementary school teacher, associates what she perceives as Jackson's patronizing demagogy with lower standards for black children in some of the local schools.

Even the most thoughtful of Coasters, forced to come to grips with the practices of the past, talk of putting the past behind them and emphasizing the color-blind present and future. They desperately want to believe that we have become a color-blind society, and react angrily to what they perceive as do-gooder whites and professional blacks who stubbornly insist on opening up old wounds. They are typical Americans, clinging to an affirmative, mythic past, blotting out unpleasant historical truths and, as such, finding that affirmative action programs, set-asides, and special scholarships all seem to violate their sense of equity. When the past is ignored except as myth, color blindness can simply be declared. Sometimes there's even a conscious effort to reverse what is viewed as reverse discrimination. Marilyn Hager, working in the casino industry, asserts, "I am anti quotas for minorities; I see white males who are more deserving of jobs that are given to other people, and I'm speaking women, blacks, Orientals, whatever. I don't like it; I'm outspoken about it at work. I find myself sometimes downgrading some women and Orientals, hoping that the white male, if they're equal . . . I will raise the white male because I don't think it's right. I think there was a time and a place for it, but it's over. No more." The middle-class suburban cocoon allows such declarations to stand unchallenged, except by untrustworthy outsiders. Within such a worldview, with the middle feeling squeezed, anger can erupt at abrasive symbols, like Jackson.

This seething racial resentment is sustained by the fact that black people, as they struggle to make lives for themselves in a formally fair system, behave with all the foibles and flaws and hypocrisies of other peoples. Many Coast baby boomers select out black deviant behaviors, for example, the lazy or deceitful fellow worker, the scholarship student who won't study, the crooked politician who claims racism to cover his shame. But similar to the heated reactions to Jesse Jackson, the resentments at perceived black violations of societal norms are intense. There is never such a volcanic outcry at the ways in which college and professional-school alumni are able to get special admissions for their children. In a meritocracy one would expect such concerns.

A significant number of Coast baby boomers interviewed have been advantaged through networks of kin and friendship: summer jobs for kids, access to the National Guard, employment opportunities with local firms. This, after all, is a region, a county, dominated by a Republican organization highly skilled at using patronage to maintain control. Many whites assumed Hap Farley's machine as part of the natural order of things—it's not what you know; it's whom you know. Or—in its modified, more honorable form, initially articulated by Tammany Hall's George Washington Plunckett—honest graft is taking the money but doing a good job. It's as if we operate with a formal and public system—merit—that we wish to believe in, and an informal, community system that we assume to be both the way the world actually operates and, within the framework of loyalty, the way it should operate. And many Coasters teeter toward hypocrisy in their selective emphasis on the formal system of equal opportunity when confronting black demands for historical redress.

The racial attitudes of 1966 graduates are simultaneously less and more prejudiced than those of their parents and grandparents. They are more willing to judge people truly as individuals. They do make significant efforts to be color-blind. But their ideological equipment, their relatively Main Street values, their belief in equal opportunity within a private, market economy, and their assumptions about self-interest and motivation make it difficult for them to make sense of the worsening economic situation of impoverished minorities without regressing to racial stereotypes. They genuinely cannot understand why someone living in Atlantic County during the boom times brought by the casino industry is not prospering.

The invisibility of past and present injustices, and the selectivity with which real and imagined examples of immoral or hypocritical black behavior are singled out, allow most Coasters to feel justified and self-satisfied in their suburban enclaves. They know racial prejudice is wrong, but simultaneously are offended by black behaviors. As a result, old-style racism leaks out in safe company, for example, jokes about the black leadership in Atlantic City or about Pleasantville schools. Some are uncomfortable with America's present racial politics. They don't know what to do; many simply run away from it altogether. Others harbor nearly forbidden thoughts about genetic inferiority. Coasters, like all other Americans, live with contradictory truths, mutually exclusive myths. And since the collapse of the welfare state, of New

Deal–style reform energies, they are left without the kinds of resources that might help them make sense of our "American dilemma."

One can feel sorrow and, indeed, empathy for Coast baby boomers struggling to live within a moral universe whose stability and self-confidence rests on closing itself off from outsiders. Over the past several decades, influenced by the civil rights revolution several steps removed, influenced by the parallel rights movements of the 1960s as well, most Coast 1966 graduates are more willing to experience black people as humans like themselves. But precisely this abstract, class-biased belief leads them to feel that things have gone too far, that reverse discimination and preferential treatment are now the rule. As such, they are responsive to conservative appeals about Middle America that zero in on such themes. And, I believe, unless those seeking to remedy racial injustices at the very least communicate some empathy for the contradictory feelings of white middle-class people such as the class of 1966 Coasters, those white middle-class people will continue to listen to the voices reenforcing their prejudices.

Profile: Tom Rogers, Family Man

Tom Rogers is a tall, handsome man, with an air of soft-spoken competence about him. He barely knew his father, an immigrant Scotsman who died of cancer when Tom was five years old. The senior Rogers ended up working in a local factory after several unsuccessful attempts at running his own business. "We were basically poor," Tom concludes, looking like he wouldn't mind changing the subject. He talks of growing up with his mother, who supported Tom and a sister, and with his grandmother, who did the cooking.

Tom was a very good student, especially in the sciences, and a varsity athlete. He was one of the guys, part of the male elite of jocks and rowdies who hung around The Nest and yet was "more on the fringe, not one of them, a little more reserved," less willing to get into trouble. Of course, he had to work after school, another factor in limiting his sociability. But mostly, Tom was a laid-back young guy who gave the impression of always having been careful. He tells me, "I don't think you're going to find anyone who's more a moderate in many ways." He doesn't recall either religion (he was raised a Methodist) or politics (both parents were conservative Republicans) touching him. In responding to questions about Cuba and civil rights, Tom confesses, "I guess I would have to be honest and say that I can't tell you that I was overly concerned with those things . . . [I was] . . . more worried about Mary Sue sitting in the next row. . . . High school is kind of a fantasy in itself; those things might be out there, [but] you didn't read the paper in the morning. I had more immediate concerns: making the ten dollars I needed, or who the date was that night, or fixing the car—really, it wasn't my concern." Reflecting on his own recollections, he notes, "I'm starting to see a trend myself in a lot of the things I'm saying; the best way to characterize it is, almost not aware of what was going on in the real world."

"Almost as a fantasy," Tom applied to several distant universities, like Clemson; he got accepted, only to discover how expensive tuition was. He jokes, "We didn't have ten cents, so I more or less rejected those acceptances and really had no plans at all." Then, during graduation week, he received two scholarship awards. Tom, with bemusement, recalls, "The next morning I'm walking down the hall, and I see my guidance counselor I hadn't seen in four years, and I say, 'Hey, I just won $450; give me the cash.' And he says, 'Oh, no, no, it goes to the college, and you're going to . . .' 'Where're you going?' he asked me. The day before graduating: 'Where are you going?' And I said, 'Oh, I'm not going anywhere,' so we made a couple of phone calls." Tom ended up at the recently opened Atlantic Community College, putting his scholarship money to use.

Tom compares himself with his daughter, now in college, who spent a year abroad and whose college plans included a family tour of campuses throughout the country: "I was just a babe in the woods as far as what the world outside of Coast was like. It was ACC for something to do, because I knew that I was a smart kid and smart kids go to college. I knew that the losers were all working the gas stations. I knew I had to do something; my mother couldn't afford to send me to college, but I knew it was a dream to send me." Tom, the first in his family to be a college graduate, found community college to be too much like Coast: "We were so homogeneous it was disgusting. I guess it was preppy; you wore sweaters and penny loafers; you wouldn't wear white socks with certain kinds of shirts. There was an in-group; there were some losers and greasers—the majority tried to act like the kids who were in power, so that the rare, rare exception was not accepted or even tolerated."

Tom wasn't particularly touched by the rock music of the times and recalls that while gradual changes in hair length and casualness began to hit ACC, there didn't seem to be any hippies "or strange people." After getting his degree, he transferred to Glassboro State College, along with his future wife, Sally. During their junior year, they married. Tom deflates Sally's recollections of antiwar activism during that late Sixties period: "You've got to realize at Glassboro we weren't exactly Kent State; we were going on a march on Trenton and carrying caskets, and a lot of people jumped on the bandwagon and said, 'Yeah, that's a neat thing to do.' How many kids were committed to it?" he asks. "It was almost an isolated event. I can't remember another event other than that one. I don't think it was that big a deal; she likes to look back on it as her radical period." Tom, as in high school, focuses on the immediate and the practical: "How I would eat that week, what I was going to do for a living, if my car wouldn't start." He does remember a Thanksgiving dinner argument with his marine-veteran father-in-law, "where he screamed, yelled, huffed off to bed—something about Vietnam; and I recall I said something like I thought it was kind of stupid they were there, something innocuous like that, and I remember it was almost like a real stereotypical reaction on his part and on my part. What I said was something I thought I was supposed to say because I was twenty-two years old and I had sideburns and I was in college, and I remember that it was not a conviction on my part; it was a feeling I was supposed to have, but it wasn't a strong feeling at all." Tom, who voted twice for Richard Nixon, says that the two families, his and Sally's, "don't hold these intellectual discussions when we all get together; we don't hold political discussions, and we don't get all riled up about these kind of things."

Tom knew a few classmates who went into the service, but he feels that he didn't really know any Vietnam veterans. "I think there was a big, big distinction at that time," he explains, "of going to college or not going to college. If you were going to college, you were not beating the draft; you weren't there for that purpose." He pauses, chuckles to himself, adding, "Perhaps, maybe you were. The kids who didn't go to college for whatever reason, that they didn't have the smarts, maybe at that time . . . I was looking back and saying maybe he wasn't smart enough to go to college. Therefore, he deserved to go into the service. I think that was a part of it." Later he recalls being uncomfortable around returning vets, wondering, "I hope he doesn't do anything, hurt anybody, or go crazy." In the last few years, however, Tom has come to work with and respect a number of Vietnam veterans, "normal human people like us."

If his son, now in high school, was faced with such choices, he would not recommend flight: "Okay, if there's no doubt that you're going into the service, let's look at the best alternatives, and if you've got this background and you apply to this school, chances are you'll be sent to Iceland to be an electronics technician—you're not going to go to Cambodia or something like that." He reflects, "I think I could intellectually analyze the situation and minimize any risk—I would definitely do that." Tom has seen and enjoyed the Rambo movies, but comments, "It's all just like a fantasy to me; it didn't really happen. I just can't believe . . . I know the atrocities; I know what happened to some of the guys; but it's just never been a part of . . . it just didn't happen in South Bay. If there was a kid from South Bay who went there, I couldn't name him."

Tom says that he "never intentionally tried to beat the draft" and would have served if called, but, he adds, sardonically, "At one point they had college deferments, so I went to college; then they eliminated college deferments. Then they had marriage deferments, so I got married—and they elimi-

nated marriage deferments. And they had deferments for
people with children, so I had a child—and they eliminated
those. Then they had deferments for teachers, and I became a
teacher—that year they eliminated those, and I said, 'OK, I
give up, you got me.' " He explored navy pilot school and
was accepted and ready to go when at an informal reunion
some of his old buddies joked about "dropping bombs on
babies in Vietnam," giving Tom second thoughts: "I remember it had an effect on me." It was a "heavy discussion about
Vietnam and killing people. Can you really do that?" Tom
reflects, honestly, "I don't know if it would have swayed me
from at that time saying I'm going into the service because
they're going to get me one way or the other and I'm going to
do what's best for me, and if that means becoming a pilot
because I can come out of it more successfully, financially, I
think I would still have done it."

Tom, whose problem was solved by a high lottery number,
adds, "I never worried about going over there and someone
giving me a gun and shooting people. I wasn't afraid of it; I
wasn't not going to do it; I wasn't going to do it; it just was
not part of my world—it just didn't affect me at all." He kids
about "the clam-digger mentality" as "almost a slur," a
"South Jersey low-key personality" that "just kind of existed
and kind of let the world take care of itself." But he admits
that he's describing himself, at least in part.

After graduating from college, Tom, who says he "never
intended to be a teacher," took a science job in a local junior
high school. After an initial rough period of being "totally
intimidated and buffaloed by a twelve-year-old kid," at a time
when standards of decorum had declined, Tom emerged as a
highly successful teacher. "I was a moderate," he explains. "I

got along with everybody; I rode the middle rail and got to like the kids and what I was doing." He recalls coming to the realization that "these kids are not like me in seventh grade; they're not going to sit in straight rows and say, 'Yes, sir; no, sir,' and I've got to relax for them and earn their respect, and they're going to respond to me, not because they respect who I am but because they respect me more personally." He believes that the progressive reforms of the late 1960s and early 1970s, for example, open campuses and relaxed rules, were "a disaster for education." He recalls the early 1970s as a time when "everybody was involved in drugs, everybody was a hippie, everybody was into rock music," including his wife's younger sister. To Tom, the Sixties counterculture is personalized by the troubled, self-destructive lives of people he knows, like his sister-in-law whose involvement in the drug subculture took her away from mainstream opportunities.

After three years, he switched over to teach high school at his alma mater Coastal, worked on a master's, took a guidance position in one of the local towns, and is now expecting to become a principal before retiring with twenty-five years of service and pension. Tom has always had ambivalence about a career in education. "I always wanted to get . . . into the real world and see what it was like, make money, and not worry about snotty-nosed little kids and complaining parents; I would keep looking but honestly never had the courage to make the break." He talks of family responsibilities, an early marriage, two kids, a mortgage, and being "a responsible person." For ten years, he supplemented his income by bartending. He recalls intensely hating it, resenting the fact that he had to engage in this kind of work because his teacher's salary wasn't sufficient to cover his family's needs.

But this is a dogged, determined man, willing to endure hardships if it means fulfilling longer-term aspirations. Tom was focused on buying the kind of home he and Sally dreamed of owning; that's all that mattered.

"I never really liked teaching," he tells me. "I'm not sure to this day that I like education, but I like a lot of things about it, and I like the kids. It sounds corny, but every year I become more comfortable in my competence. I was a good teacher; I was well thought of, well respected." He complains of some of his colleagues' "lack of dedication," charging, "I think we're looking at ourselves as a union now, the money we're making. We're not bricklayers, and too many of us are looking at ourselves as bricklayers; it's 3:15 and 'Don't bother me; I'm out the door; I'm not paid for that.' The kids pick that up."

Tom and Sally Rogers chose to live in "the warm, caring environment" of South Bay, not as academically strong as the more prestigious Channing next door, but "a situation where a teacher would stop in your house and shoot the breeze and have a beer." He contrasts this with the cooler atmosphere of nearby and more affluent Channing. Sally, who also taught, now earns good money working an evening shift for the casinos, a decision collaboratively made to allow them to achieve the kind of standard of living they desired.

Tom believes that he is "pretty much the same person" he was as a high schooler: "I don't think I've changed my values, my philosophy of life. When you're seventeen, eighteen, twenty-one, you like to think you're wild and radical, raising hell and all that, but inside you've got certain ways of looking at things and certain ideas which I don't think have changed." For Tom, who never seems to have been particularly wild and radical, "number one, it's got to be the kids; it's been the kids, such a joy from the day they were born; I think it's kept our marriage together. Looking back I wish I had ten kids. I'm motivated by . . . almost everything I do is related to the kids. If I walk the straight and narrow, in the back of my mind I think, 'Well, I better do what I think I should do because of the kids.' " He admits, "I'm motivated by money, success, no doubt about it. I'd grown up, I don't want to say poor—obviously just a mother working in a factory . . . I had to work myself to bring in a few bucks, and I guess I made a vow to myself that I was never going to be poor."

Tom is a computer buff, restricting his reading to computer magazines; he watches television sports and plays golf several times a week. He talks of all of the divorce and infidelity and temptations that seem to be part of his generation's experience: "The most difficult thing in life is to stay happily married these days. A good marriage doesn't just happen; you've got to work at it." He talks honestly about growing in directions different from Sally: "I wonder if we're just sitting here seven nights a week, looking at each other, trying to entertain each other, put up with each other." But he adds, "We're still here twenty years, which is more than I can say for most people."

Tom Rogers, with his daughter in college and his son soon to graduate high school, with retirement at age forty-seven on the horizon, asks, "What are you working for? Now I can do something I want to do, something for myself, more than something I was supposed to do." But what? Characteristically, he ponders, "If we're living in a fantasy world, I guess the thing I'd do is go back to school, full-time, and get a degree in civil engineering." "I'm not going to do it," he concludes, "but that's what I would do."

Politically, he jokes about shifting from "JFK, all the way, my main man, to okay Reagan, let's cut some taxes back," though he has always voted conservative Republican. But he now lives in a less homogeneous environment: "Recently my wife and I went to a bar mitzvah, and one day we went to a Greek festival, to an Italian wedding the other day. I think at this point I accept other groups and can appreciate and enjoy other cultures." "In fact," he adds, "we wish we were of another culture, because they have traditions, the family ties, things like that that we might miss, being the WASP mentality."

Tom remembers how he looked at the world when he was just out of college in the early and middle 1970s, when so many others seemed to be experimenting and rebelling: "I could identify with it, around the edges, identify with it, physically, but still totally aware of my position as a husband, father, community-type person, teacher. I realized the bounds, that I was supposed to stay within. The temptation, the fantasy, was there when I was twenty-three, and it's there at thirty-nine, and it hasn't changed. There were a thousand times when you wanted to say, 'I don't want to play the straight and narrow; I don't want to do what people expect me to do; I want to go, live in the woods, eat roots and berries.' I thought it and said it a thousand times, but I guess, given the background, the responsibility, because I went to Sunday school for years, I knew what I was supposed to do, whatever it took, courage or stupidity, to do anything different." Tom Rogers has experienced great success within the bounds he confronted and has accepted. There's an itch that he hasn't scratched, several desires that he has felt but stored away. It wouldn't be fair to called him trapped, but perhaps one might conclude that he is resigned to his relatively comfortable, successful life.

Profile: Pam Baird Lane, Do-er

Pam Baird Lane lives in a comfortable ranch in the Oxley section of South Bay with her husband and son. She gives the immediate impression of being a direct, confident, and lively woman. She is described by several of her Coast classmates as having been a preppie within the academic elite. Sometimes Coasters confer preppie status with contempt, but in Pam's case, there seems to be only respect, perhaps even envy. The Pam Baird of the Sixties was very popular at Coastal.

Pam moved to Wilbur in eighth grade, when her dad was transferred from a South Jersey suburb of Philadelphia to the Atlantic County office of the utility he worked for. She recalls wondering, "What is this godforsaken place?" and indeed, at the time, considered it to be the boondocks relative to the more sophisticated environment her family was leaving. At the same time, she was so nervous about not finding new friends, not being accepted, being the only eighth grader with braces, that she didn't sleep well until Christmas and was throwing up regularly. While her mom took her to the doctor, she thought, "Oh, my God, what have you dealt me?" And yet it turned out to be, she wistfully notes, "the greatest year of my life"; she was voted most popular, nicest, friendliest, and most likely to succeed. The thirteen-year-old Pam Baird "felt like a queen."

Her father was a college graduate from a wealthy family; he was a conservative Republican. She describes her mom as "one of the United States' first liberated women" and a Stevensonian Democrat: "The women in my family were all extremely independent; it's got to be in the genes." Her mom's dad emigrated from Great Britain, scrimped and saved, only to be wiped out by the stock market crash: "Meanwhile, Nana [her grandmother on her mother's side] was abroad, with two young girls, working when women didn't work," and then finally arrived in the States.

Pam's mother had "desperately wanted to go to college," but the grandfather's ill health forced her to seek ways of immediately contributing to the family. Indeed, shrewdly joining practical necessity with a desire for travel and adventure, she served in the military during World War II. But peacetime, marriage, and the arrival of children brought her back to domestic duties. Mrs. Baird was a voracious reader; it was her escape from boredom and routine. When the children—Pam has a sister two years younger—entered school, Mrs. Baird "wanted to work; she wanted to be useful, to have conversations with grown-up people." Mr. Baird at first resisted, but when both girls needed braces, he relented but set the terms of compromise: "You go to work, that's fine, but nothing in this house will change. My children will be taken care of, my dinner will remain the same, this house will be clean, and the wash will be done." Mrs. Baird worked as secretary at an area college, and the job yielded the bonus of both girls transferring to a special, college-administered school with state-of-the-art equipment and enthusiastic, youthful teachers.

Part of Pam's immediate success first at Wilbur's Pinetree School and then at Coastal was the superior preparation she received at her previous school. At Coastal she was often in advanced classes with upperclassmen and participated in choir, Latin, and French clubs, theater, the literary magazine, the yearbook, and the prom committee, where she worked with many of the Wilbur rowdies: "It was Bill [Green] and

Bobby [Green], and it was [Joey] Campion, and it was all those kids who had the muscle; they had the energy; they had the class prestige to pull off" what she calls "the cause célèbre of our four years," the much celebrated prom. And yet despite being voted "best conversationalist," Pam emphasizes, "my consuming thought about high school" was "to be the best academic person that I could be." She adds, "If my friends had to be put on the side for me to study, I never really made a conscious decision about that, but I knew that's how it was going to go." She was a fully active and nevertheless popular student whose aesthetic interests and skills led her to an early expectation of becoming an arts teacher.

Pam confirms that at the time of graduation from Coastal, the Sixties had yet to occur: no one had long hair, did drugs, or paid much attention to public events like the battle next door in Atlantic City over the seating of the Mississippi Freedom Democratic Party delegation in 1964. As in most cases, politics and public affairs were "not dinner table discussion" to Pam's parents. The possibility of conflict seems to have been an anathema in many Coast households. "We had a nonfighting household," Pam recalls. "I never saw my parents fight." Pam is certainly no shrinking violet, but such family and community silences have their powerful if subtle weight. At the very least they direct conversation to the ephemera of everyday life.

Going to college set off old anxieties similar to those Pam experienced in eighth grade. Her dad wanted her to go to MIT—an interesting fatherly preference in a prefeminist time—but given her art interests, she explored Pratt and Moore, which were vetoed by her folks, who insisted, "You will not be a kooky art beatnik," before a compromise was reached on an art major at a conservative private college in the South. Pam, who wanted academic excellence but wasn't "a big risk taker," yielded to parental pressures: "I felt that I wanted to rebel, but didn't know anything; I never went against my parents. I thought they were right most of the time, and they were always there for me, so I would never dare tread upon that. I owed them."

Once she arrived at college, Pam "found out what fun really was," admitting, "I probably did myself a disservice in college; I didn't study as well as I should; I didn't take as demanding a course load as I could have. I made the dean's list every semester because you could cut classes if you were on the dean's list. It came to me easily, much too easily." Unlike many of her Coast classmates who floundered and failed in college, Pam speaks highly of her high school preparation, especially in English. In addition, she felt special as one of the Northern girls, flaunting Northern sophistication below the Mason-Dixon. Pam, as in high school, worked to pay part of her way, including her sorority dues.

There is a contradiction between Pam's obvious and attractive buoyancy and air of confidence, on the one hand, and her seeming timidity, on the other. How did such tensions play out on a late 1960s college campus? She was a talented young woman, able to function as a liquor-store bookkeeper while still in high school, successful as a display designer at a campus shop in her college years, impatient with the slow, amiable pace of Southern mercantile practices. "They were wimping along and I was accomplished," she asserts with some pride and a touch of arrogance. She clearly enjoyed setting herself off against Southern sloth. Yet this talented, seemingly confident young woman, who had once dreamed of becoming an artist, who had considered architecture at one point, abandoned it upon discovering how much schooling was involved: "I realized that I wasn't good enough; I couldn't be competitive." Pam offers an honest self-analysis: "I stopped running for class office when I was afraid of being beaten—it didn't mean that I would have been beaten, but I didn't even want to come close. I just never wanted to be a loser in any way." The Coast environment wasn't particularly conducive to risk taking, especially for women.

George McGovern was her college's graduation speaker in 1970. Pam and many of her classmates wore black armbands as an indication of concern over the Kent State killings. But she didn't consider herself to be an activist or even antiwar. "I was antiauthority," she declares, "more than anything; that's what I was, and who knows why you're antiauthority? At that time was it because you're just at that age and you would have been antiauthority anyway, or was it the time too?" Pam, intellectually vital and analytic, sees herself reacting against her strict Presbyterian background but, after a pause, adds a caveat: "But I was away at school and my parents would never find out. I'm sure they didn't like the way I looked, but there again, I was at a conservative school—we weren't allowed to wear slacks on campus; we were allowed to wear jeans in the dorms but not in class."

She describes her sorority sisters and herself as "hippies," noting that she had long straight hair and wore cutoffs when she could, but at the same time, she emphasizes that she was not "a druggie": "I didn't know many people who were, although I went to parties, and if some kind of joint was getting passed, I didn't want to look ridiculous, so I would do something and go, ahhoom!" But her standards remained high, if somewhat covert: "I thought that everybody who did that was a loser. Who wants to escape the real world? Again, you're not productive." Whereas Pam loved dance music as a teen, by college rock 'n' roll "was not important" to her: "I didn't like acid rock! I hated it! I don't like 'ugly'; I can't tolerate ugly anything, so the music was ugly."

Within my sample of Coast graduates, fewer than half went on to college. Of those, probably no more than a quarter graduated, and mostly from either New Jersey state teachers colleges like Glassboro, small, often church-affiliated colleges, or large state schools in the South. Few went to elite institutions, even fewer to the kinds of colleges at the center of campus activism—for example, Rutgers, Michigan, Columbia, and Swarthmore. Pam Baird Lane was one of Coast's most accomplished students. But her college experiences, while touched by the eruptions of the era, remained muted, at some distance, and shaped by her established values and predispositions about truth, beauty, and success.

After graduation, Pam went off for a summer in Europe with many of her classmates, anticipating a career as a window designer in New York City. But she discovered that Manhattan was a tough nut to crack: "It was an interesting year, I learned a lot and felt that I had conquered the city; I felt that there wasn't anything that I couldn't do in that town, except," she adds sardonically, "make money." She was told that only men were hired as window designers because of the dangers of night work, and ended up a research assistant at a Manhattan investment house, quickly losing her romantic vision of the city: "It was kind of fake; you went to these bars and you never believed anything people ever told you." At the same time, she notes, "I was twenty two and I thought, 'Am I ever going to get married?' For the first in my life, I was manless."

Pam, needless to say, was not caught up in the women's movement at that time: "I always felt that what I wanted I was going to get anyway—that was not an issue for me. It was, 'So what is this?' I never felt reluctant to compete with a man for anything." She recalls being aware of a developing feminism around her but declares, "I thought bra burning and that type of thing was ridiculous; only later did I realize that you have to, as in draft-card burning; you must go to visible extremes to make your point. And you never get that far, you always come back to here, but you're at least farther than from where you started out—but I didn't respect that at the time." At the time, Pam was preparing to return to the offshore area to get a teaching job.

Pam Baird Lane's reflections ring true for a considerable number of more conventional, middle-class baby boomers. We hear a great deal of "big chilling," of Sixties radicals becoming yuppies; in fact, the more significant phenomenon may be the "warming," the radiating outward from a red-hot activist center of waves of cooler but still significant transformations in consciousness and behavior regarding race, gender, and lifestyle. As is often the case, agitators provoke new issues that over time allow less adventurous souls to incorporate new truths. Certainly in areas of gender, the center has shifted left. Were the 1960s a watershed or at least a critical extension and deepening of modernizing, liberating currents? Pam Lane's life thus far suggests so.

Pam met her husband, Robert Lane, at the Coast elementary school where both of them were teaching. They married in 1973 and settled in South Bay, where they still live: "I would say that fifteen years ago, when we first moved here, I would not have said, 'Oh, I'm from South Bay,' and volunteered that information, nor would we have volunteered that I taught in the school system. Now I am proud of what South Bay has to offer, and I don't care what other people's perceptions are—I know we have a fine, progressive school district and a fine community-education and recreation-support system." Both Pam and her husband are very active in the community, serving and sometimes heading several important town agencies: "It all goes back, I guess, to why I didn't want to be in New York; I didn't want to be a little fish in a big pond."

"At heart," she says, "I am a Democrat," placing her at odds with both area and peer loyalties. But, she adds, "I'm apolitical." What she means is that the interest-group realities of electoral politics offend her. To win her loyalty, the Democratic Party would have to be less wedded to brokering the interests of organized labor, minorities, and other distinct interest blocs. She finds no political organization sufficiently committed to the public interest. Therefore, her intelligence and her energies go into her career, her community, and, primarily, her family.

In South Bay, Pam is definitely a winner. She has played a leadership role as a grants writer and administrator, developed a writing curriculum well before such things were mainstream, and, except for a belated and much desired pregnancy in the early eighties, would have advanced to a countywide administrative position. With the birth of her son, her priorities shifted, even as she returned to her elementary school position. His future, in significant ways, shapes her present. She thinks a great deal about helping her son become a decision maker: "I want to teach him to make it in the world, not just to survive—yes, you have to be a survivor no matter what is dealt to you—but also how to gain control, too." She worries about the passivities engendered by television watching, because "where there's television, there's no reading, and where there's no reading, there is no intellec-

tual stimulation, there is no fantasy, there is no anything!"
The Baird genes allow for no couch potatoes.

This is a doer who has found her niche. Niches, however,
while allowing, even encouraging, one to "act locally," tend
to restrict one from, as the slogan goes, "thinking globally."
Pam Baird Lane has never thought globally—she is suspicious
of foreign policy adventurism and ferociously asserts that she
would send her son to Canada in the event of another
Vietnam in Central America. But her instincts, her comforts,
are local: "Do what affects you directly; work with what
affects you directly; to me, it's a rather practical thing to do."
She thoughtfully asks, "Is it a human characteristic to be
capable of worrying about global issues? Number one, you've
got your own backyard to worry about, and you're a fool if
you don't; number two, a human being feels basically power-
less to do anything about it." Many Coast graduates, and not
necessarily highly educated people like Pam Baird Lane, have
this local commitment and invest considerable energy and
meaning in community affairs ranging from Little League to
Girl Scouts to school board membership. At least in these
communities, what Robert Bellah calls a utilitarian individualism does not nearly approach the totality.[3] People, many of
them with old-fashioned commitments to work, family, and
community, rarely stretch outside of their own suburbs. They
resist coming to grips with the increasing interdependence of
the larger world. In addition, in valuing winners and avoiding
losers, Coasters tend to block out issues of poverty, homelessness, and racism.

There are conflicting images of baby boomers. The reality,
I suspect, is that these Coasters are more characteristic of at
least the white middle-class segments of the 1960s than what
we see on *thirtysomething* or in *The Big Chill.* Coast's class of

1966 graduates have changed; they are more tolerant, less racist, less sexist than their parents. But they were not hippies, rebels, or activists in the 1960s and are not, outside of the acceptable forms of community involvements, political or cultural rebels or activists today. But, like Pam Baird Lane, some look for some attractive voice representing what they consider to be the public interest. It's a broader public interest than that of their childhoods; it now includes at least some sensitivity to issues of gender and race and environment. But it is an interest tempered by political cynicism and apathy. Meanwhile, suburban middle-class baby boomers like Pam Baird involve themselves in local matters and attempt to teach their children how to make it in this less-than-perfect world.

Each suburban wife struggled with it alone.
As she made the beds, shopped the groceries,
matched slipcover material, ate peanut butter
sandwiches with the children, chauffeured Cub
Scouts and Brownies, lay beside her husband at
night—she was afraid to ask even of herself the
silent question—"Is this all?"
  —Betty Friedan

Growing Up Female

As late as 1970, Coasters were being told, "While carpenters
are hammering nails, businessmen are reading statistical reports, and spies are out spying, most American girls will be
baking cakes, sterilizing bottles, and waxing floors. To them
fall the responsibilities of homemaking, child rearing, and
morale boosting."[1] So it is prudent to begin with the assumption that what was called the women's liberation movement,
modern feminism, reached southern Jersey towns with, at the
least, some cultural lag.

Fully one-half of female graduates' mothers worked, in
addition to taking care of household and child rearing,
although most worked part-time and often only after the
children were teens. At the patriarchal extremity, Linda
Duncan Gent recalls her Southern grandmother telling her
mom how to cope with her son, Linda's father: "Don't worry,
Albert is fine, and you should just leave him alone. He's just a

boy." Some of the Southern good old boys who migrated to the offshore towns carried with them traditional attitudes about male prerogatives. They were to bring home the bacon and do the home repairs befitting a man, but beyond those essential tasks, wives were to expect nothing further from them. For some, such an apology as "Boys will be boys" worked. But it was made more difficult if fathers were like Linda's: "always angry, always yelling and screaming," drinking too much, getting abusive and assuming that it was a woman's place to take it.

The Coast norm was a marriage based on companionship, yet one within which women, mothers, and daughters had to struggle for equity.[2] Meg Judson deeply resented the ways in which her five younger brothers demanded to be served. "It was always, 'Get me an ashtray,' " she exclaims, adding, "Females have to do all the cooking, the cleaning, the laundry; they have to wait on the men; and I was not going to play that role, if I could get around it somehow." For some young women, getting around it was the key; none lived within an environment supportive of more-open forms of rebellion. In fact, in the period between World War II and the revival of feminism in the late 1960s, several steps had been taken backward toward domesticity.

Most rebellion, as in Melanie Combs Wayne's case, was social and sexual—and covert. Many Coast females grew up like Carol Smith Rizzo, who heard from her strict father that whereas it was assumed that her brother would go on to college, "it wasn't important" for her. Carol notes, "I was going to be a housewife, I guess, like my mother." It isn't surprising that she describes her adolescent self as "this cute little thing that ran around the school and knew all the teachers—I passed, but I just passed."

Carol's yearbook reflects a patriarchal structure. Not only are the Future Teachers of America, and the Health Careers Club mostly female, but there is something called Student Secretaries, all female, "a group of seniors enrolled in senior Office Practice classes," as clerks, typists, secretaries, "gaining valuable experience for future employment" (96–99). Many a female graduate, like Linda Duncan Gent, "just wanted to be a secretary," find a husband, and have a family. Running against this current often were legacies passed from frustrated mothers to their ambitious daughters. The mothers of Sally Vincent Rogers and Pam Baird Lane had wanted to go on to college, but circumstances had diverted them; their bright daughters, however, could now serve as surrogates for such educational ambitions.

Some girls had unique female role models: Maria Haratzi, whose mother (a Central European émigré) was a scientist, or Ann Dietrich Holvi, whose grandmother on her father's side did "scientific hand analysis, palm readings," for a host of prominent artists in her Manhattan apartment. Ann remembers the excitement of visiting her rather exotic grandmother when she was thirteen—being taken to a television studio, learning how to get around on the buses and subway of Manhattan. Marilyn Hager's mom, thrice divorced and ably managing a career, gave Marilyn a very real sense of women managing without men. But most Coast girls grew up without direct experiences that could subvert conventional sex-role expectations.

Mary Perle Ives

Mary Ives is a compact, high energy woman; she is a competitive runner. Born in Atlantic City, she grew up on Channing's affluent Gold Coast. Her father ran the family business, while her mother was in charge of the household of three children. The Perles were among the more prosperous and locally rooted families, conservative Republican members of Channing's prestigious Methodist Church.

Mary jokes, "I was boring as a teen. I was a good student, honor society; I was what they called a 'jockette' at the time." She played field hockey, basketball, and softball. Chatting on the front porch of her comfortable home, she comes across as a confident, direct woman. Was she at all influenced by the women's movement that emerged during her collegiate years? "I didn't know," she ponders. "I was growing up that way until ten, maybe fifteen years ago; but man, I got screwed!" Mary explodes in a laugh less bitter than ironic. She believes that she received equal treatment within her family but tells a story about her law school aspirations being put down by her dad, who advised her to take a typing course. It runs against Mary's character to reflect on her past; her style is to get on with it, not to dwell on what can't be changed. Moreover, she hasn't maintained any significant ties with high school chums. The past is, simply, the past.

Mary describes herself in high school as "more aloof," goal oriented, oblivious to the world outside of the Coast area, and focused on preparing for college. She was and is a very self-contained person.

She went to a small private liberal arts college in upstate New York, where she majored in history because, she says defensively, "It seemed the best thing to pick at the time; I was always good at history. I just thought, 'That looks nice, okay"—I thought I'd teach." But Mary wasn't sure that this was what she wanted for herself. Despite being an accomplished and enthusiastic athlete, she rejected a career in physical education: "That was a no-no for a girl, because you had that stigmata if you were to go be a phys. ed.; that was just understood." You would be perceived as a lesbian, a "dyke." Mary talks about how female athletes compensated for their sports abilities by highlighting their good looks, how they made sure they dated guys with some regularity, and she offers one counterexample of an unattractive, heavyset, verbal female assumed to be a lesbian because of her aggressiveness.

Mary was not allowed to join the Little League, nor was she placated by the new girls' softball league started a few years later. She still resents the fact that "the boys always had the use of the gym in the high school, and the girls had to get out"; and she would "bitch and moan" about girls' scholastic sports results not appearing in the local press.

Mary communicates an intense competitiveness but, at the same time, harbors no wellspring of anger or rage about such inequities. Part of the reason for her equanimity is the changed climate today, which she welcomes as "begrudgingly great." But more to the point is her sense of place: she is a well-born, comfortable woman, now married to a man whose family business is flourishing, living in a lovely home off the bay, with two children. She seems comfortable, at one with her environment, exchanging pleasantries with neighbors out for an after-dinner stroll.

Mary was insulated from most of the 1960s movements and challenges. She describes her college as "yuppie heaven, very preppie," observing, "I think I just continued four years of Coastal; I felt at home." More diverse and energized SUNY branches were close by, but were viewed as "weird," as "staties," with snobbish disdain. She had no experience with the recreational drugs also prevalent on many campuses at that time. But at college she became more outgoing, enjoyed partying, and was elected president of her sorority. She suggests that it was unusual for her to get so involved. Mary completed college with a minimal sense of the larger events occurring in the late 1960s.

With graduation approaching, she felt no pressure to marry, but had concerns about work. She ended up moving to suburban Pennsylvania with two friends to take a job with a large insurance company, a job that led to what she describes as a "dead end" as an associate manager in personnel.

How did this accomplished, seemingly confident, competitive, and athletic woman react to the emergence of feminism as she was finishing college and entering the work world? She felt and still feels distant from the woman's movement and would be offended if called a "woman's libber." It was "too outspoken for me," Mary replies, adding, "I agree with what you're saying, but I don't agree with the way you're saying it." She talks of the environment within which she grew up, which made activism of any kind difficult. People became wary and timid, she explains, "from being put down too many times, by parents, all the adults, the teachers." She speaks of how this conformity increases in the corporate world, where "if you said the wrong thing, you suffered the consequences." Mary explains her own passivity in the face of such pressures: "Probably because I thought I had no control over it; if I were to say something, I didn't feel as if it mattered. What control do I have?" She understood that outspokenness involved risks.

Mary admits that she was oblivious to civil rights, poverty, and the Vietnam War. She dated, one time, a Vietnam veteran, but had no friends who served and knew no one who was wounded or killed. This former history major seems defensive but complacent about her ignorance of the public events that have shaped the world during her life. Her explanation for her insensitivity to civil rights—"because it didn't apply here"—epitomizes what one Coaster, Mac Schmidt, calls the "cocoon," the suburban ability to insulate oneself and one's family from social problems regarding "the other," whether it be the homeless, the minorities, or the working-class stiffs sent off to fight our wars.

Mary married at twenty-six and had her two children in her mid-thirties. Although now an accomplished runner starting to earn some prize money, she views her sports activities as an avocation. She thinks of working in her husband's successful family business—he is also a competitive runner—or possibly following a path chosen by a number of her friends, going to law school. Although fairly oblivious to politics, she's always voted Republican: "All I know is, I just don't like the Democrats."

Among the twenty-two women interviewed, nearly half completed college, a significantly higher percentage than among the female graduates as a whole. But few shared Mary Ives's experience of attending an expensive, private liberal arts college out of state. Indeed, eight of ten majored in education, mostly at New Jersey teachers colleges.

Polly Bain Smythe

Polly Bain Smythe's high school yearbook pictures and commentary suggest a tall, awkward, unsophisticated girl still struggling to become comfortable with her size. She was born and bred in Wilbur, within a deeply religious, Methodist family. No drinking was allowed, and Polly recalls her parents finally, reluctantly allowing her to go to school-sponsored canteens on Friday nights when she reached junior high school. Her father and his brothers were involved in construction; her mother's family was more Pine Barrens rural folk. Despite their own limited educations, the Bain family was deeply committed to the value of formal schooling, including for their daughters.

They were conservative Republican, middle-class, and traditional. "When dinner was over," Polly recalls, "the men got up and went into the living room; the women got up and did the dishes." No one was "outgoing" or "talkative," perhaps in part because "everyone seemed to have the same values, the same standards." Janet can't remember ever hearing arguments or seeing controversy; concerning her childhood, she notes, "I saw the world in white and black." Life was simple and unreflective, but honest and respectful.

Polly describes herself in high school as "quiet, shy, a very good student." One of the best parts of high school, she jokes, was that "all of a sudden guys were the same height as I was." She was especially interested in the sciences and mathematics and dreamed of becoming an engineer. But despite outstanding accomplishments in those male-dominated disciplines, she was discouraged from pursuing a career in engineering or any other science-based profession. Instead, she was told that teaching science "was a good career for a woman" planning to marry and have a family. Polly Bain Smythe, now a teacher, reflects, "Some of my best feelings now are [for] the ladies who go on to be engineers." She has never heard of the Peggy Seeger song "I Want to Be an Engineer," a witty feminist tale of ambition subverted by gender, but the fact of its existence delights her.

College was a revelation to Polly: "I began to challenge everything that I had been taught, politically." She met her first black people at college. Previously, she had considered Martin Luther King Jr. to be someone "really hung up" on race. She recalls, "It didn't affect us; we didn't feel that blacks were treated that different than whites." College opened up a whole new world to her, "listening to Bob Dylan," being attracted to the various protest movements on campus. But Polly Bain Smythe, whose future husband was sent to Vietnam, a war she strongly opposed, apologizes for the fact that she stayed on the sidelines. "It wasn't my nature," she says, to protest. She found herself attracted to the hippie cultural rebels—"I wanted to be seen as a hippie," she confesses—but "didn't have the guts to go out and join the marches." In her recollections, the antiwar activists and the countercultural hippies are one. All forms of rebellion merge.

It isn't so easy to imagine this thoughtful, bright woman standing on the sidelines of dissent at college. She has a businesslike demeanor offset by a confident, easy laugh. For many years Polly has been representing her teacher's association across the bargaining table with consummate skill. Often elected as association president, she is a tough negotiator. It's not difficult imagining her turned off by the excesses of Sixties rebellion; timidity, however, seems out of character.

Polly began teaching in her home town's middle school and has remained there since college. There was "a teacher that we had in town for a few years," she tells me, "very liberal," whom she identified with. The teacher is Andrea Spencer, now an area social worker. "Andrea and I," she continues, "were very close at that time. I liked her a great deal, felt very close to her, and almost felt, 'Why is she teaching here?'" Indeed, so did the politically active Andrea Spencer, who soon left the system, frustrated by its seeming stick-in-the-mud resistance to reform. Polly indicates that many townspeople criticized Andrea, charging her with being a radical, a Communist. Polly indignantly responds, "What if she is? Hey, I liked Andrea."

Polly Bain Smythe has become a swan—a highly respected computer teacher/educator, a respected leader among her fellow teachers. She married the Vietnam veteran she met right after graduating from high school; he is a local contractor. They have no children. Other than teaching, most of Polly's enthusiasm is for golf, a sport she pursues passionately and, almost needless to say, successfully. She feels obligated to add that although there has been an upsurge of better female golfers in the last decade, she plays mostly with men.

Polly is a good and deeply moral human being. Within the parochial context of her upbringing, her Bain family Methodism taught her to accept all people, regardless of race or any other classification, as children of God. She isn't a regular Sunday churchgoer, but remains a believer. Indeed, as opposed to Mary Ives, Polly Smythe experienced a version of values transformation during the late 1960s. But it remains more latent than lived; she wanted to be an engineer, a hippie, a protester. But she wasn't able to find a way to join the Sixties movements she clearly admired. On the other hand, what she has accomplished in her working life as teacher and leader remains impressive. She declares that she doesn't view herself as a liberal, but suggests that "the Democrats should be targeting me" because she likes to vote against the prevailing current. Her heart remains with those who challenge authority.

Within Coastal, affluent girls with social skills like Mary Perle Ives ranked higher in the pecking order than old-fashioned, awkward types like Polly Bain Smythe. But in both cases, these were academically accomplished, college prep students whose lives would be significantly touched by higher education. Most Coastal girls, however, didn't go on to college; they went to work, usually in gender-defined jobs like secretary, bookkeeper, phone operator, retail clerk. And they married, sometimes immediately after graduating, sometimes within a few years. Children arrived early.

Nora Reilly Bennett

Nora Bennett has been, for a time, a persistent speaker at school board meetings, politely if forcefully asking for remedies to a host of what she perceives as pressing problems. She is a spirited woman. Some Coast baby boomers seem to have already settled into middle age. Nora, however, declares, "I don't feel that old [as she approaches forty]; I feel like I'm still in my twenties."

She talks little of her father, described as "a very quiet man," "very devoted," a hard worker who was killed on the job. She comes alive in presenting her mother, forty-one years old at her birth, as "the pillar of the church," "a very strong personality, a "staunch Republican." Nora was not "one of the 'in' crowd" in high school, but her friends, not as affluent as Channing preppies or as unregulated as some of the rowdy Wilbur or South Bay guys, went to dances, occasionally dated, and felt the constant eyes of parents ready to pounce on any untoward behavior. Nora jokingly recalls, "I can't say that I was truly chicken, but my mother instilled in me that if I did something wrong, eventually she would find out about it, and that was always back here," pointing to the rear of her head. "If anybody in the whole crowd was caught," she asserts with nostalgic relish, "it's gonna be me. I always thought I had the guilty face." She went out in guys' cars a few times, with a six-pack or two, and recalls, trying hard not to laugh, "they're all making like they're falling down drunk, and you know darn well that they're not; everybody maybe had three sips." To Nora, it wasn't worth it, especially since she was allowed modest amounts of beer or wine at home.

Nora was an average student and admits to not working hard enough. "I wanted something in the business world, preferably working with figures or machines, so I said, 'Let me take my business courses—the ones I liked I did excel in, bookkeeping.' " When she graduated, she worked at a local retail store in the auditing department.

Were there any ways that she was affected by the tumult of the 1960s? Nora loved the music of the times, including the Beatles and Rolling Stones, but says, defensively, "I don't know if you consider me an airhead or what. I enjoyed the music; I never looked for a deep meaning; half the time I didn't even know the words." She claims to have taken the period "in stride" and, by way of example, asserts, "I didn't see anything wrong smoking pot; I didn't do it; I was always under the impression that if you're a strong enough person, it's the same as drinking." On the other hand, to her, anyone doing LSD, given its well-publicized dangers, was "mental."

The period's most direct effect on her occurred when her boyfriend's National Guard unit was activated during the Pueblo crisis in early 1968. They were planning on marriage at the time, and, as Nora angrily recalls, "I got hot; I found a letter I wrote to Senator [Clifford] Case [R-N.J.] about the whole thing. I felt they were activated under false pretenses; they needed fresh troops." Nora could never understand why the United States was in Vietnam and remembers asking,

"We're going to lose some face because we just pull out? We're not cowards—pull out of there and just chalk it up to a bad venture." At the time, she says, "everyone was holding out for hope that when Nixon got in, he would end it. I couldn't stand Johnson; I thought he was a very crude, rotten person. People I knew and talked to [said,] 'Nixon is going to be the salvation.' " She concludes, "I would have voted for anyone who would have said 'I'm going to stop the war.' "

Nora Reilly Bennett doesn't remember much about Gene McCarthy or George McGovern. She found George Wallace to be too "radical," "a hothead," and for the most part mistrusted all politicians and disliked politics in general. She remembers being careful in voicing her opposition to the war, "but the bottom line was, they shouldn't have been there." At the same time, Nora, who has vivid memories of all of the families welcoming the returnees, including her husband, Rob, from Vietnam, felt no love for the protesters, declaring, "Demonstrations and all that is mass hysteria, and you can't really get wrapped up in that." So Rob Bennett, a skilled worker, returned to a "red-white-and-blue" crowd, a band playing, banners and flags waving. He married Nora Reilly soon after his return in 1970. She kept her job until the first of her two children arrived four years later.

Nora and Rob bought a fix-up house in Wilbur. "He does the construction," she notes; "I do the painting." Rob, whom Nora affectionately describes as "a country boy," would prefer living in a more rural spot, but she resists, feeling more comfortable with the school system and support networks within Wilbur. Nora remains close with her mother and her sister Lorraine, for a time a Manhattan model, now living in a wealthy shoreline suburb, who still considers Wilbur to be "country." "I've always had close family ties," Nora concludes.

Nora stayed at home with the kids until they began school but adds, "I'm not the typical housewife; I don't like just getting up and cleaning." During that time, she and Rob went out with other couples, but Nora felt that she had little to contribute. "I felt dull," she recalls, signaling an impatience with routine that is a part of Nora Bennett's personality. She began to work part-time at the local mall; presently she is an aide at a child-care center.

When asked about feminism, Nora responds, "I've gotten mouthier; I always had a mouth. There again, I wasn't a sign carrier, burning-the-bra-type thing." Having a mouth juxtaposes with being an activist or a troublemaker. Nora claims that she wasn't really affected by the women's movement: "I still like being treated like a lady; I like a door held for me; I like when my husband . . . of course, he knows that I'm a clutz—if there's a high step, I like someone to hold their hand out and say, 'Can I help you down?' " She denies being independent and switches the topic of the conversation toward what she perceives as a congenital rudeness in our society.

But quickly—Nora talks in spurts—she returns to gender: "I felt that if a man and a woman go up for a job, regardless of the sex, let them both try out for it, and let the better person get it. Then again, you can say that if it's a woman that she just wants to go out and be a plumber and her husband's working and has a good job; and you have a man plumber, and he needs that for the livelihood of his family—yes, it should go to the man. If it's a woman that's divorced or unmarried, and that's going to be her sole support, then let's just let them go against each other, regardless of their sex."

Nora characteristically avoids the abstract, ethical approach, focusing on situations, on consequences, on the particular. And she has more to say about feminists: "We've had the Miss America pageant, and it's a nice thing. Why does someone have to get up there and say, 'All they're just doing is displaying and degrading that woman's body'? To me, that's bull; I couldn't waste my time protesting that; it's a tradition. Why should these people be over there protesting about it? It's going to keep going on, and a lot of time it's a shame because that handful could spoil it—to me, that's an Atlantic City tradition." To Nora Bennett, tradition matters; yet the force of her reaction depends on her not being persuaded that such contests are sexist, although, she is quick to add, "if I had a daughter, I don't think I would groom her to be a beauty queen, but some mothers get a great thrill out of that—if they want to torment their kids with that, I guess that's their view; there's nothing I can do about it." So Nora separates herself out from tormenting mothers—concluding that it's both none of her business and out of her control—but comes down hard on outsiders who protest, because they may be subverting a tradition valued by locals. Like many working-class people, Nora Bennett places considerable value on loyalty to one's own and can fend off criticisms by focusing on "these people," the deracinated naysayers.

Yet she relishes the more liberal gender roles she sees in her sons, who have girls as friends, not exclusively as girlfriends, something not typical of her own adolescence. She's concerned about parents pushing their children too early into dating and pairing up, adding somewhat defensively, "I'm not a prude in any sense of the word." On marriage, she believes in a fifty–fifty partnership, with no dominant partner. Nora recoils at being told what to do. She sees herself as similar to her mother: "She was always happy for him [her father] to have the few pleasantries he had, but she might take control of a situation. I have a tendency to do that, but I would never do it in front of the kids." She talks of the delicacy of intervention: "The only thing he's ever told me I can't do is, on my bowling night, if it's snowing and there's ten feet of snow on the ground, he'll say, 'Don't go bowling.' Don't tell me not to go! Just ask me to please not go, because I'll get my back up. I know I shouldn't go, but don't tell me I can't go." She adds, "He duck hunts, and we have hurricane-force winds, and it's dark, and I'll say, 'I don't want you to go; please, don't go hunting.' And he goes."

Nora, who perceives herself as "not that independent" yet hates to be ordered around, and whose "mouthiness" contrasts with her husband's laconic nature, thinks that "with the women's movement, some of them, the power went to their heads." She is quick to add, "I believe that women have gotten crapped on, to put it plainly. I'm glad that some things have come on out through this," noting how good it is for women to be chemists or construction workers, or for men to be nurses. But there is a part of Nora Reilly Bennett that "stands by her man," perhaps never without some lip, but nevertheless loyal, especially in front of the kids.

Of the twenty-two women I have interviewed, all but one married. Seventeen remain with their first husbands; there have been three divorces, one with a second marriage; and there is one widow. Those who went off to college, typically to become teachers, returned to mix family with career. The most notable exception to the Coast norm is Maria Haratzi, daughter of prominent Central European refugees from Stalinism, bright, attractive enough to be Miss Channing, an Ivy

Leaguer who is now vice-president of a large New York advertising agency. Her husband holds the same position in another firm. They live in a stylish apartment across from Lincoln Center. Maria and her husband, childless by choice, are the only people I have encountered who could be labeled Yuppies. They live very well, are cultured and worldly, and are at more than a geographic distance from the offshore towns.

The other women, both those with careers and college degrees and those who married soon after high school and work to supplement their husbands' incomes, have little contact with that more sophisticated, urbane environment. In fact, several had their taste of it and then turned away.

Ann Dietrich Holvi

Ann Dietrich Holvi is a tall, slender woman voted "best looking" in her yearbook. She began modeling while in high school. After graduating Coast, she went off to college but quit at twenty-one to marry a stockbroker. When he was transferred to New York, Ann's modelling career began to take off. The marriage, however, collapsed. She then lived for about five years with a hospital administrator, Harvey, who introduced her to a different world.

"He was political," she tells me. "He asked me once, 'Who was César Chavez?' and I said I didn't know, and he said, 'You don't know!'" The Jewish New Yorker played political and cultural Henry Higgins to Ann's mainstream Eliza Doolittle. She liked his outspokenness but adds, "We fought all the time; there were good things, but he also wanted me under his thumb; he was very controlling." Harvey was divorced, with two kids; Ann found herself modeling, playing mother, and beginning to become more assertive, in part through the encouragement of Harvey's feminist women friends.

Ann, with "the women's movement and the equality thing" pushing her toward sharing, had to deal with Harvey's jealous demands that she quit modeling. He told her, "You got more brains than this; why don't you do something?" However, she adds, with a cynical laugh, that with his own job in jeopardy, he implored her to help him get into show business. Welcome to the Big Apple.

During her early years there, Ann found the city to be "terribly exciting" and thought, "I can never be outside of New York; [I'll have] a place in the country and a place in the city, a career and children, all." But some rocky experiences in her career and in her personal life led her back home. As she admits, "I was never very good at pushing myself all the time, driving myself," adding, "I started realizing how much you really have to sacrifice to do it." She began modeling less and waitressing more and, after dumping Harvey, fell in love with Mark Holvi, a Brooklyn-born and-bred artist who was making more money as a restaurant captain than on the stage.

Both Ann and Mark decided it was time to start a family. So, with Mark eventually finding work as an artisan, they returned to the shore area and had a boy. Ann reflects, "For a long time I was thinking about doing it all and having it all; I see people working and juggling jobs and managing a home, and I don't have the way to do it." She concludes, "Now I'm very old-fashioned. Can the career! I want to be home with my child until he's well on his way—then maybe I'll think of doing something." As she speaks, her son, Ira, comes in and out of the room. Ann gently suggests things for him to do until she is finished with the interview. She explains, "It's such a short time when you have them; it goes so fast; it really does. I grew up with a mother at home. It's the hardest job I ever had."

She rarely visits New York anymore—"It's not home." She's now close with her mother and family and occasionally attends church. She reads mystery novels and often finds herself disgusted with the television news; she tells Ira, when he is watching a Rambo cartoon, "You're watching garbage." Ann is not a political person, although her New York experiences have made her more cosmopolitan than many of her Coast classmates. For example, she is tolerant of homosexuality, having had gay and lesbian friends in the theater world; indeed, her history of working and becoming friends with some black artists makes her a rare Coaster. And she still finds Vietnam to have been "a senseless war." But despite having lived on the edge of Manhattan's fast lane, Ann Holvi reflects, "I guess I've always been kind of old-fashioned."

At the beginning of the interview, Ann spoke of her earlier interests in psychology and children. In many ways, this former Manhattan model, now doting mother, has come home, albeit with the contradictory richness of her experiences, to the Coast mainstream.

Ann Holvi achieved more success than most in the Big Apple, as well as some battle wounds and scars; she's certainly a wiser person as a result. Her old boyfriend, Harvey, is merely a variation on the theme of manipulative men, self-described as liberated, still seeking the same old end. Coastal women have experienced the difficulties in establishing genuinely egalitarian marriages that equitably address child rearing, household duties, and work. Maria Haratzi's solution is not having children; others, like Mary Ives and Ann Holvi, have not worked while raising their kids. A few, like Meg

Judson and Elaine Kraus, chose jobs or careers, like running a nursery or child-care center, that allow them better to integrate family and work. Some, like Rachel Barnes, a devout Protestant, believe that certain jobs are for men only. Another born-again woman, Sue Ellen Bach, sees feminism as wrongheaded, even immoral on the abortion issue, and supports the Moral Majority and candidates like Pat Robertson. Her life revolves around her family—her husband's business, in which she works, and her five children, all in a local Christian academy, whom she organizes for school, sports practices, and church youth activities.

Sue Ellen Bach and Rachel Barnes are the most conservative women interviewed, struggling to preserve traditional family values and behavior from the onslaught of what they perceive as secular humanism, decadence, and permissiveness. Most of the other women—less religious than their parents, more affected, albeit at several steps removed, by feminism's call for an expansion of rights and opportunities—have made forays into more truly companionate marriages. But given the absence of reasonably priced or government-subsidized high quality child care, of flexible and equitable work situations to accommodate pregnancy and maternity or paternity leave, most Coast baby-boomer women make the best of things.

The area is only beginning to respond to the realities of two-income households. One local principal, for example, views before- and after-school child-care programs as legitimation of parental irresponsibility. Few have the social-class resources and background to take advantage of the opportunities in law, medicine, and corporate business that upper-middle-class women like Mary Ives can expect. A few, like Sally Rogers, can choose a high-paying casino job (unique to the area) on the evening shift and maintain family life by waking midday to greet her children after school, go to their games (both, a girl and a boy, are talented athletes), make their dinners, eat, and then rush off at seven to work.

Aggie Jones Rizzuto

Aggie Jones Rizzuto's situation is probably most representative. She has two young boys, eleven and six. Her husband, Tony, whom she began dating right after high school, works for one of the local public utilities and is passionately involved in Wilbur's community efforts. Many afternoons and weekends, one can watch Tony down at the local playing fields, mowing the grass or putting on the sideline markers. Aggie is equally civic-minded; after staying at home with the kids for ten years, she began working as a part-time crossing guard at her sons' elementary school. She also is an officer of a community beautification organization. In addition, Aggie now coaches her younger son's soccer team. Aggie was the organizer, the moving spirit, behind a unique Pinetree School eighth-grade twentieth reunion. Understandably, Aggie sometimes looks frazzled, although she is remarkably cheerful.

She feels that she is part of an in-between generation: "With your parents, it was, the wife stays home, the husband went out to work. Now it's, the wife works full-time, which is really most of the time—it's a necessity; the wife works and the husband works, and they share the housework and raising the children. But we're kind of caught in the middle, where the wife gets the full-time job plus the kids plus the house, and the husband kind of wants it both ways and yet still likes the old lifestyle where the wife does the cooking and the cleaning up and the washing and the vacuuming." Aggie feels that some couples have made the adjustment, but the men tend to backslide, and tensions result: "The woman feels like she's being asked to carry everything, and the husband doesn't want to take on any more, but he doesn't quite realize that the woman is taking on more." At this point in the conversation, Aggie, after expressing hope that her children will handle this better, shifts her frustration to rising auto-insurance rates and how the middle-class is always asked to pay for the deadbeats.

Things have changed since 1966 for Coast women. More of them work; there is opportunity, if not for them, for their daughters in careers previously closed. Sally Rogers, for example, speaks with pride about her daughter, Cheryl, on a sports scholarship at a prestigious Southern college, who anticipates a career in law or diplomacy. But for many parents, particularly those without college educations, their lives have more typically been like the Rizzutos. Wives work more; husbands help out more; but for the most part, when the women come home, instead of dinner, television, and a beer, they find themselves on a second shift, taking care of the kids, doing the dishes, cleaning the house.[3]

Billie Dixon

Billie Dixon is attractive, slim, and deeply tanned from spending lots of time out on the golf course. But this is not an upper-middle-class woman; Billie, a mother of two, divorced and now remarried, has been working as a waitress at a popular local restaurant for almost twenty years. Her upbeat athleticism only partially obscures the facial lines of worry and stress.

Billie's parents were from the Philadelphia area; she lived there until at age eleven the family moved to South Bay. She reflects, "There's a lot of history about my parents I don't know for one reason or another." She has two half brothers, her mother's children, but says, "It was something that was never explained to me, and I was never able to get any answers." Her mom's parents had retired to the Jersey shore, and Billie's dad, in the restaurant business after driving a bus for many years, and an avid sportsman, decided it was a good place to resettle.

Billie's mom "was definitely English"; indeed, "she was always sorry that she didn't end up in the upper echelon. That bothered her." When I ask about her mother's early life, Billie tells me, "My mother was very smart in school, but she got married young. She used to get mad at me because I didn't associate, you know . . . [she'd say,] 'Why don't you go out with those two girls?' " referring to socially prominent Sea-viewers from Channing. Whatever tensions existed in the marriage over social-class aspirations were compounded by Mr. Dixon's drinking. "He was a nasty drunk," Billie recalls, with some anguish.

She tells me that she was spoiled, growing up as an only child in a typically middle-middle, suburban household. She weighed 150 pounds at the time the family moved to South Bay. "Kids made fun of me," Billie states, stopping to remember those not quite buried pains. "I wasn't used to that, like I kind of fit in with everybody when I was a kid in Doylestown." The shore kids seemed more aloof, more prone to sarcastic put-downs about appearance, fashion. Billie adjusted by strenuous dieting: "I swore I'd never be fat again." And she hasn't been.

In school "what mattered were my grades." She recounts proudly, "I think I graduated thirty-ninth in the class." Her future seemed bright: "I was going to college, the whole bit, I was going to go into teaching." Billie's scholastic accomplishments rested on hard work. She admits, "I have never been a reader; I think that's why I had to work a lot harder to keep my grades. I would have to read something twice to get something out of it. In English I had a terrible time; because of my grades I was kept in the higher English, and they got into this reading and symbolism. I was, like, you know . . . "She stops, trying to explain the frustrations she felt in an advanced class, then continues, "All I know is, I read something, I either like it or I don't like it—the story—and that's all. I wasn't into authors and all that, and I'm still not." But she did have her passions: "When I was a kid, I read the Nancy Drew mysteries and horses; anything that had to do with horses I read." Billie loved to ride: "I'm a frustrated cowgirl; I should have been born a hundred years before, ride off into the sunset kind of thing."

Billie was a quiet teenager who never smoked or touched a drink. Although usually placed in the classes of the more preppie students, she "felt very insecure among that group. A lot of my friends weren't in that group, and that made them look down on me more, I think." In addition, she had to devote many of her after hours to part-time jobs, especially after her parents separated and divorced. At the time, she was sixteen. "I had to kind of take over my own financial responsibilities; my mother couldn't afford to, and that kind of made me different." Billie doesn't have the fond memories about school social life that some of her peers have; she was forced to grow up quickly at a time when she was feeling insecure and lost. After her parents' separation, she and her mom had to move into an apartment. Money became tight, and Billie felt that she had to put her college dreams on hold.

Back in her freshman year of high school she had started dating Joey, then a senior. Her parents did not approve, refusing to even meet him; her mother, in particular, disapproved of Joey's background and plebeian aspirations: "My parents, especially my mother, were great class dividers." Joey didn't graduate but got into one of the building-trade unions. "I was still talking about going to school, but he was pushing; he wanted to get married because he was older." Given the financial realities at home, Billie's mother allowed her to take a job with a local company right out of high school. College was deferred; instead, she married Joey. He wanted kids right away, so Billie got pregnant, left work, and found herself alone at home much of the time. A second child soon followed, but by this time Joey's work had become intermittent, and financial pressures forced her to consider returning to work.

The company for which she had last worked wouldn't take her back on a part-time basis, but a girlfriend helped Billie get the waitressing job she still holds: "It wasn't feasible for me to work days, because my husband worked days, my mother worked, I had nobody to watch my children, and I didn't just want to dump them." She quickly adds, "They didn't have the child care that they have today." The waitressing, at a restaurant minutes from her home—"If anything went wrong, I could run out"—has allowed Billie to be a mom to her kids through a divorce, a period living back with her mother, and now a second marriage. "I like what I do," she proclaims. "I've met a lot of great people; I work with a lot of nice people and the owners have been super to me. I've been involved with them longer than anything else in my life. There's a lot of regular customers that I've become personal friends with outside of the restaurant, and I like that."

Through marriage and divorce and two children, Billie did not have much involvement with the more dramatic happenings of the 1960s. Regarding hippies, she notes, "I was in a different world from them; I thought a lot of them were freaky; I just stayed away. I associated a lot of those people with trouble." She didn't know any cultural rebels but recalls seeing some of them hanging around the local nightlife spots. "You figured they were up to no good," she concludes; "they're wasting their life away." Much of her concern focused on her children. She would see some hippies and she would think, "My son is never going to look like that!" Billie loved music and dancing, but says she never liked hard rock; her present tastes run to Whitney Houston and Gloria Estafan.

Like most Coast women, Billie has never defined herself as a feminist or woman's liberationist. She tells me, "This business of bra burning and all that type of thing, I thought it was a little ridiculous." Reflecting on her own experience, Billie tells me, "I never considered that I was belittled because I was a woman, and even to this day I still think it's very nice to have a man open a door." At the same time, she believes in equal pay for equal work and relates her pro-abortion feelings to the needless death, shortly after graduation, of a pregnant classmate from an illegal abortion. As with hippies and activists, Billie hasn't known any feminists but believes "they were getting a little pushy."

Billie, divorced in the late Seventies, recalls that she and her first husband "had a lot of problems with arguing." "I am not an arguer," she adds; "I will swallow a lot." Billie pauses to ponder something and then says, "I guess that's another thing with the woman's lib—I will hold back to try and stop trouble. I don't like fighting; I don't like a lot of aggravation. I don't see any reason for screaming and yelling, ranting and raving—that doesn't get you anywhere." Given her descriptions, it's easy to see why Billie wouldn't consider herself a feminist.

She sees her daughter as similar to her in many ways: "She's very independent and she's got a lot of common sense." Billie adds, "I don't attribute it all to me, because there's a lot of people that can do the best for their kids, and they still don't turn out right." But she likes and trusts her own children. Her daughter, now out of school, is working locally. Billie wants her to go to college, but "we differed there a lot." Her son, on the other hand, attends college: "He picked that up, thank God; if it had to come right down to it, women are the ones who have children; there's still a period of time . . . they don't have to be the sole support in a lot of cases." She searches for the right words and concludes, "So if it's going to be one or the other, I still think it's more important for the man to have the higher thing."

She was pleased that her son did not choose to go to a notorious party school with what she calls "fast-laners." Interestingly, she connects such concerns with the demonstrations against tuition increases at her son's college: "I told my son, I said, 'I'll kill you if I catch you in any of that; I don't believe in that type of thing.' " To Billie, "that doesn't get you anywhere and these kids, the kids that get involved in a lot of this, I always considered they're not learning about consequences. And they're more of a chance-taking type; they're always going against the grain." Billie conflates partying preppies with student activists, seeing the irresponsibility of both as resting on their social-class privileges.

At the same time, Billie has raised her children to be independent, to be prepared to cope with life's realities if and when she isn't there to support them. But independence, to Billie Dixon, has little to do with nonconformity. It's more of a quiet, stubborn determination to manage your own life and to be more responsible to those in your charge.

Billie, who once tried running a small coffee shop, admits, "I'm not a risk taker, never have been. I want it in black and white: this is what is going to happen." She is always focused on paying her bills and emphatically declares, "I am very money orientated; I want to know what bills are going to be paid. I'm fanatical about my credit." She has no interest in shifting over to casino work either. She tells me, "I don't get along with those people; they're too fast for me; it's a different type of world." She worries about the rising cost of living in the area, to a large extent caused by the rise of the casino industry, and expresses concern about how it will affect her children's economic futures.

Billie Dixon rarely votes. She admits, "I have a very poor attitude on politics—all these people who promise, one way or another they're going to get you." No names come to mind when she reviews the past several decades for public figures she admires: "They're still out for themselves, especially the higher up you get." Billie lives as if the larger public world doesn't exist. Her instincts are essentially conservative, especially regarding issues like welfare. But she carefully distinguishes the "completely different class" of inner-city blacks from the two well-respected, minority families in her Pennsylvania hometown. She is presently without any medical insurance—the restaurant stopped offering such benefits several years ago—but offers no complaints directed either toward her employer or toward the government. Instead, she seems to accept this harsh reality and searches for reasonably priced private health-care coverage.

When Billie was a high school senior, ranked thirty-ninth in her graduating class, she worked in the guidance office with

Mr. Travis. Back then, he encouraged her to go on to college. She recalls, "He was very disappointed that I didn't go; he did get me a scholarship. He pushed me constantly, and he did everything he could to help me. And he kept in touch with me for some time." Billie pauses and then tells me with some mixture of pride, regret, and nostalgia that Mr. Travis would come into the restaurant and "he'd have a fit; he'd say, 'You're still carrying trays!' " Billie laughs.

She's a good mom, a hard worker, and has been able to cope with a lifetime of troubles, from an alcoholic father to a very ill husband. Billie doesn't look backward at missed opportunities. But she still has visions of living in the country, riding horses. That's her dream, her sense of the good life. But for now, for the present, she sustains her family, waits tables, and gets out to the golf course, often with customers who are now friends, as often as time permits.

Mac and Vicki Lewis Schmidt

Among the 246 graduates of Coastal's class of 1966, there are, at the very least, thirteen marriages between high school sweethearts. Four ended in divorce, one with an accidental death. Of the eight extant couples, I have interviewed five, all now entering their forties and approaching their silver wedding anniversaries, often with children completing high school or in college.

In their yearbook, Mac Schmidt and Vicki Lewis were voted the "cutest couple." They started dating at the beginning of their junior year. At the time, Vicki was a cheerleader, and she was captain in her senior year; Mac, a burly young man always larger than most of his classmates—he shaved as a freshman—was a guard/linebacker on the football team.

Victoria Lewis's grandfather on her father's side had been a handsome, well-known lifeguard. He married a Southern entrant in the Miss America Pageant in the 1920s; Vicki describes her grandmother, who played piano for silent movies, as "very theatrical, a character." Both her mom and dad were Atlantic City High School graduates. Her dad worked for a local utility; her mom waited until her three kids (Vicki was the middle child and only girl) were teenagers before taking a job. As in a surprising number of cases, Vicki's parents compromised on religion, with her Methodist mother yielding to her father's Catholicism.

Vicki grew up in South Bay in a middle-class household. Although she inherited her beauty queen grandma's good looks, she doesn't seem to have much of her flamboyance or theatricality. Vicki claims that she has a terrible memory and it wouldn't be very useful to interview her. She seems comfortable with herself and yet maintains a reserve, a shyness, which makes her appear still girlish at forty. She reflects, "I can't really say that I was popular, but everybody knew me—I was captain of the cheerleaders. Mac was very popular; he was always outgoing—I was quiet." Mac, although from a Channing Seaview family, was a bit of a roughneck; one gets the sense that Vicki's steadiness has helped to draw in and almost, but not quite, civilize some of Mac's mustang wildness.

Vicki was a good student with thoughts of going to art school, but during her senior year, already thinking of marriage, she decided that she had enough of the classroom, at least for a while. Mac lasted five weeks in his first and only experience of college.

Mac's great-grandfather was prominent in the development of Atlantic City as a resort town in the late nineteenth century. The family roots are Swiss and German. Mac speaks sarcastically of his family leaving Atlantic City to move to Channing "because the Italians were moving in. Oh, they were great Christians! They discovered Jesus and lived by the Bible, but they had to get out of Ducktown [an Atlantic City neighborhood] because the Italians were moving in." He is a bearded, forceful man who gives an immediate impression of both decisiveness and merriment. He isn't likely to suffer fools gladly.

"I grew up in a German household, with a very autocratic father," Mac states. His dad had a successful business. Like Vicki, a middle child, he has two sisters, both college graduates. Mac, however, was more rebellious toward teachers, less willing to play the scholastic game. He felt considerable contempt for many of his teachers. He felt, "I'm a whole lot smarter than you are, so why should I work hard to prove to you how smart I am so that you can give me some artificial grade that who's going to care about anyhow?" He recalls, still with a seething resentment, his biology teacher, on the first day of class during his sophomore year, looking around the room for the biggest kid, finding Mac, and ordering, "You, you're going to erase the boards all year." Mac, becoming animated in the telling of this story, continues, "He threw the eraser at me; and I said, 'No, I'm not.' And then he said, 'Then you're going to fail.' And I said, 'Guess I'm going to fail,' and I failed. Screw him! I wouldn't erase his chalkboards." Mac proceeds to tell me, with obvious relish, about his suspension for mooning drivers on County Road from the bleachers across from the high school. He still seems to be a roustabout.

Mac describes his upbringing as upper-middle-class, but adds that there wasn't a caste system in the area: "Channing was not the terrifically wealthy place then that it is now."

Vicki interjects, "Still a big difference from South Bay." Nick agrees. As is so often the case, those with disadvantages, albeit slight, are more in tune with the subtleties of status, the hidden injuries of social class, the long remembered snubs, than those who can blithely assume themselves as the norm.

In his senior year, Mac put his nose to the grindstone, studied, earned nothing less than a B, and went off to a junior college, but, to his dismay, found "it was high school all over again." After five weeks he quit, with his dad's support, on condition that he join the service. His father had been a gung ho marine who served in World War II. Mac, however, not so gung ho and sensitive to possible Vietnam assignments, was relieved when he failed physicals for both the Navy Reserve and the army: he had, among other ailments, an old football knee problem, a deviated septum, and flat feet.

Vicki initially worked for a local company and then as a dentist's secretary. With possible military service out of the way, Mac and Vicki, both nineteen years old, married in March of 1968. Mac's dad wanted him to join his firm, but instead, seeking his own path, he took a job with a major utility. He stood out sufficiently to quickly become the company's youngest supervisor and with in-house training earned the equivalent of an engineering degree. He has built a successful career. Vicki devoted most of her time during their first decade of marriage to raising their two children, a boy and a girl.

The Schmidts live in the house they purchased in Channing in the early years of their marriage. It is a simple, traditional home, one of the oldest in the area, renovated with loving and competent care over the years. As Vicki proudly asserts, "This was our main thing, restoring the house. And the children; we were just totally wrapped up in that, totally." With the children grown, Vicki returned to her earlier interests, establishing her own commercial art business.

The Schmidts are attractive, bright people who have created an oasis of simplicity and charm, a domestic haven on a quiet shaded street. They don't seem to have been touched in any significant way by the eruptions of the Sixties and Seventies. Vicki admits that public events weren't important to her, "I doubt that I read the newspaper, to be honest; and I didn't watch the news that much." Like many of her apolitical classmates, she most remembers the Kennedy assassination, although little of Kennedy's politics; she does recall that her staunchly Republican father voted for him. Mac also grew up in a "totally nonpolitical" household: "My father was a real conservative guy, called black people niggers. He doesn't really dislike black people; if a black man moved next door, and he was a decent guy, he'd probably lend him his lawnmower. But their generation called every black person a nigger; that's just the way it was." Vicki, who was born in Atlantic City, attended a predominantly black elementary school in Pleasantville until she was nine: "I never got to dislike any of the black children; [but] I remember that we weren't supposed to bring them home as friends." Her older brother once brought home a black classmate to the dismay of Mrs. Lewis. Vicki's parents moved from Pleasantville to South Bay to escape what they perceived as deteriorating conditions. In the Coast communities, the white flight certainly included, although it was not limited to, racial prejudice.

Mac grew up in "a totally lily-white environment" and believes that, as in his father's generation, "it wasn't necessarily a bad thing to be calling [a black person] a nigger; it was the way it was." It would be easy to reduce Mac's rationalization to stereotype. Like most Coasters, Mac rarely questions prevailing mores; in fact, he barely pays attention to them at all. His interests in life are elsewhere, and such community ways of thinking tend to rest, semiconsciously, away from the personal stage of making a life. The Schmidts, for example, can recall few feelings about the civil rights movement or any thoughts they had at that time about Martin Luther King Jr. Mac, admirably direct, offers, "I would probably have said something about [him] being an oversexed nigger or something like that, a troublemaker, yeah." Mac extends this honest recollection, admitting that he and his crowd probably had several dozen slang epithets for black people. Then he adds, "You look back on those things, and probably—what was the woman's name, Mrs. Parks?—we probably thought she was a no good son of a bitch; but today I think, 'Way to go, Rosa!' In fact, when I see her, I give a little clap. Now I have the ability to put myself in her mocassins. We've done a major turn, when it comes to those things; we were in our own lily-white world and influenced by our parents."

Vicki was concerned about Vietnam mostly as it affected Mac: "I was always in my own little world anyway." Nonetheless, she viewed Vietnam as "a lot different from World War II," since nobody, including Mac, had much enthusiasm to volunteer for combat duty. Yet at the same time, she can't think of anyone she knew who was actively against the war; she never knew an antiwar protester. Mac interjects, "This was a very nontraditional war; if we were invaded in Bakersfield, I'd have been down there myself, but this was a very remote war, and I wasn't sure why in the hell we were there. I don't really know if I cared. All I can remember is worrying about my friends who were there, getting killed, and really, for what? What are we there for? We're there because we're defending democracy, an all-encompassing statement—what the hell does that mean?" Some of Mac's friends and class-mates served in Vietnam, a few of whom returned in bad shape and remained so. He concludes, "I didn't really feel an overwhelming sense of pride in going over there; if I could get out honorably . . . you know, I wouldn't burn my draft-card or anything like that, because I really want to be honorable about it."

So, to Mac Schmidt, a self-described "isolationist," to burn draft cards, to protest, was morally questionable. He stopped watching the news on television because, he says, "I'm a very contented person, happy-go-lucky-type guy; I'd have a nice day at work, come home, and watch this crap on the news, and it would screw me up—I depressed myself. So why expose to that?" Vicki adds, "We just wrapped up in our own little world with our kids." Mac asserts that later, when he learned of the wastefulness of the war, it made him angry. At the time, back in 1968, he supported Nixon, finding Bobby Kennedy and Gene McCarthy on the Left and George Wallace on the Right too extreme. But, he adds, "I really did not have real strong political beliefs, ties, feelings; we didn't get involved, still don't." Vicki reminds him that he is on the zoning board; Mac responds by emphasizing its thankless nature, but con-cludes, "But I said that I'd do it, and I do—once I commit, I commit."

Both Mac and Vicki Schmidt are very good at whatever they commit themselves to. Their commitments are certainly narrow, but it's difficult not to admire their solidity, their integrity. They don't seem to have been affected at all by the countercultural currents of the 1960s. Vicki loved the Beatles while in high school; Mac preferred the Beach Boys. But in neither case were such tastes prominent in their respective lives. Her description of high school reenforces the stereotype of suburban conformity: "Everybody tried to look the same; we all tried to dress the same." After the Schmidts finished high school and found themselves socializing mostly with other young marrieds, rock 'n' roll became simply "background music," to be turned on the radio—"and if you liked it, fine; but if you didn't, fine." She doesn't see the music as having any significance in her life, adding, "We certainly weren't interested in drugs or anything." Within the media-shaped packaging of a Woodstock generation, baby boomers like Mac and Vicki Schmidt remain invisible. Their youth ended in 1966, upon their entry into marriage and work.

Mac remembers that some of the academically accomplished Coast graduates who went off to elite, Ivy colleges "ended up getting screwed up, off on drugs, LSD—you know, this is the stuff you heard." So, to the Schmidts, the Sixties were either remote or destructive. "I didn't want to get really involved with any of that stuff," Mac offers. "My purpose was to come back and get a good job, get ahead in my job, have a house and . . ." He has remained close friends to this day with old Channing elementary school buddies: "We weren't really political and we didn't have strong feelings about political things; I think our perception of the whole thing was, I realized I can't do anything about this, so why question myself." Mac chooses to construct well-crafted environments within which he can exert control.

Yet Mac can become passionate about what's happening in the environment within which his children are growing up, particularly the rising proportion of broken marriages. He bemoans what he sees as a decline: "I think we're all soft, we're soft everywhere, we're soft middle. We don't have real good workers anymore; the old 'made-in-America' doesn't mean good anymore. We've flip-flopped, we're fat, we're lethargic, we don't really make strong commitments." But he sets himself and Vicki apart as different. Vicki emphasizes that he's of German descent, which he affirms, "I'm a very hard worker and I take a lot of pride in my work." He scornfully concludes, "We had it too easy, we were on the top of the heap, and we're so rich, and then . . . that's eroding; our riches are all false; we're all self-centered, spoiled-rotten brats." Mac's analysis is broadly puritanical but includes a swipe at the 1960s for giving additional encouragement to an already permissive culture.

Mac seems comfortable but is hardly what one would call mellow. "My relaxation," he says, "is working; I'm doing a kit car, a model of a 356 Porsche; I just rebuilt my Dodge. I like to do things like that; I rebuilt this room, rebuilt my barn. I always plan to have projects to keep me busy, because I'm afraid of being bored." Vicki adds that they have always loved to travel, to stop at bed-and-breakfasts, to visit historical places. They will soon have an empty nest for the first time since their first year of marriage. Mac declares, a bit too emphatically, that he isn't concerned about his kids. His son, like Mac, not an academic, is in one of the building trades. Vicki adds, "He lives at home; she [the daughter] is a junior at Coastal, hates school. They both hated school." The Schmidt children's aversion to the classroom seems to run deeper than that of their more old-fashioned folks. They are, after all, part of the cultural decline that Mac bemoans.

The Schmidts are Methodist but nonchurchgoers. When not working around the house, Mac likes to read mysteries. He brags about putting one over on the teacher living next door, who likes to rag him about his pedestrian, lowbrow reading tastes: "She read a book that Stephen King wrote under a pen name and said, 'Here's a really good book.' And [I said,] 'Guess what! Stephen King! Ha, ha!' " He prides himself on watching little television: "One day there was a discussion about 'Wheel of Fortune' with Vanna White, and I said that I'd never seen any of that crap; now if I watch 'Jeopardy,' if you'll leave it on, you'll hear 'Wheel, of . . .' and I quick jump up to hit the button." It would be of some interest to know how many "Jeopardy" freaks take pride in that same quick, contemptuous flick.

Vicki is very proud of Mac and self-effacing about her own talents. It's not that she doesn't take pride in her recent career; it's more that she has tremendous admiration for her husband's abilities and accomplishments. Discussing their respective scholastic careers, she declares, "He was a lot more intelligent than his grades showed; I know what he's going to tell you, that it had no meaning to him whatsoever—he could have gotten straight As; I can't think of the word he always uses; it just wasn't real. The only thing I can say about him is, even in the standings I'm higher than he was, and yet he has absorbed everything that he learned in high school, and me, I've forgotten it all: I studied it for the exams and I knew it, but then it was gone." In many ways the Schmidts fit snugly into many of our stereotypical, gendered images of the mainstream, white middle-class couple: artistic versus analytic, nice versus rebellious, soft-spoken and shy versus garrulous and cocky.

Mac's present thoughts about Vietnam are, perhaps, the most self-revelatory. He has ignored the war, including the Hollywood films about it, for years. Recently he rented *Platoon,* but couldn't finish it: "It got too heavy. This is horrible: these poor guys are sloshing through the mud; people are being cut up; and when I finally turned it off, it was when they went into the village, and one of the soldiers beat a young boy to death with the butt of his rifle. I could sense the frustration of not being able to identify who the enemy was, but I can't believe we were there to abuse those people like that. You have this wonderful little village, this idyllic night, and we're going to go over and rape the women and beat them to death and kill their pigs—I'm sure a pig was worth quite a bit." He was deeply shocked and surprised by such atrocities: "Yeah, I'd avoided the whole thing. I'd just as soon not know really; it's too heavy. Same attitude I had in '68—Why screw up my life?"

So Mac Schmidt remains within his "Channing cocoon," with his sweet, talented wife and two kids, his Germanic and quite admirable work ethic, his stubborn pride, his impatience with fools, and his emotions under control—though occasionally leaking out at New York Giant football games he attends—sublimated into his sense of craft both at work and in the garage working on motorcycles and old cars.

The world outside of Channing, outside of the offshore suburbs of Atlantic County, is too "heavy." It isn't relieved by the simple application of intelligence to a technical problem, or by good will. Indeed, it isn't fair to lay the burden for racism, poverty, or Atlantic City homelessness, on people like the Schmidts. They have constructed a life of integrity and meaning for themselves and their children; they are good, upstanding local citizens. But their accomplishments seem to require a blocking off of any unbearable emotional heaviness that is beyond their everyday lives and experiences.

A citizen is by definition a citizen among
citizens of a country among countries.
  —Hannah Arendt

[L]oyalty, which asserts the continuity of
past and future, binding time into a whole,
is the root of human strength; there is no
good to be done without it.
  —Ursula K. Le Guin

7

Career, Family, Community

During a quintessential moment in the mythmaking of the
Sixties, a guest leaned over to Dustin Hoffman's Benjamin in
The Graduate and whispered, "Plastics." When one imagines
or reconstructs that scene, one can almost hear the audience
chuckling, even smirking, at what was presumed to be a
ludicrous offer. Yet our imaginings rest on implicit assumptions concerning the Sixties generation: for one, the belief that
young Benjamin personifies baby-boom resistance to, if not
contempt for, mainstream business careers and opportunities.

Joey Campion

The career of Joey Campion suggests one silent majority
alternative to *The Graduate*. Joey got married shortly after
finishing high school; two children arrived before the decade
was out. While others went off to college, Joey started at the

bottom at one of the major glass-and-plastics plants in the region, sweeping floors. Within a short period of time, he was respected and popular enough to be elected to union office and, by 1969, had moved over to the management side to become the company's youngest shift supervisor ever. He was aggressive and talented but felt increasing frustration at work; he felt stymied by what he perceived as limited opportunity. It was a family business reluctant to promote outsiders to upper management positions. Joey, son of Italian immigrants, was, despite his talents, still an outsider.

He was working late shifts and hardly seeing his children. In fact, he still tended to hang out at the local bars with his old crew of rowdies. He wasn't yet ready completely to let go of his more rambunctious, carefree youth. But in 1971 he received an offer to come to work for a new plastics manufacturer; his five-year work experience had provided him with highly marketable expertise in a new, rapidly growing industry. Joe Campion took the offer and almost immediately became an international trade representative, traveling throughout the world over the next half-dozen years to make purchases, establish new plants, develop sales. He rose to be a well-paid executive with what became a large plastics conglomerate.

Joseph Campion, president, sits at his impressive desk, reflecting on his achievements: "If I went to college, I wouldn't be where I am today." He has become a fairly cosmopolitan person, pleased with his access to luxurious corporate facilities around the globe. Yet in some ways he is still wide-eyed and boyish about his leap from his immigrant dad's luncheonette to an executive office. He remains in close contact with many of his old high school buddies. This former union business manager is now a staunchly conservative

Republican. "The union protects the lazy worker," he asserts. Joey also complains about the younger generation's refusal to pay their dues. He contrasts the Western European tool-makers he brings over to work in his plants with young Americans unwilling to take apprenticeships that require "dirty work." Although he admits to "living for today" as a youth, he views himself as having been "a workaholic" for nearly two decades, putting in eighty-hour weeks until fairly recently. He has just begun to allow more time for relaxation and for his family.

When Joey Campion looks around him, he sees too many of his peers who settled for unchallenging jobs. He speaks of a few classmates "still back in the Sixties," unable to get past partying and too mellow to make their way in the real world of competition and bottom lines. Almost casually, he adds that the Sixties didn't have "a big impact on me." He was too busy working and supporting a family. But he quickly adds that from his worldwide contacts he now has "a broader look at how people look at different things"; his experience has "taught me how to reason" and how to "think in terms of other people." He is proud of the ways in which he has become a more cosmopolitan person.

Joey lives a few blocks from where his father's store used to be; he is a hometown boy who made good. He loves to talk about the old days, about his rowdy friends, and certainly relishes his own success in the telling. Joe tells me that "somebody should make a movie" about his Wilbur crew, about The Nest, about their schoolboy adventures. When he talks about those schoolboy days, he becomes highly animated, excited, and occasionally somewhat wistful. He doesn't live in the past, but the past provides the essential setting for his own success story.

Mike Nichols's *The Graduate* opened in December of 1967, two months after the Pentagon march, and was a box-office smash in the cataclysmic year of 1968: Clean Gene, Tet, King and RFK, Columbia, Prague Spring, Chicago, Mexico City, and, finally, "Nixon's the One." But most Coast graduates from the class of 1966 were more open to careers in plastics or to any other means of making a decent living than our images of the era would suggest. And they certainly weren't yet sensitive to issues of environmental impact; the word "ecology" was not part of anyone's vocabulary at that time.

They were coming of age at the tail end of an national economic boom, a veritable golden age of postwar American capitalism, but were living in the midst of a local economic decline rooted in Atlantic City's misfortunes. Social-class estimates are, at best, approximations. By rough calculation, Coast baby-boom parents distributed into 11 percent working class (factory workers, housepainters), 31 percent lower middle class (small storeowners, postal workers, mechanics), 31 percent middle middle class (principals, insurance agents, middle managers), and 27 percent upper middle class (medium-size business persons, chemists, engineers). Only one in eight fathers were college graduates. Among the baby-boom children, there was a complicated upward mobility. Approximately 40 percent within an extended sample of ninety-nine graduates completed college; closer to 45 percent had some significant post–high school education, most often associate degrees from local community colleges. Professionals with long experience at Coastal High School indicate that approximately 50 percent of graduates over the years go on to college, but only about 20 percent, maybe 25 percent, earn bachelor's degrees. Thus, both my interview and extended-outreach samples are skewed toward the more successful graduates.

Among the forty-seven Coastal graduates interviewed, twenty-one completed college, ten from state teachers colleges and three from prestigious institutions. As Joey Campion's story suggests, a college education is not a sufficient indicator of social class. Some studies suggest that only those attending the three hundred or more "good" colleges and universities show a significant income differential from those not going on to college at all.[1] Several Coaster cases—Campion, Bill Green, Mac Schmidt, among others—indicate that upper- and middle-middle-class incomes are available to those without bachelor's degrees.

Comparing graduates' social class positions with those of their parents suggests a flattening toward the middle, with somewhat fewer upper-middle-class but considerably fewer lower-middle- and working-class. One must be cautious with such limited data. The 1966 graduates were approaching forty at the time of most interviews, and some mobility, more likely upward, may occur over the next decade or so. In addition, one must note the complications that tend to be obscured by aggregate data. For example, Ernest Bond grew up quite affluent, but saw his family descend to near poverty after his father abandoned them. Marital breakup had a similar effect on several graduates' family fortunes. Also, several graduates have experienced roller-coaster lives that make social-class categorizations problematic. There have been shifts from low to middle-middle with the coming of well-paying casino jobs. Bill Green, for example, went from unstable bartending work to a well-paid casino position, more than doubling his income.

In many ways, with the exception of a few Coasters firmly planted in the upper middle class—especially those born there, like Seaviewer Mary Ives, or those, like Maria Haratzi, achieving corporate success in Manhattan—and those unfortunate enough to have fallen on hard times, often exacerbated by alcoholism, there is a predominant clustering about the middle range of the middle classes, which translates into home ownership, health care and life insurance, a general sense of economic security, credit-card debt, and salaries instead of hourly wages. In this all-white suburban environment, the rich and the poor are at the margins of the great American middle.

Twelve graduates operate within some version of corporate America, usually at the middle-management level. Mel Farmer came back from Vietnam and put in applications at several local companies. Finally an entry-level job with a public utility company came through: "At that time [1969], any physical job you'd have to start as a janitor, for a year. Whenever jobs are posted on the board, off you go. I did that for a year, four to twelve, and [then] went into the overhead lines department, started out as a helper, and worked my way up to a truck driver." Farmer then moved up to being a lineman, but after seeing a fellow worker electrocuted, he switched to another department. Opportunity knocked out of the blue: "The company was starting a program to investigate people who were stealing, and I volunteered." Within a year, a new investigations department was created, with Mel was its only investigator. Soon, with the hiring of other investigators and clerical help, Mel became a supervisor: "I got the company car and everything." That was five years before the interview. Mel Farmer, like several of his classmates, has moved up the ladder over twenty years of service. He reflects, "I lucked out, that's all," but then adds that "it wasn't given to me." Most Coast baby boomers in middle management are college graduates, but high school grads like Mel Farmer or Mac Schmidt (see profile) have had room to advance.

Another twelve are part of the entrepreneurial middle class, owning small and middle-sized businesses in the area. Jack Claire has a home services business, Davy Hunter works in the family business, and Melanie Wayne runs a fitness center. The boom generated by the casino industry has bolstered an assortment of small service-oriented businesses, for example, restaurants, travel agencies, boutiques. Such people worry about the downturns in the economy, especially the leveling off of casino growth. Their businesses are highly sensitive to the ups and downs of the area economy.

There are seven teachers, several of them moving up to administrative positions. Within the larger outreach sample, there were three more teachers (one a principal), five nurses, and nine involved in criminal justice, mostly police officers. Al and Meg Judson, high school sweethearts—she's from the class of 1967—both teach in local public schools and, to supplement income, operate a preschool. In the case of Tom and Sally Rogers, they made a decision to bring in more money: "We kind of tossed a coin, and whoever won or lost, however you want to look at it, would try out for the casinos." Both were offered jobs; Sally was the one to leave teaching: "We knew one of us had to stay normal, while the other one tried the other career." Initially, she planned to work for the casinos for about five years, but it's now clearly her career.

Baby-boom wives are more likely to work than their mothers. In many instances, women left the labor force to raise kids, only returning to work when the children either entered school or, less often, became adolescents. In about a quarter of the families, the wife's income is essential to maintaining a middle-class lifestyle, usually middle-middle, with a few cases of upper-middle. In all such instances, the wife is a college graduate. In a larger number of families, more than half, the wife supplements the husband's income, usually working part-time for hourly rates close to the minimum wage. Such jobs often provide whatever disposable income families closer to the lower-middle possess. In the case of Susan Dennis, the stress of work led to a decision to leave a well-paying position for a less prestigious part-time job, and the Dennises agreed to scale down their lives to accommodate the loss of income. In other families, like the Rogerses, two full-time jobs, including night-shift work, are carefully calibrated to ensure that the needs of children are met. In the Coast communities, as in much of America, the reality of women working hasn't easily translated into supportive institutions and benefits, for example, pre- and postschool child care or maternity leave with pay. The towns finally established after-school programs in 1991.

At the bottom end of Coast graduates, there are at least four instances of people down-and-out, chronically unemployed, sometimes alcoholic, emotionally unstable. A number of graduates talk sadly of Willie Jones, often seen down at one of the area taverns; Jack Claire was shocked one evening to run into him and say hello, only to discover that the chronically enebriated Willie couldn't remember who he was.

Several graduates are no longer alive. One was killed in a motorcycle accident. Two graduates apparently drank themselves to death; another is felt to have intentionally killed himself in an automobile accident. There was one other reported suicide. One of the most tragic stories was of a young graduate who died from an illegal abortion. There has also been one recent death from cancer.

Nearly half of those interviewed still live in one of the three Coast towns (eight in Wilbur, five in Channing, ten in South Bay); all but four have remained in the county or have crossed over to nearby Cape May County. Within an extended outreach sample of 129, more than half of the class of 1966, 91 (71 percent) have remained in the area and 35 have dispersed throughout the country, 12 in the Southern states. Some, like Ann Holvi and Marilyn Hager, have returned after long absences. Several, like the Waynes, talk of moving to a less congested area, like the rural South. But a remarkably high percentage of 1966 graduates have remained in and around the three Coast towns.

They live, for the most part, in comfortable but modest suburban houses—ranches, split-levels, bungalows. To Tom and Sally Rogers, married while in college, saving for their own home was a central preoccupation in their early married years: "This is where we want to live; to me, this is a dream home; it's got everything I want; [it's a] quiet neighborhood." Like many Coasters, the Rogerses have put a lot of care and work into improving their home, for example, redoing hardwood floors. Coast baby boomers often take care of their own home improvements: new rooms, basements, drywall, sound systems.

Marriage and family are central to their values and concerns, but baby boomers have had to struggle in the face of changing social and sexual mores. Within their parents' generation, there were fewer divorces, slightly less than 10 percent, although Coasters tend to exaggerate the permanence of pre-Sixties marriages. Within the class of 1966, there are twenty-one known divorces, with at least half a dozen cases of multiple divorce. Certainly there is a perception that divorce is more frequent and, what is important, more acceptable. Coasters have mixed feelings about this; on the one hand, they bemoan declining moral standards and the threat to the family, but at the same time, most admit that the unhappy marriages within their parents' generation might have been better off ended.

There are a few instances of men blaming "feminist," or "women's lib," wives for the breakup of marriages, but more typically, one hears the standard refrain of incompatibility. Within the sample there are five divorced people (three men, two women) and one widow, and all the others are married. In a few cases, like that of Harry Kearns, an initial unhappy marriage was followed by a divorce and then a more successful marriage. Of those married, all but four have children. In fact, Kearns's divorce was precipitated by his first wife's resistance to having a child. Two couples have decided not to have children; in two other cases, the initial marriages, occurring in the mid-eighties, followed protracted bachelorhood, with children likely to follow.

Among those married with children, almost two-thirds (20) have two kids; more than a quarter have one. In the latter case, given several late marriages, more two-children families are likely. Of the three "larger" families, the two with four children are, perhaps not coincidentally, born-again Christian households. Baby-boom families are significantly smaller (mean size, 1.48 children) than the households of their parents (mean size, 2.78 children).

To many Coast families, their children are the focal point of their lives. Coasters are, mostly, church members, but at lower levels of participation and intensity than their parents. As Sally Rogers affirms, "Church doesn't play a big role in our lives, like it may have years ago." The centerpiece of activity within the Rogers family has been sports, from the local peewee leagues through high school varsity competition. I had great difficult establishing interview appointments during the period of local baseball play-offs; many of the parents were scheduled in for most weekday evenings. Sometimes the sports activities of the children reflect the stereotype of overbearing parents getting too caught up in winning. But there is also the sense of a community coming out to ensure that their children have wholesome activities that keep them out of trouble. Parents know enough from their own generation, albeit at some distance, and especially from their siblings closer up, to seek to protect their own children from what they see as self-destructive drug experimentation.

Parents worry about the rapid development within the county spawned by the casinos. Some speak of the increasing pressure on their children to dress up for school. Some, like Stan Burke, blame that pressure on more affluent, recently arrived parents, "They're very standoffish and snippy, a lot of backbiting and dog eat dog; [it's] the haves and the have-nots. People who have lived here a long time see people who have just come in and working in the casinos, driving around in Porsches and Mercedes and BMWs." He's unhappy about how classmates treat his daughter: "They're all over her case, about the way she dresses." One hears many complaints about how difficult it is to cope with school fashion pressures. In several interviews, one heard of conflicts over peer pressure to purchase expensive, stylish clothes. Parents also worry about drugs, drinking, and sex. There is a fast-lane element associated with casino culture, which concerns parents seeking security and stability for their children. But given how many baby boomers have derived economic advantage from the casinos, directly and indirectly, there remains an ambivalence characteristic of American middle-class culture. Coasters want to preserve old-fashioned ways and values and yet encourage the market forces, the very idea of progress that inevitably uproots tradition. In an area with a delayed entry into suburbanization, pushed forward by a glitzy casino industry, such ambivalence is heightened.

Because of their characteristic insularity, Coast baby boomers lack a means effectively to criticize those forces putting their family lives at risk. They know little of the world around them, tend to cling to the myths of American uniqueness so effectively evoked by Ronald Reagan, and, consequently, move back and forth between a congenital buoyancy and an occasional griping about declining standards. Successful businessmen like Joe Campion and the technically skilled Mac Schmidt see America losing her competitive edge and, to some extent, blame the Sixties and its permissiveness for the decline in craftsmanship. They zero in on presumed welfare indulgences, but do not recognize that the European societies they admire for sustaining workmanship have much more extensive social welfare programs than the United States.

Coast baby boomers, in the face of a "heartless world," focus attention on their havens of work, family, and local community. At least half bring considerable enthusiasm to their work. In about three-quarters of these cases, there is a definite and intense pride in one's skill, in one's craft, either in creating goods or in delivering a service like education. In the other quarter of those voicing significant satisfaction with their work, being self-employed, being one's own boss, is central. The remaining third to a half, to whom work seems to be more of a means to an end, are split between those relatively content with career achievements and the material rewards that result, and those who work because there is no other choice. Jack Claire, who keeps dreaming of sailing away from the increasingly hectic pace of the area, is more than aware that "to move to Pittsburgh and not have a job would be a terrible thing." He knows that the South Jersey shore area is, as of 1988, booming, with almost fifty thousand new jobs created by the casino industry. Many Coasters retain a somewhat nervous optimism about the economy and their children's futures, remembering the tough precasino times, aware of other, less fortunate job markets, and worrying about the decline of a once supreme American economy. But the present, their own personal and family present, is sufficiently secure to keep such anxieties under control.

Coast families, in their leisure, like to travel; many vacations center on camping, visiting historical sites, trips to Disneyworld. They watch television, but it doesn't seem to be more than a filler except for the sports viewing of most of the men; there were few instances of any passionate identification with television shows, including the soaps. In most homes, a television occupied center space in the living room, but it wasn't always on. At the same time, few Coasters are readers. Only one baby boomer, Roy Smiley, a divorced executive and "history buff," was a vociferous reader. Those who read tend to enjoy popular novels, the men leaning toward detective and adventure, the women toward romance. The main nonfiction readings are how-to books, self-improvement books, some pop psychology, and biographies of celebrities. Mostly, Coasters engage in activities relating to their children or focus on improving the appearance of their homes. Some of the men love to work on cars and motorcycles or, more recently, hack away at their personal computers. Golf, skiing, and, in a few lower-middle instances, bowling generate enthusiasm. There aren't many health spa regulars or joggers.

The class of 1966 takes on a goodly amount of volunteerism and community service. Many of the activities center on children, for example, Little League, scouts, the school board, and parent-teacher organizations. There are also people serving on the various community boards—for example, zoning and environmental—and active in their churches or with the various charitable organizations in the area. It would hardly be accurate to characterize Coast baby boomers as selfish or self-centered, although it is clear that their generosity of time and heart tends to remain within conventional and local boundaries.

Family matters include not only one's own nuclear household, but often one's parents, brothers and sisters, and other relatives. On several occasions during interviews, relatives dropped by. There are families who rarely make contact with one another, but the most typical behaviors include fairly regularized visits, certainly on the major holidays, and family picnics. Geographic mobility sometimes limits such contact, but among Coasters, with so many remaining in the area, family get-togethers are close to the top of leisure activities.

Within the framework of diverse, blurred middle classes, there certainly is some envy and conflict. Jack Claire recalls that after returning from his wealthy brother's sumptuous home, "it used to bother me that I could walk in the front door and see the back door; for a long time I couldn't deal with it." In an area culture personified by Donald Trump, it is likely that such resentments are widespread. But they are tempered, albeit rationalized as well, by people's professed satisfactions with their own version of middle-class living.

George Evanson, a successful middle manager, speaks of his sister: "She's the brains of the family, and she's just too way above me. She lives upstate with her lawyer husband. We talk different; she's a yuppie girl." What does George mean by such a characterization? "She knows everything, from how to raise kids . . . they got a Corvette, a Mercedes, and they're into skiing and playing tennis." George is uneasy about his criticism: "I like my sister and her husband very much, but we're very different," and he repeats a reference to her sports activities. Then he explains, "We were at a picnic this past week when we all got together, she tripped over the picnic bench, which is the third year in a row that I can remember, and I just can't imagine her playing tennis or skiing." With yuppies, George continues, "it isn't strictly income. I think it's just an air—it's strange I can't put my finger on what it is; it's just the manner in which they carry themselves, the way they talk." George, who makes a good living, without any defensiveness, says, "I would not consider myself a yuppie," and, as an explanation, begins to describe his 1966 Triumph Spitfire and his love of boats: "I would say a yuppie is someone who has a boat and doesn't know how to drive it. I've got my sixteen-foot fiberglass boat. I don't do it for show; I do it because I enjoy it." So, to George Evanson, yuppies engage in conspicuous consumption, of commodities and of culture. They have "an air" of what middle-middle Coasters experience as snobbery and pretense. Within the Coast sample, only Maria Haratzi, living in an expensive apartment in Manhattan, married without children, cultured and sophisticated, would be designated as a yuppie.

The essential intraclass distinctions separate cosmopolitans from locals, upper-middle from middle-middle, consumers from producers. George Evanson's sister, married to an attorney, living in a prestigious upscale community, talks differently and has different tastes. The implication is that yuppies only engage in activities that raise their status, but one must note, at the least, that the activities all involve considerable disposable income, college (often elite) education, and leisure and often suggest matters of taste and refinement.[2] To whatever extent such activities exist within America's middle classes, they are a rare phenomenon among Coast's baby boomers. Coasters are essentially middlebrow, insular, and mainstream and are often culturally conformist. They tend to ignore everything outside of their own communities, everything they believe they cannot control or, often, understand. But within these tunnel-vision limits, they work hard to do good work, to maintain stable families, and to build comunities. It is to their credit that they have constructed lives rather than lifestyles.

Germany has declared war on Russia
—Swimming in the afternoon.
  —Franz Kafka, August 2, 1914

Conclusion

As we approach the twenty-first century, for the first time in American political history more than half of the electorate will be suburban.[1] I cannot make the claim that the 1966 graduates of Coastal High School represent that suburban reality. I would, however, suggest that these particular baby boomers reflect significant components of the American suburban middle classes that too often are obscured and misrepresented in much that passes for political and cultural criticism.

I wish to challenge two myths: one, concerning what might be called the yuppification of the middle class; two, concerning the same yuppification of baby boomers. There is a certain dovetailing of myths, in both instances, resting on a tendency to reduce the most varied middle classes to a segment of the professional and clearly upper middle class. After all, the percentage of baby boomers who might be categorized as young urban professionals is, according to one study, between 1.1 and 2.4 percent.[2]

I am interested in those middle-class, suburban white baby boomers who are not usefully categorized as yuppies. It would be excessive for me to claim that the 1966 Coastal graduates represent, in any statistically valid manner, that group. In fact, one can argue that by choosing a relatively early baby boomer group, born mostly in 1948, I have minimized the impact of the 1960s.[3] Indeed, there is some truth in such a claim; the younger siblings of 1966 graduates did, in fact, partake of more of the countercultural aspects of the era. But the longer-term effect remains uncertain. My own focus was to demonstrate that at least for those baby boomers coming of age at the time the Vietnam War was becoming highly visible, living in a mainstream middle-class suburban environment at some distance from cosmopolitan urban centers, the impact of the 1960s was at the margins.

In fact, the stories told within this study demonstrate that the Sixties had barely reached Coastal High School by 1966. In most ways, its adolescent subculture remained consistent with the suburban dynamics of the postwar period. By 1966, in effect, "the Sixties" had barely begun in the three Coast towns. There were no hippies, no drug experimentation, no long hair, no civil rights or peace activists, no SDS. In fact, it's important to emphasize that there were also no "beatniks," no small pockets of anti-middle class, bohemian cultural rebelliousness, although there were some incipient and closet Holden Caulfields.

The class of 1966 grew up during the second Red Scare of McCarthyism, in an era shaped by a "politics of growth" that offered the carrot of a rising standard of living to offset the sticks of Cold War witch hunts and cultural conformity.[4] And it did so in an area where it was unlikely for a school board to employ a teacher alleged to be a Communist and, therefore, subject to dismissal; where there were few industrial unions needing to be purged of their radicals; where there were few liberals to charge with being pinkos. Coastal teachers and administrators reflected the conformist culture of the 1950s. The postwar Coast culture believed in the air-brushed, middle-class suburban environment mythologized by popular television shows like *Father Knows Best*.

But, at the same time, the three Coast towns were part and parcel of larger forces that they tended to downplay and, at times, deny. Coast baby boomers recall childhoods as essentially stable, even pastoral. Yet up to one-third of them were born in nearby urban ethnic areas like Atlantic City that were experiencing economic decline and African-American migration. Their parents, often Irish or Italian Catholic first-generation Americans, were in flight from what they perceived as threats to their upward mobility. And yet their flight was also a quest to achieve that same mobility, to continue the search for better lives that began with the journey to America.

And this suburban migration would deliver on much of its promise during the golden age of American capitalism, the twenty-seven-year economic boom that began after World War II.[5] By the time Coasters were sophomores in high school, fully 44 percent of Americans, many of them living in suburbs, defined themselves as middle class and up.

Coastal 1966 graduates were ill equipped to come to grips with the hurricane that blew through the middle and late 1960s. They were oblivious, even insensitive, to civil rights, ignorant of foreign affairs and essentially conformist in adhering to Cold War anti-Communist shibboleths, and remote from any dissenting or rebellious cultural traditions. Even those most predisposed to challenging mainstream values lacked any framework of ideas or associations that might have assisted them in traversing rebellious paths. In many ways, even those Coasters who went off to college fit pollster Daniel Yankelovich's description of "the vast majority of Americans going about their daily routines unruffled, their outlook on life hardly touched by these momentous happenings."[6] One must keep in mind that as late as 1966, 72 percent of the students at the progressive, activist University of Wisconsin campus in Madison approved of the Vietnam War.[7] For most Americans, what we call the 1960s didn't arrive until 1967 or 1968; for some, it never arrived.

It is useful to break down the subgroups within the baby-boom generation. Sociologist Michael Delli Carpini distinguishes between "ambivalent," "experienced," and "socialized" subcategories within the Sixties generation. The ambivalent element, those between twenty-five and thirty-six years old from 1964 to 1973, presumably had grown up during the 1950s and had mixed feelings about the events impacting on them during the Sixties. The experienced subgeneration, thirteen to twenty-four years old in that same period, faced the challenges as they were growing up, although their earliest socialization was rooted in the 1950s. The socialized element, only one to twelve years old at that time, were most affected by the 1960s in the sense that their very socialization occurred in the midst of the tumult. In effect, they never knew the pre-Sixties.[8]

Delli Carpini's model is useful but must be tempered by issues of locale. In more-backwater areas like South Jersey, those who were formally "experienced," like the Coast class of 1966, shared more of the characteristics of the "ambivalent" group. They carried a sizable cultural baggage from the postwar culture as they confronted issues like the Vietnam draft, cultural rebellion, and the challenges posed by blacks, women, and other aggrieved parties. Especially for those who married right out of high school, whose adulthood began in 1966, the Sixties were experienced several steps removed.

And yet at the same time, there would be transformation. In criticizing some of the myths concerning the Sixties generation, I do not wish to construct new ones. Even these marginally touched baby boomers, isolated in suburban milieus, were shaped by the rights revolutions of the period, which continued building momentum into the 1970s. They became more tolerant, less prejudiced, more culturally pluralist.

Social Class: In the Middle

The most influential analyses of the Sixties generation and its impact on culture and character suffer from a tendency to exaggerate both the nature and the pace of change. Much of this distortion rests on a privileging of one kind of upper-middle-class experience. It would be a relief if the explorations of social class were any less treacherous than those of generations, but they are not. One is tempted to join sociologist Herbert J. Gans in considering the concept of middle class as "virtually meaningless."[9]

Gans seeks to distinguish working- and lower-middle-class culture and values from middle and upper-middle yet at the same time confesses that there is a considerable stretch upward. Barbara Ehrenreich represents, in her study of "the inner life of the middle class," a model more skewed toward the upper-middle. Her criteria of occupational autonomy, credentialing, discretionary income, and a consequent upscale lifestyle. limit her model to the professional middle class, which she perceives as the cutting edge of middle-class culture. Indeed, she specifically rejects any consideration of the more numerous suburban middle classes, curtly indicating that their insularity sets them off as politically hopeless.[10] Such a perspective, which underestimates the degree to which the culture has been profoundly transformed by the 1960s movements, is at the heart of what this study attempts to critique.

Coasters, for the most part, stand closer to Gans's model but extend well into the middle and upper middle classes. For example, of ninety-eight Coastal graduates, approximately 18 percent are upper middle class. Of the forty-seven interviewed, twelve worked as middle managers for corporations, another twelve were small businesspeople, and seven were teachers.

Educational levels certainly matter in establishing social class on the Coast; cultural markers distinguish high school from college graduates. But several success stories suggest that the absence of a college education isn't the definitive distinguishing mark between working class and middle class or within the middle classes. Most Coast college graduates attended nonelite state institutions for teachers training; others graduated from less prestigious out-of-state colleges. Only a very few attended top-ranking institutions.

The larger middle-class environment, what Gans calls the microsociety, tends to shape the experiences of individuals with diverse educational and social-class credentials.[11] Indeed, the state of mind of the middle classes includes an awareness of, even an assumption of, social networks available to assist in finding employment. Such are the very real, if unnoticed, benefits of all white people raised within a middle-class milieu. Job-referral networks based on kin and community offer a real safety net not available to most minorities and the poor. These networks were especially important to the non–college graduates in the Coast group who used such connections to gain access to jobs from major local employers—even though the jobs by no means guaranteed upward mobility. Two Coasters started as floor sweepers, janitors with no promises of promotion. But, as with many other graduates, they got "in," and that was the key.

Issues of income matter in understanding the social class of Coasters, but income needs to be qualified by the variations that occur over the life cycle and by the number of income producers within the household. The Coast shares with the nation the phenomenon of more wives and mothers entering and staying within the workforce. Coast women are more likely to work for wages than their mothers were. Characteristically, women left the work force to have and raise their children, only returning when the children either entered school or, less often, reached adolescence. In about one-quarter of the families, the woman's income is essential to maintaining a middle- or upper-middle-class lifestyle—vacations, new cars, mortgage payments. In all such instances, the woman is a college graduate. In more than half of the households, the wife supplements her husband's income with part-time work compensated at hourly rates close to minimum wage.

The Great Debate: Whither the Middle Class?

Many critics have sought to capture post-Sixties culture and personality as it shapes middle-class behavior and values. Indeed, the experiences of white middle-class baby boomers seem to be a national preoccupation. There are three points of view. Two of them share a common set of observations but diverge sharply in how they interpret the behaviors cited. The third offers a different, at times contradictory, set of observations. The first two stories, one hopeful, the other gloomy, tell of a transformed middle class. The pessimists—including Christopher Lasch, Robert Bellah, and Barbara Ehrenreich— tend to see a middle class, particularly its baby-boom subset, as tending toward narcissistic shallowness, an anomic rootlessness, and yuppie selfishness. The pessimists continue a long tradition in American cultural criticism—including such diverse works as those of David Reisman, Philip Reiff, and Philip Slater—that sees a deterioration in the integrity of middle-class life.[12]

The optimists, best represented by the works of Daniel Yankelovich and Peter Clecak, translate as hopeful virtually the same cultural phenomena bemoaned by the pessimists. Where some see selfishness, Yankelovich sees versions of self-fulfillment, self-actualization, a growth of possibilities for previously constrained individuals.[13]

The third group of critics deny the centrality of both pessimist and optimist models of middle-class development. In fact, these critics—including Herbert J. Gans and the Middletown follow-up team headed by Theodore Caplow— deny that there have been fundamental changes in behavior and values within the American middle classes, at least in the period since the 1960s. They argue for greater continuity in middle-class culture. This study clearly leans toward this third position, recognizing significant transformations in attitudes about race and gender, in tolerance, but argues for more continuity than either the pessimists like Lasch or the optimists like Yankelovich consider.[14]

Lasch's suggestive but highly speculative argument framed much of the discourse about contemporary culture following the 1960s. Unfortunately, Lasch's polemical and impressionistic approach also led many of his critics to confuse the concept of the narcissistic personality with a kind of fast-lane, trendy selfishness. Yankelovich, for example, charged Lasch with accentuating the negative and less significant aspects of "a search for fulfillment." He argued that since the 1960s, we have been in the midst of "a genuine cultural revolution" involving as much as 80 percent of our adult population, "with evidence of startling cultural changes . . . that penetrate to the core of American life. . . . What is different about contemporary American culture is precisely the fact that private conceptions of fulfillment hitherto confined to the upper crust have become democratized and now find their way into all social classes." Like the pessimists, Yankelovich worries about the diminution of social conscience and ethical commitment, but his essential argument is for a transformed culture, properly modified by his suggestion that there is both a strong and a weak form of this revolutionary search for fulfillment.[15] Certainly there are elements of such a weak form in some Coasters, more willing and able than their parents to throw off the historical burdens of guilt in seeking new pleasures, sexual and otherwise, in their lives.

Probably the most widely discussed analysis of American national character affected by the 1960s has been Robert Bellah's influential *Habits of the Heart,* an examination of the limitations of individualism, especially as traditional forms of communitarianism—biblical, republican—erode.[16] Bellah and associates focus on "our cardinal sin: we have put our own good, as individuals, as groups, as a nation, ahead of the common good." At the same time, Bellah denies that the issue

is one of selfishness, or narcissism; instead, his study emphasizes the ways in which forms of individualism—expressive
and utilitarian—hamper the development of an ethic of social
responsibility.[17]

My primary concern with the pessimists is with their unit of
analysis. Bellah, for example, disproportionately emphasizes
upper-middle-class lives, those lives more typically touched
by the cultural rebellions associated with the 1960s. Barbara
Ehrenreich explicitly links the yuppification of what she calls
the professional middle class to "that last period of youthful
assertiveness, the sixties."[18] Ehrenreich's professional middle
class includes that 20 percent of managers and professionals
whose fears of falling into economic insecurity reflects "inner
weakness," fears of "growing soft, of failing to strive, of
losing discipline and will," of being threatened by "hedonism
and self-indulgence." Freed by Reaganite greed to aspire
toward upper-class wealth, these yuppies become a "new
class."[19]

It's interesting how concepts of a new class arise from both
radical and conservative critics. Conservatives write as if Dan
Rather epitomizes media types, professors, and liberal professionals. Radicals turn things back by associating yuppie greed
with the Reaganite 1980s. But radicals tend toward distinguishing upper-middle-class yuppies from more-worthy
lower-middle-class, working-class, and poor people. As opposed to conservatives who express an abstract fealty to
Middle Americans, radicals tend to dismiss or ignore them.

Ehrenreich, for example, dismisses "the suburban middle
class" as "long since withdrawn" from the "challenges of a
diverse and unequal society." They are presumed to be
unworthy of consideration. One could not find a better
shorthand to the irrelevancy of much of the American Left

than Ehrenreich's contempt for the lives of most middle-class people.[20]

The Coastal class of 1966 includes few yuppies or professional middle-class people like those Lasch, Bellah, Yankelovich, or Ehrenreich describe. Like the images from the mass media, accounts of middle-class life and culture suffer from a narrowness of focus. It's what might be called the Woody Allen view of the United States: a barbell with weights at both coasts—Manhattan and L.A.—with the bar, the rest of the country, Middle America, as merely a long, thin, and scarcely noticed connector. Indeed, there seem to be few narcissists, yuppies, cultural experimenters, and therapeutic personalities in the Coastal towns; mostly there are suburban, mainstream Middle Americans of the quite variegated middle classes.

Cosmopolitans and Locals

The controversies concerning the nature and direction of U.S. national character often turn on interpretations of social class and generational dynamics. All too often the discussions, as Christopher Lasch asserts, are decidedly ahistorical, accepting uncritically a premodern, "old-fashioned" backdrop from which emerged a more hedonistic, anomic culture. The focus on a much-publicized segment of the upper middle class, as well as the assumption that that segment stands as a vanguard of cultural change, has obscured the complexities of whatever transformations have actually taken place.[21]

There is a half-full, half-empty quality to a major part of the debate between the optimists and pessimists. What is liberatory and self-actualizing to one critic may be self-destructive and narcissistic to another. But the more significant discrepancy is between those who see major change, either positively or negatively, and those who offer an alternative picture of relative continuity and stability.

My own sense, confirmed by this book, is a cautious skepticism about major cultural changes associated with narcissism, selfishness, or regarding the collapse or radical transformation of the everyday middle class existence. For one, those arguing for such transformations tend to fixate on professional upper-middle-class people living in the most sophisticated metropolitan areas. If academic psychologists tend to study mostly undergraduates in researching human behavior, academic and more journalistic cultural critics tend to substitute California, eastern megalopolis, and campus-town sophisticates for the more diverse middle-class people living in less urbane environments. In brief, they too often study themselves.

It may make more sense to examine American middle-class culture in terms of the consequences of a historically evolving abundance based on extensive natural resources, an educated, literate workforce, and an emerging mass-production economy consequently requiring mass consumption. As historian Warren I. Susman notes, critics of what he calls a "culture of abundance," whether radical, liberal, or conservative, adhere to the Weberian vision of economic rationalization as forming an "iron cage." They share a contempt for mass culture and its products, a dread of the "technological and bureaucratic organization of life," a conviction that modern communications manipulates and distorts honest discourse, and a sense that the culture has brought a marked decrease in human freedom. Susman shrewdly critiqued those who "are clearly unhappy living in this country," with "little sympathy for anything that is for the masses, seeing always some sort of fascism or Stalinism around the corner."[22] Critiques of the "ticky-tacky" tract homes of suburbia often reek of such nasty snobbery. Most of all they obfuscate the variety of ways in which middle-class people have adapted to a culture of abundance.

In fact, the cultural optimists seem to make a better case, at least when temperate, tentative, and cognizant of the contradictory dimensions of greater freedom and choice. Coast's class of 1966 offers some support for Yankelovich's argument of "a weak form of self-fulfillment search" and for a greater tolerance of difference. There *has* been an erosion of moral absolutism, a greater acceptance of pursuing one's own pleasure, and perhaps, most important, a greater willingness to include marginalized groups in a truly pluralistic culture.[23] Coasters are less religiously dogmatic than their parents and less prone to racial, religious, or ethnic prejudice. At the same time, it makes no sense to sterotype Coast baby boomers' parents as old-fashioned. Certainly 1966 grads tend to exaggerate their parents' traditionalism. After all, those World War II marriages were consummated in a cultural context of Frank Sinatra's crooning and Betty Grable's and Rita Hayworth's pinups. We tend to exaggerate the uniqueness of an emerging television generation; weren't their parents already quite absorbed with commercial radio shows and Hollywood movies? Historian Elaine Tyler May persuasively suggests that the kinds of cultural counteroffensives of the 1950s arose precisely because of the liberatory trends baby-boomer parents had experienced in their own youths.[24]

Theodore Caplow and his associates, in their follow-up to the Lynds' Middletown studies, strongly argue that a more modern, culturally relativistic society that was more sexually permissive and more tolerant of divorce had already taken root by the 1920s. Middletowners, according to Caplow, "hold to much the same values as their grandparents held two generations ago," but "they are much less eager to impose them on other people and much more tolerant of beliefs and life-styles that differ from their own."[25] Coast baby boomers, building on changes experienced by both their parents and grandparents, have teased out those aspects of transformation associated with the 1960s that they have felt comfortable absorbing over time: tolerance, especially racial tolerance; sexual equality; environmental sensitivity; reduced sexual inhibition; greater individuality in clothing and hairstyles; greater skepticism about the honesty and good intentions of government officials. The changes seem dramatic precisely because of the especially conservative, often reactionary qualities of postwar Fifties culture and politics. Coast baby boomers, reacting to some of the conformist excesses of the Fifties, although never accepting the cutting-edge political or cultural radicalism of the period, selected out the less risky, more absorbable pieces of it. These have become a part of a constantly reconstructed common sense of behavior, values, and morality. The most significant changes occurred earlier in the century with the convergent rise of assembly-line production, advertising and credit buying, a fun morality, and the beginning of a national mass culture of movies, music, and radio.

Coasters share with Caplow's Middletowners a commitment to the nuclear family, including extensive outreach to parents and relatives. Most of them engage in routine visits and contacts with parents and siblings. There is little to suggest the kinds of anomic loneliness and isolation offered by so many cultural critics, especially those left of center. There *is* more divorce and, in most households, what sociologist Arlie Hochschild has termed "the second shift"; the double duty of the woman as worker and housewife seems dominant.[26] It is possible that cultural alienation predominates within the most cosmopolitan elements of the upper or professional middle class, but Coasters have over time adapted to our culture of abundance through work, family, and the local community. Their family lives are less patriarchal, more egalitarian, and more stressful.

Coasters, for the most part, remain locals, resisting the cosmopolitan culture of the professional middle classes. No more than 10 percent of Coasters from the class of 1966 have become more cosmopolitan; those who have did so usually through a combination of college education and migration to more sophisticated places like Manhattan, Boston, Chicago, San Francisco. But the overwhelming majority of Coasters, including most of those who left the area, have remained local in their cultural values and behaviors. Indeed, nearly three-quarters of 1966 graduates have remained in the area, and among those who have departed, fully one-third have moved to the South.

Few Coasters express any interest in the arts. They don't often attend concerts or visit museums. Their reading habits are limited to the daily newspaper, job- or hobby-related materials, and popular fiction. Many never visit nearby Philadelphia or New York City. In all of my interviews, I heard little of psychotherapy; the few exceptions were marriage encounters sponsored by local churches. Eating tastes are middlebrow, with few indications of haute cuisine. Home furnishings are tasteful and simple, with leanings toward country and colonial styles; few homes have extensive book cases and anything but the most conventional artwork. There is little of the garish and tasteless; mostly one finds signs of domesticity and lots of do-it-yourself home improvements.

To say that the Coast lifestyle differs from that of upscale communities like Marin County in California or Colorado's Vail would be putting it mildly. There is little pretense and much comfort; much craft, if little art.

Coastal graduate George Evanson's thoughts about his yuppie sister suggest the contrasting realities. He buys things because he likes to tinker and because he enjoys owning quality products. He assumes that she and her attorney husband purchase strictly for conspicuous display. George loves working on his motorcycle or his sailboat or building a new recreation room for his home. He sees his sister and brother-in-law as unable to fix things and, therefore, as unable to appreciate quality. At the same time, George is intimidated by and ambivalent about their lives in their more cultured, urbane, sophisticated—and wealthier—suburb. They're cosmopolitan; he's local.

To most Coasters, there are actually three alternative lifestyles. Nora Bennett's husband, Rob, would prefer to live in the country, hunting and fishing, restricting social life to family and friends. He hates life in what he considers to be too crowded, too noisy, too dirty suburban communities, not to speak of cities. He's a country boy, more a provincial than a local, in the sense that he remains essentially detached from most mass media and suburban consumer habits and desires. Nora's sister, on the other hand, who once lived in Manhattan and now resides in a nearby and very affluent shore town, regards middlebrow, suburban Wilbur as the sticks, the boonies. She's cosmopolitan and more upper-middle-class in her values, style, and behavior. Nora, who feels that she would go nuts if forced to live in the country and who lacks the social graces to be comfortable in the more cultured world her sister inhabits, is a local, a middle-class, suburban local.

Like her cosmopolitan sister, she is fully a part of the culture of abundance, but like her husband, she stands apart from its most sophisticated, urbane qualities.

The Suburban Cocoon

The suburban milieu, critical to an understanding of Coast culture, both distances and obscures social-class dynamics. Suburbia flattens out the social-class tensions, often exacerbated by ethnic ones, of smokestack or mill towns and sections of cities. There is no clear "other side of the tracks" where immigrant-stock factory workers live, divided from Anglo owners and managers. Nor are there the interethnic and racial tensions so characteristic of city neighborhoods, where, for example, an Italian crossing over onto Irish or Polish turf means trouble.[27] The towns of Wilbur, Channing, and South Bay, which experienced suburbanization following the end of World War II, have successfully walled themselves off from the social-class and racial conflicts that mark urban and smokestack America. Some people recall childhoods in a declining section of Atlantic City or recall stories from relatives about neighborhood deterioration, but for the most part Coasters are comfortably oblivious to such urban woes. In fact, if there is any trend, it is to move further out, away from the rising property taxes and the increasingly congested roads of the Coast. The city collapses from afar, and some of the suburban promise sours with congestion, traffic jams, and rising anxieties about the spilling over of violent crime.

Within the diverse Coaster middle classes, the wealthy, although certainly envied and sometimes resented, are at the margins, on Channing's Seaview section or across the bay in the exclusive seaside towns. The poor and the minorities—

black and Hispanic—are in Atlantic City, Pleasantville, or isolated rural pockets. The suburban cocoon, even within a stagnant economy, sustains the Coast illusion about the totally middle-class nature of the United States. The American utopia, after all, is universal middle-classness. And in the everyday life of most Coasters, retreating to the ranch or the colonial-style home or the bungalow box, spatially removed from both *The Lifestyles of the Rich and Famous* and the realities of an urban underclass, the norm is varieties of middle-classness.

The suburban cocoon protects the American middle classes from most threats to their well-being. It helps Coasters sustain an insularity from social and global problems they perceive as beyond their control. It constructs what one critic calls "suburban pastoralism—nostalgia for the supposedly stable, prosperous white suburban way of life we associated with the 1950s."[28]

Within the cocoon, Coasters sustain as much personal control and security as they can through family activities, home ownership, and networks of small groups. Their sense of public participation and social responsibility is characteristically circumscribed by locale. There is a love of country that, except when undermined by a morally problematic and financially and humanly costly war like that we fought in Indochina, transcends locale.

But the active involvement in public affairs—becoming an activist or even, for most, paying attention to larger, global affairs—is experienced as alien, even by most of those who flirted with dissent during their more rebellious college years. Their comparative successes, at work, in constructing families, or participating in most child-centered aspects of their communities, reinforce a resistance to larger commitments. At least within work, the family, and the community, there seems to be some possibility of exerting control. Within their vision of the world, walled off as the suburban cocoon, Coasters believe that they do shape their futures.

What they attempt to control is parochial, although deserving of our utmost respect. Coasters remain locals rather than cosomopolitans, in part because the latter requires, at the least, some gloss of the high culture, an awareness of and an ability to manipulate cultural artifacts, to master the cues and symbols essential to the elite world of ideas and, perhaps more important, taste. As locals, as, at their most admirable, practitioners of crafts, as personifications of Thorstein Veblen's "instinct of workmanship," Coast baby boomers are able to exert some control over their lives, if not over their destinies. They are competent within their microsociety.

They are not conventionally selfish; many give considerable time to community activities, ranging from charities to local boards to child-centered activities, often sports supervision. They are not advocates of the individualism associated with free-market conservatives; Herbert Gans is quite right in distinguishing a popular, middle-class individualism committed more to security than to risk, more to the family than to the firm.[29]

The dilemma is that as the nation and the world become more and more interdependent, as we move toward whatever model of "new world order" we choose, the kinds of localized community investments Coasters are willing to make allow for control over fewer and fewer domains. Their competence is necessary but not sufficient. In effect, Coast havens face an increasingly heartless world. Externalities spill over, from polluted ocean waters and freshwater rivers, to drug- and poverty-driven burglaries and violent crimes, to consequences of the United States' relative economic and technological decline in the world. Since Chernobyl, one cannot consider energy policies as bound by national boundaries. The collapse of the Berlin Wall suggests more than the pathos of Communist Party irrelevancy; it reflects the ways in which an electronically based communications revolution drives interdependence. But as they have tended to do since adolescence, Coasters live and act as if the larger world does not exist. They are a perfect fit for the contemporary contradiction of people with hope and optimism about their own personal and family prospects but a deep pessimism concerning the ability of the nation or the international community to resolve macro-level problems. If economic stagnation continues, if the squeeze on the middle class tightens, it will be more difficult to maintain such a dichotomy.

A Personal Note

I am technically not a baby boomer, having been born too early, but am nevertheless what my students call "a Sixties person." I was propelled by the civil rights movements and the Vietnam War toward both political activism and scholarship. My values have often brought me into conflict with mainstream American culture, something I share with previous generations of radicals and dissenters. Indeed, in my first major study, I examined the ways in which a previous generation of Communist Party activists sustained deviant values and behaviors over a lifetime.[30]

This story, on the other hand, seeks to make sense of aspects of that mainstream culture which political radicals have rarely understood and, therefore, have rarely influenced. The Marxian tradition has been all too quick to reduce the issue of American exceptionalism—the emphasis on our historical uniqueness among modern societies in not having a mass-based Left, or socialist movement—to class or racial privilege. Yet it has been apparent for some time, at least to me, that a democratic transformation necessitates a movement that includes much of the American middle classes.

In the attention paid to issues of social class in the United States, academically as well as within the mass media, entirely too much focus has been paid to "yuppies," the professional middle class or "new class." Our most polemical cultural analysts seem to fixate on what is after all a relatively small group. Demographers limit the category of yuppies to less than 3 percent of the baby-boom generation; Barbara Ehrenreich's professional middle class can only be stretched to roughly 20 percent of the population by including its less prestigious vocations, for example, groups like public school teachers who don't seem to fit much of her analytic framework.[31]

We remained mesmerized by what are all too convenient categories: the black underclass, urban ethnic blue-collars, affluent suburban yuppies. Such triangles are decidedly subversive of any effort to make sense of the landscape that has been emerging in the United States since at least the end of World War II. And now, since we may be moving, according to a number of recent and influential studies, into a postsuburban environment, we at the very least owe it to ourselves to make some sense of the suburban realities without falling back on social-class clichés.[32]

This study of a suburban middle-class group of baby boomers reinforces my own disposition toward caution in fine-tuning social-class categorizations. At least outside of the more metropolitan areas, there seem to be many middle-class people who are neither yuppies nor a new class nor a professional middle class in matters of values, behavior, or lifestyle. And their middle-classness is accentuated by the suburban milieu in the sense that such an environment tends to reduce a variety of social-class tensions more typical of smokestack towns and cities. This is not to deny the realities of labor conflicts, the importance of battles of unionization, the very real friction between the affluent and those struggling to tread water. But it is to suggest that the suburban environment, in contributing to an erosion of ethnic solidarity, in often lacking an ethnically defined other side of the tracks, produces a consumer-driven, domestically focused middle-class culture participated in by a continuum of families ranging from the upper middle class to the working class. All have been affected in significant ways by secularizing and culturally relativizing trends and by the erosion of a more repressive sexual and cultural standard. But at the same time, they have struggled to maintain core values, to make adjustments as a means of remaining the same.

I believe that the suburban context of their lives is a critical ingredient in such struggles, mostly in helping to make less visible many of the contradictions and fissures within our society. The cocoon often succeeds in insulating suburbanites from the uglier and more painful realities of injustice, oppression, and just plain misery both in America and throughout the world. It distances. Recall Mac Schmidt's aversion to coming to grips with the Vietnam War experience. Such feelings are compounded by an environment monopolized by microsocietal, local concerns. As Coast baby boomers grew up, they could keep issues of race and poverty at a distance;

facing the Vietnam War, many men who neither protested nor served could opt for National Guard or reserve duty to avoid possibilities of combat.

Ernest Bond, one of those who left the Coast area to pursue a writing career in the big city, understood that "if I stayed here, this thing would nail me to the ground; I would be stuck here the rest of my life." He was too much of a dreamer, too ambitious, too restless, to stay put. Ernest felt he had to leave, "to cut it," so that he could become an artist, an urbane person. He is not exaggerating when he adds, "If I would have stuck here, I would have been dead." His options may have differed if he had grown up in a more cosmopolitan suburb or in a suburb or "technoburb" generating its own cultural life. But that was not the case in the Coast area.

And yet Ernest Bond strongly identifies with his roots, with the Coast towns and their people. He sees the Coast as the mother lode out of which his creativity flows. The Coast towns, to Ernest, stand for what is decent and good. When asked how he reconciles seemingly contradictory views of the Coast as both source of creativity and yet spiritually deadening, Ernest hesitates, ponders before responding, "This place is comforting. As a writer, I don't want to be comforted; I want to be challenged and excited." He knows that the kinds of conversations and activities he now takes for granted aren't possible in the Coast towns.

In the presidential elections of the 1980s, class of 1966 Coasters voted overwhelmingly for Republicans Ronald Reagan and George Bush. In 1980, there were three votes for Jimmy Carter, one for independent John Anderson; in 1984, two for Walter Mondale, one for Barry Commoner. In the 1988 election, the sentiment was clearly in favor of Bush by a margin of four to one.

But a survey of respondents indicates a significant shift in the 1992 elections. First of all, support for Bush collapsed, dropping from nearly 80 percent down to below 40 percent. Coasters, most of whom have consistently voted Republican since coming of age, gave Democrat Bill Clinton close to half of their votes; one in six supported independent Ross Perot. At least half of those who voted for Bush were tempted by Perot. Perhaps most strikingly, the swing away from Bush was most marked among Coast women, several of whom stated that Republican opposition to abortion was critical.

One must be cautious about such seemingly significant changes. First of all, the sample is small. Second, it is far from clear whether a longer-term trend is at work. But one can certainly state with some confidence that such voting shifts bolster my argument about the ways in which ideas associated with the 1960s have impacted on Coasters. Coast women stand away from the label of "feminism," but their voting suggests significant influence.

Coast baby boomers share a political skepticism and a psychological withdrawal with their generational peers. Most remain Republican, but there are few GOP enthusiasts. Even though most Coasters vote, they exhibit little belief in the integrity of the electoral process. Many express a cynicism about the excessive materialism of the society and relate this to the political climate. As Coaster Jack Clair bemoans, "Money's a problem in America; it's the basis of everything. It seems like all the leaders, the way America has turned, we're real capitalists." He states this with resignation, as if it's the only game in town. Like most Coasters, the Dennises don't talk politics much, but their differences tell us much about this pervasive cynicism. Judd Dennis asserts, "She's more Democratic and I'm more Republican. I see Republicans supporting big business; without big business, the little guy's not going to have any jobs to do. I see the Democrats—now this could be wrong—as spending, spending, spending, on good social programs, wonderful things, but the money's not there—and if they do keep with this, I'm not going to have any money for my savings account." Susan Dennis, ostensibly the Democrat, responds, "I see it differently, to the point that regardless of whether you're taxed for the money or big business is taxed, you're going to pay, because big business is not going to suffer a loss. It doesn't matter."

It is this sense that one can't really fight—not city hall, which is amenable to local middle-class influence—but larger forces that mark Coast baby boomers' political attitudes. One may gripe about declining standards, one may worry about the fast-lane hedonism of the casinos, one may recognize the political power game as tilted toward those with the most chips, but given that the system has been essentially good to them, Coasters see no need for significant involvement.

Significant economic downturns may affect both political loyalties and levels of involvement. But if the furious responses to Democratic governor James Florio's tax package is at all indicative, it is likely that Coasters will rally more to suburban-centered tax revolts than to challenges to the most powerful and privileged. To the extent that liberal reformers persist in holding "suburban" as a synonym for "affluent," they will risk maximizing such disaffections.

I conclude this story with ambivalent feelings about Coasters. I admire their decency and integrity and am most grateful for their friendliness, their willingness to welcome me into their homes and their lives. But I remain concerned about the consequences of their insularity, about the ways in which the suburban cocoon allows them to avoid coming to grips with the realities of the increasing interdependence of modern life. Sometimes their seeming obliviousness to the larger world frustrated and angered me. I could feel my self-righteousness rising.

I would like to think that more often than not my curiosity about Coast baby boomers and my respect for their essential integrity got the better of my ideological intolerance and self-righteousness. After all, I came into their lives to seek understanding, to learn, to listen to mainstream voices. I know enough to know that it is easy to vent frustrations at the comfortable, to cast aspersions at those living "in little boxes, all made out of ticky-tacky," which "all look just the same". We've had enough of that. Finally, such perspectives are snobbish and one-sided. I wanted to pay attention, to focus on questions rather than answers, to begin with the assumption that any reconstruction of a politics seeking to address our fundamental problems—for example, homelessness, poverty, environmental deterioration—must begin with a respect for the people inevitably needed to embrace such a politics as in the public interest.

There has been much public discussion of the centrality of the middle class in any challenge to conservative Republican electoral dominance. Minimally, we need to move toward a clearer definition of that middle. We need, for example, to reject the linkage of suburbia with upper-middle- or professional-class incomes and lifestyles. The suburbs, now including more than one-half of our voting population, range throughout the income continuum with heavy concentration in that middle middle range. The clumsy phrase "working middle class" suggests the appropriate terrain. Conservatives, especially Republicans and more recently Ross Perot, have been working that terrain with great success since George

Wallace instructed them in its nuances. Richard Nixon referred to them as "the great silent majority" of Americans. Democrats have only recently discovered the importance of such middle-middle-class voters, at least in rhetoric. Bill Clinton's claim to be a New Democrat rests, in large part, on his claim to return his party to the service of such voters.

It is unfortunate that the bulk of our most perceptive recent studies remain focused on the cosmopolitan professional middle-class suburbanites. It is questionable how representative upper-middle-class people from the New York City or San Francisco suburbs are of the far less cosmopolitan suburbanites living at some distance from elite campuses and from our most sophisticated cities.[33]

Coast baby boomers are part of that silent majority which has dominated the political landscape from the late 1960s until, at the least, the early 1990s. Myths about the Sixties generation are not helpful in coming to understand such silence and such contradictory responses to cultural change. The beginning of wisdom, at least to me, is to come to grips with the very middle-classness of American culture. Somewhere between the much publicized upper middle class and the alternatively romanticized and denigrated working class—between, if you will, *thirtysomething* and *Roseanne*—is a nonelite, hardworking, family-centered middle class, whose members are either ridiculed or ignored by media and academic elites, convinced that the American way of life, with all its flaws, remains the best available option. Such is not the case, it goes without saying, for those left out of the suburban cocoon, living in the ghettos and barrios and in the impoverished parts of the Third World.

I would like to believe that education might contribute to the broadening of middle-class perspective and generosity.

Unfortunately, middle-class schooling often reinforces rather than challenges suburban parochialism. One cannot be sanguine about the relatively weak reed that our educational system truly is; schools tend to reflect culture and society. At the same time, one should not underestimate the extraordinary transformations spawned by the movements of the 1960s to extend legitimacy to a variety of excluded and aggrieved groups and to sensitize people to environmental issues.

Our political culture remains the contested terrain. The good news is that the transformation going back to early in this century and heightened by the movements of the 1960s and early 1970s has enriched, slowly and in contradictory ways, the lives of the middle classes. Middle-class baby boomers, like Coast's class of 1966, are more open-minded, more tolerant, less racially prejudiced, more accommodating of a variety of differences, than their parents. They *have* been influenced by the 1960s, if several steps removed. But their half-full cup of greater tolerance and environmental sensitivity stands next to the half-empty one of two nations: one white, one dark; one affluent, one poor. And their cocoon muffles the cries for help.

While some of their thoughts and feelings about "the other" reflect this insularity from, if not insensitivity to, human suffering, they also raise valid questions and have legitimate concerns about what has come to be called "political correctness." To be opposed to affirmative action is not necessarily to be a racist; to value work over welfare is not inherently to be "blaming the victim." My own feeling is that we've been asking people to make incredible adjustments in their values, their behavior, and their identities over the past thirty-odd years—adjustments from smoke-free environments to gays in the military, from recycling garbage to MTV. The silent-majority baby boomers have observed from the sidelines many of the movements calling for change; sometimes they have reacted with hostility, even contempt. But as the movements faded, many of the challenges they provoked remained—modified, mainstreamed, absorbed, unevenly and contradictorily, but nevertheless absorbed.

Such absorption may be little comfort to those outside the suburban cocoon, with little time for the slow pace of cultural change. How to translate the suburban middle classes' still predominant silences into the sounds of justice and compassion remains our most pressing agenda.

Methodological Appendix

When I decided to study the Coastal High School class of 1966, I began with an examination, what I like to call "swimming" in the local milieu. I have spoken to many dozens of people with various levels of knowledge and experience about the area and have read as much as seems to be available from local newspapers, county and town records, historical libraries, and materials existing at the high school. At certain points in my research, particularly after I had engaged in perhaps two dozen interviews, I began to feel almost as if I were a 1966 Coastal graduate.

At the same time, I tried to place my local research within a context of the issues that drove me to Coastal High School: the nature of American middle-class culture, generational change, the baby boom, the significance of the 1960s, and especially conflicts over race, gender, morality, and patriotism.

Oral history needs to be grounded in the historical context to protect itself from the seductive illusion that interviewees' reflections and memories, although clearly central in decoding historical meaning, tell the whole story. One is always working at that extraordinary border area where perception and reality engage in a dance, where truth and meaning lie. As such, the oral historian is always a cultural historian, seeking to uncover the fundamental assumptions shared and disputed by participants in a culture.

The establishment of a sample began rather conventionally, with the yearbook, newspapers, and magazines of the Coastal class of 1966. I expected to track down a few of the graduates, to interview them, with good fortune winning their trust, and, consequently, to build a more extensive sample as I proceeded. In fact, a serendipitous event facilitated a smoother than expected process. I discovered, in browsing through the yearbook, that I was in regular contact unknowingly with an officer of the 1966 class. He was gracious enough to offer me assistance at this early and crucial stage of contact gathering, supplying me with approximately a dozen names and, importantly, with the use of his name in reducing understandable suspicions among potential subjects about the good intentions of a complete stranger.

The sample of 47 from a class of 246, obviously, is not random. To approach representativeness I sought a distribution of subjects proportional to town residence, and I tried to be sensitive to issues of social class, ethnicity, religion, and gender and to friendship patterns. My initial contacts were mostly males from one of the key social groups, but I worked very consciously to ensure maximum heterogeneity, to include those who didn't fit into any of the cliques. This was particularly important in protecting against a snowball effect, that is, the tilt of a sample toward the social network of those interviewed early. My initial respondents tended to provide me with contacts from their own cliques; I had to limit interviews in some instances to ensure that I included enough women, enough members of less prestigious groupings, and individuals outside of all groupings. There is always a certain bias in such a study toward geographical stability; that is, it is easier to trace and interview those who have remained living in the area. I have tried to temper such a bias with several interviews of those graduates who chose to leave the area. Women are more difficult to trace because of name changes via marriage, but the sample does reflect the sexual distribution of graduates.

The taped interviews, for the most part, were conducted in the homes of graduates, usually one-on-one, but in a few instances the interviews included both husband and wife. The sessions lasted anywhere from ninety minutes to four hours, averaging between two and three hours. I also asked graduates to fill out a brief two-page information sheet, including basic information about schooling, parents, religion, marriage and children, work, political affiliations, and voting record. Most complied.

A few graduates chose not to be interviewed, and several were halfhearted in their interviews, too obviously self-serving or self-protective. For the most part, however, I was struck by the generosity and curiosity of most graduates interviewed. As is often the case in oral history, many began by wondering what there could possibly be in their lives that would prove interesting to a researcher. And, as is almost always the case, the telling of one's story, the rekindling of memories, opens the floodgates.

My approach was essentially autobiographical: I would begin with questions about their parents and their childhoods, focusing on what it was like growing up in their respective suburban towns and on the kind of adolescents they were as high school graduation approached. I wanted to know how they perceived the world in 1966, what they knew, what they were ignorant of, how prepared they were for both the adult life and for the cultural challenges that would follow. The interviews explored how, if at all, they were affected by the civil rights revolution, the Vietnam War, antiwar and student-based activism, hippie rebellion, rock 'n' roll, feminism, the environmental movement, and so on. I was interested in seeing how their post–high school lives—immediate marriage and children versus extended singles living, college versus work, military service versus civilian life—correlated with their Sixties experiences. As the interviews proceeded toward the present, toward career and family, one framing question was asked: "Do you identify more with your parents, or with your children?"

Respondents provided me with a rapidly expanding file of leads and information on graduates. One particular gold mine was a set of index cards on graduates compiled for an eighth-grade reunion in one of the area's middle schools. I ended up with some usable information on approximately 175 of the 246 graduates, more detailed data on approximately 100, in addition to the 47 interviews.

How do I know that those I interviewed provided accurate recollections about how they felt, thought, and acted more than twenty years ago? My own approach is to analyze interviews along parallel tracks. One track is the meaning of past experience to the present; in this regard, what matters is how a graduate shapes and gives meaning to past experiences.

Distortion is assumed. The other track is what I can establish as the historical record within which an interviewee lived. This is the "swimming," both an immersion in the locale and a sensitive cross-referencing of interviewees' recollections. It's what Theodore Reik used to call listening with "the third ear." When there's a discrepant voice, a hint of exaggeration, of defensiveness, of boasting, of embarrassment, of any sign of the false, my own third ear relayed a signal to make a note, keep that in mind in further interviews.

There are no guarantees in this business. As Warren I. Susman suggests, the historian "must be able always to take words seriously but not always literally."[1] To be successful, on the other hand, the historian's own words must be taken both seriously and literally. But that's, finally, part of the reader's story.

Notes

All quotations and references to Coast baby boomers in the text are from interviews conducted in 1988, 1989, and 1990. Also interviewed were the 1966 principal and a teacher/counselor. During the week of September 6–10, 1993, I followed up telephone interviews regarding 1988 and 1992 voting patterns. In addition, I have spoken to dozens of area residents who either graduated from Coastal High School in the baby-boom years of 1963–81 or were attending other nearby high schools in that period, and to longer-time residents with knowledge and experience about the area.

Introduction

1. Jack Whalen and Richard Flacks, *Beyond the Barricades: The Sixties Generation Grows Up* (Philadelphia: Temple University Press, 1989), and Doug McAdams, *Freedom Summer* (New York: Oxford University Press, 1988).

2. Herbert J. Gans, *Middle American Individualism: The Future of Liberal Democracy* (New York: Free Press, 1988).

3. Loren Baritz, *The Good Life: The Meaning of Success for the American Middle Class* (New York: Knopf, 1989).

4. Good examples would be PBS's six-hour series *Making Sense of the Sixties;* Katherine S. Newman's *Declining Fortunes: The Withering of the American Dream* (New York: Basic Books, 1993); Donald Katz's *Home Fires: An Intimate Portrait of One Middle-Class Family in Postwar America* (New York: Harper Perennial, 1993).

Chapter I

1. Elaine Abrahamson, *Atlantic County: A Pictorial History* (Norfolk: Donning Company, 1987), 172–92; Charles E. Funnell, *By the Beautiful Sea: The Rise and High Times of That Great American Resort, Atlantic City* (New Brunswick, N.J.: Rutgers University Press, 1983), 142–56.

2. Elwood G. Davis, "Poverty in Atlantic City and Atlantic County" (Atlantic Human Resources, May 1965), 1–7.

3. Such sample data are consistent with the scattered reports about area migrations; see Richard F. Feathers and Philip C. Shaak, "Developing Employment Opportunities" (Atlantic Human Resources, n.d.), and Community Housing and Planning Associates, Atlantic County Planning Board, "Population Report: A Master Plan for the Atlantic County, New Jersey, Planning Board," (1969).

4. Funnell, *By the Beautiful Sea,* 142; Davis, "Poverty,' T-2, T-24.

5. "History of Channing" (n.d.), 11, "Short History of Wilbur" (n.d.), "Short History of South Bay" (n.d.)—all in the Atlantic County Historical Museum Archives.

6. Abrahamson, *Atlantic County,* 172.

7. Atlantic County Economic Development Commission, "Facts and Figures of the Economy of Atlantic County," (n.d.).

8. Diane Ravitch, *The Troubled Crusade: American Education, 1945–1980* (New York: Basic Books, 1983), 12–15.

9. (Atlantic City) *Press,* January 15, 1961; April 1, 1965, 1; June 6, 1966, 13; June 13, 1966, 6; *Coast Journal,* March 31, 1966, 813; April 28, 1966, 20; May 5, 1966, 1–2; June 2, 1966, 2; June 16, 1966; July 14, 1966; August 8, 1966.

10. Abrahamson, *Atlantic County,* 171; Funnell, *By the Beautiful Sea,* 145.

11. Abrahamson, *Atlantic County,* 161.

12. Ibid., 162–63.

13. For the best studies of the new middle-class suburban subculture, see Kenneth T. Jackson, *Crabgrass Frontier: The Suburbanization of the United States* (New York: Oxford University Press, 1985), chaps. 13–14; William M. Dobriner, *Class in Suburbia* (Englewood Cliffs, N.J.: Prentice-Hall, 1963), esp. part 1, chap. 2; and Gans, *Middle American Individualism.*

14. On social class and prestige, see A. B. Hollingshead, *Elmtown's Youth* (New York: John Wiley, 1961), chaps. 4–5.

15. Hollingshead labels them Class III, 95–102; see also Dobriner, *Class in Suburbia,* esp. chap. 2.

16. In the years that the class of 1966 was moving through the school system, two Jewish families, both headed by professionals, lived within the three Coast towns.

17. Coast *Journal,* April 7, 1966, religion section.

18. *Coastal High School Literary Magazine,* April 1964, 7.

19. Alan Wolfe, *America's Impasse: The Rise and Fall of the Politics of Growth* (New York: Pantheon Books, 1981).

20. Elaine Tyler May, *Homeward Bound: American Families in the Cold War Era* (New York: Basic Books, 1988), 20.

21. Robert Bellah et al., *Habits of the Heart: Individualism and Commitment in American Life* (New York: Perennial Library, Harper & Row, 1985).

22. See Garry Wills, *Reagan's America: Innocents at Home* (Garden City, N.Y.: Doubleday, 1987), chap. 14, "Sports."

23. Bellah et al., *Habits of the Heart,* 32–35.

Chapter 2

1. (Atlantic City) *Press*, June 6–13, 1966; May 5, 1966, 1; July 14, 1966, 1; November 10, 1966, 1.
2. Scrapbook, Coastal High School Library collection, n.d.
3. Robert S. Lynd and Helen M. Lynd, *Middletown: A Study in Modern American Culture* (New York: Harcourt, Brace & World, 1956), 212.
4. *Coastal High School Literary Magazine*, November 1963, 5.
5. Ibid., October 1964, 7.

Chapter 3

1. James Fallows, "What Did You Do in the Class War, Daddy?" *The Washington Monthly*, October 1975.
2. Stone's 1987 movie, starring Tom Berenger, Willem Dafoe, and Charley Sheen (Orion Pictures), eschewed facile attacks on student protesters.
3. In addition to Fallows's article, the most influential such study is Myra MacPherson, *Long Time Passing* (New York: Signet Books, 1984).
4. Nancy Zaroulis and Gerald Sullivan, *Who Spoke Up?* (Garden City, N.Y.: Doubleday, 1984).
5. John Mueller, *War, Presidents, and Public Opinion* (New York: John Wiley, 1973).
6. Atlantic County Department of Regional Planning and Development, May, 1985, "Atlantic County Census Trends, 1970–1980," 28.
7. "U.S. Military Personnel Who Died . . . in the Vietnam War, 1957–1986," reprint from "Combat Area Casualties, 1957–1986," records of the Office of the Secretary of Defense, Record Group 330, National Archives, Washington, D.C.; (Philadelphia) *Inquirer*, November 27, 1990, 1-B.
8. *Coast Journal*, June 2, 1966, 7b.

9. Lawrence M. Baskir and William S. Strauss, *Chance and Circumstance: The Draft, the War, and the Vietnam Generation* (New York: Vintage Books, 1978), xvi.

10. At the time of the controversy over Dan Quayle's draft status I did an editorial called "Quayling" for both the Canadian Broadcasting System, August 25, 1988, and for National Public Radio's *Morning Edition,* August 26, 1988, which argued that the central issue was "the privilege of the affluent . . . within a safety net of family and business connections which assist them in making it."

Chapter 4

1. (Philadelphia) *Inquirer,* August 3, 1989.

2. Lance Morrow, introduction to "Pictorial History of 1968: The Year That Shaped a Generation," *Time,* Special Collector's Edition, Spring, 1989, 8.

3. See Kenneth Kenniston, *Youth and Dissent: The Rise of a New Opposition* (New York: Harcourt Brace Jovanovich, 1971), prologue, "Youth as a Stage of Life," 3–21.

4. (Atlantic City) *Press,* August 1, 1969, 1.

5. Ibid., August 4, 1969, 1.

6. Ibid., August 5, 1969, 1, August 7, 1969, editorial page.

7. Barbara Ehrenreich, *The Hearts of Men: American Dreams and the Flight from Commitment* (Garden City, N.Y.: Anchor Books, Doubleday, 1984); see also Paul Goodman, *Growing Up Absurd* (New York: Vintage, 1960).

8. Richard Flacks, *Making History: The Radical Tradition in American Life* (New York: Columbia University Press, 1988), 5, 8.

9. It is interesting to see how such Popular Front images collapsed in the post–World War II Cold War and Red Scare period. The Century of the Common Man then confronted Tennessee Williams's Stanley Kowalski, arguably the first Polish joke or, more tellingly, the beginning of the conversion of working people from "salt of the earth" to "Joe six-pack Archie Bunkers."

10. See Jack Newfield, *A Prophetic Minority* (New York: Signet, NAL, 1966), for one of the earliest and best considerations of the distinction between those on the freedom road and those on the liberation road.

11. Coastal High School Yearbook, 69.

12. See James Webb, *Fields of Fire* (Englewood Cliffs, N.J.: Prentice-Hall, 1978).

13. See Donald Warren, *The Radical Center: Middle Americans and the Politics of Alienation* (South Bend, Ind.: University of Notre Dame Press, 1976), for analysis of support for the Alabama governor.

14. See Norman Mailer, *Miami and the Seige of Chicago* (New York: Bantam Books, 1969), for what the Walker Commission called a police riot.

15. This skepticism remains the bottom-line commonality among most baby boomers, according to Michael X. Delli Carpini, *Stability and Change in American Politics: The Coming of Age of the Generation of the 1960s* (New York: New York University Press, 1986), xxiii, 84, 87, 150, 243, 325–26.

16. "Will We Ever Get Over the '60s?" *Newsweek,* September 5, 1988, 14.

17. "Portrait of a Generation," *Rolling Stone,* April 7, 1988, 53.

18. Ibid., 38.

Chapter 5

1. Herbert J. Foster, "Institutional Development in the Black Community of Atlantic City, New Jersey: 1850–1930," in *The Black Experience in Southern New Jersey,* papers presented at a symposium, February 11 and 12, 1984 (Camden, N.J.: Camden County Historical Society, 1985), 43. See also idem, "The Urban Experience of Blacks in Atlantic City, New Jersey: 1850–1915," Ph.D. diss., Rutgers University, 1981.

2. (Atlantic City) *Press,* July 24, 1964, 22.

3. Bellah et al., *Habits of the Heart,* 32–35.

Chapter 6

1. Yearbook of the class of 1970 at Coastal High School.

2. See Michael Young and Peter Willmot, *The Symmetrical Family* (London: Penguin, 1973), 28–33; Glen H. Elder, *Children of the Great Depression: Social Change in Life Experience* (Chicago: University of Chicago Press, 1974), 287; and Elizabeth Bott, *Family and Social Network* (London: Tavistock, 1957), 92–96.

3. See Arlie Russell Hochchild, *The Second Shift: Working Parents and the Revolution at Home* (Berkeley and Los Angeles: University of California Press, 1989), and Judith Stacey, *Brave New Families: Stories of Domestic Upheaval in Late Twentieth Century America* (New York: Basic Books, 1990), for the most recent and insightful studies of modern families struggling to balance work, child care, and household chores.

Chapter 7

1. Richard D. Coleman and Lee Rainwater (with Kent A. McClelland), *Social Standing in America,* as quoted in Paul Fussell, *Class* (New York: Ballantine Books, 1983), 153–54.

2. See my "Yuppie: A Contemporary American Keyword," *Socialist Review* 19 (January–March 1989): 111–22, for an analysis of the history and contradictory meanings of this 1980s term.

Conclusion

1. Thomas Byrne Edsall and Mary Edsall, *Chain Reaction: The Impact of Race, Rights, and Taxes on American Politics* (New York: W. W. Norton, 1991), 29; William Schneider, "The Dawn of the Suburban Era in American Politics," *Atlantic,* July 1992, 33–44.

2. Michael X. Delli Carpini and Lee Sigelman, "Do Yuppies Matter?" *Public Opinion Quarterly* 50 (1986): 502–18; John Y. Hammond, "Yuppies," *Public Opinion Quarterly* 50 (1986): 488–501.

3. See Delli Carpini, *Stability and Change in American Politics,* 15–18. Katherine Newman, in her *Declining Fortunes,* 26–27, 172–173, makes a persuasive case for distinguishing older from younger baby boomers.

4. Wolfe, *America's Impasse.*

5. Baritz, *The Good Life,* 196; Jackson, *Crabgrass Frontier,* 4, chap. 13.

6. Daniel Yankelovich, *New Rules: Searching for Self-Fulfillment in a World Turned Upside Down* (New York: Bantam Books, 1982), xi.

7. Baritz, *The Good Life,* 257.

8. Delli Carpini, *Stability and Change in American Politics,* 18; Baritz, *The Good Life,* 227.

9. Gans, *Middle American Individualism,* 8.

10. Barbara Ehrenreich, *Fear of Falling: The Inner Life of the Middle Class* (New York: Pantheon Books, 1989), 13–14, 249.

11. Gans, *Middle American Individualism,* 4, 64–66.

12. Christopher Lasch, *The Culture of Narcissism: American Life in an Age of Diminishing Expectations* (New York: W. W. Norton, 1978); Bellah et al., *Habits of the Heart;* Ehrenreich, *Fear of Falling;* Philip Reiff, *Triumph of the Therapeutic: Uses of Faith After Freud* (New York: Harper & Row, 1966); David Reisman, Nathan Glazer, and Reuel Denney, *The Lonely Crowd: A Study of the Changing American Character* (New Haven, Conn.: Yale University Press, 1950); Philip Slater, *The Pursuit of Loneliness* (Boston: Beacon Press, 1970).

13. Yankelovich, *New Rules;* Peter Clecak, *America's Quest for the Ideal Self: Dissent and Fulfillment in the 60s and 70s* (New York: Oxford University Press, 1983.

14. Gans, *Middle American Individualism;* Theodore Caplow et al., *Middletown Families: Fifty Years of Change and Continuity* (Minneapolis: University of Minnesota Press, 1982).

15. Yankelovich, *New Rules,* 30–32, xix, 7, 57, 89, 130–131.

16. Bellah et al., *Habits of the Heart,* 25, 283–86, chap. 11.

17. Ibid., viii.

18. Ehrenreich, *Fear of Falling*, 198.

19. Ibid., 12, 15, 22, 31–32, 231, and esp. chaps. 3, 4, 5.

20. Ibid., 67, 249.

21. See Lasch's review of Yankelovich's *New Rules* in the *New York Review of Books*, December 3, 1981, 22–24, for a critique of ahistorical survey analysis. The focus on upper-middle-class culture makes it difficult to understand that middle-class Americans constitute two-thirds (57.3 million of 86.4 million) of the dwelling units that, according to Kenneth Jackson, consist of "a single family living in a single dwelling surrounded by an ornamental yard" (*Crabgrass Frontier*, 7).

22. Warren I. Susman, *Culture as History: The Transformation of American Society in the Twentieth Century* (New York: Pantheon Books, 1988), xxviii, xxix.

23. Yankelovich, *New Rules*, 89.

24. May, *Homeward Bound*, 9.

25. Caplow et al., *Middletown Families*, 31.

26. Ibid., esp. chap. 13; Hochchild, *The Second Shift*.

27. See Joseph I. Illick, *At Liberty: The Story of a Community and a Generation: The Bethlehem, Pennsylvania, High School Class of 1952* (Knoxville: University of Tennessee Press, 1989), and Jonathan Rieder, *Canarsie: The Jews and Italians of Brooklyn Against Liberalism* (Cambridge: Harvard University Press, 1985), for insightful considerations of the role of ethnicity in two very different urban communities.

28. Ehrenreich, *Fear of Falling*, citing historian Allen Hunter, 181.

29. Gans, *Middle American Individualism*, 3.

30. Paul Lyons, *Philadelphia Communists, 1936–1956* (Philadelphia: Temple University Press, 1982).

31. Delli Carpini and Sigelman, "Do Yuppies Matter?" and Hammond, "Yuppies"; Ehrenreich, *Fear of Falling*, 12–14.

32. See Robert Fishman, *Bourgeois Utopias: The Rise and Fall of Suburbia* (New York: Basic Books, 1987).

33. See Edsall and Edsall, *Chain Reaction;* see also Newman, *Declining Fortunes,* and Katz, *Home Fires.* For an interesting portrait of pre–baby boomers within the middle-class mainstream, see Larry Colton's impressive *Goat Brothers* (New York: Doubleday, 1993), a study of fraternity brothers from the University of California at Berkeley.

Methodological Appendix

1. *Culture as History* (New York: Pantheon Books, 1984), xi.

Bibliography

Abrahamson, Elaine. *Atlantic County: A Pictorial History*. Norfolk: Donning Company, 1987.

Appy, Christian. *Working-Class War: American Combat Soldiers and Vietnam*. Chapel Hill: University of North Carolina Press, 1993.

Atlantic County Department of Regional Planning and Development. "Atlantic County Census Trends, 1970–1980." May 1985.

Atlantic County Economic Development Commission. "Facts and Figures of the Economy of Atlantic County." N.d.

Baritz, Loren. *The Good Life: The Meaning of Success for the American Middle Class*. New York: Knopf, 1989.

Baskir, Lawrence M., and William S. Strauss. *Chance and Circumstance: The Draft, the War, and the Vietnam Generation*. New York: Vintage Books, 1978.

Bellah, Robert, Richard Madsen, William M. Sullivan, Ann Swidler, and Steven M. Tipton. *Habits of the Heart: Individualism and Commitment in American Life*. New York: Perennial Library, Harper & Row, 1985.

Bott, Elizabeth. *Family and Social Network*. London: Tavistock, 1957.

Caplow, Theodore, Howard M. Bahr, Bruce A. Chadwick, Reubin Hill, and Margaret Holmes Williamson. *Middletown Families: Fifty Years of Change and Continuity*. Minneapolis: University of Minnesota Press, 1982.

Clecak, Peter. *America's Quest for the Ideal Self: Dissent and Fulfillment in the 60s and 70s*. New York: Oxford University Press, 1983.

Colton, Larry. *Goat Brothers*. New York: Doubleday, 1993.

Community Housing and Planning Associates, Atlantic County Planning Board. "Population Report: A Master Plan for the Atlantic County, New Jersey, Planning Board." 1969.

Davis, Elwood G. "Poverty in Atlantic City and Atlantic County." Atlantic Human Resources. May 1965.

Delli Carpini, Michael X. *Stability and Change in American Politics: The Coming of Age of the Generation of the 1960s*. New York: New York University Press, 1986.

Delli Carpini, Michael X., and Lee Sigelman. "Do Yuppies Matter?" *Public Opinion Quarterly* 50 (1986): 502–18.

Dionne, E. J. *Why Americans Hate Politics*. New York: Simon & Schuster, 1992.

Dobriner, William M. *Class in Suburbia*. Englewood Cliffs, N.J.: Prentice-Hall, 1963.

Edsall, Thomas Byrne, and Mary Edsall. *Chain Reaction: The Impact of Race, Rights, and Taxes on American Politics*. New York: W. W. Norton, 1991.

Ehrenreich, Barbara. *Fear of Falling: The Inner Life of the Middle Class*. New York: Pantheon Books, 1989.

———. *The Hearts of Men: American Dreams and the Flight from Commitment*. Garden City, N.Y.: Anchor Books, Doubleday, 1984.

Elder, Glen H. *Children of the Great Depression: Social Change in Life Experience*. Chicago: University of Chicago Press, 1974.

Fallows, James. "What Did You Do in the Class War, Daddy?" *Washington Monthly,* October 1975, 5–19.

Feathers, Richard F., and Philip C. Shaak, "Developing Employment Opportunities." Atlantic Human Resources, n.d.

Fishman, Robert. *Bourgeois Utopias: The Rise and Fall of Suburbia.* New York: Basic Books, 1987.

Flacks, Richard. *Making History: The Radical Tradition in American Life.* New York: Columbia University Press, 1988.

Foster, Herbert J. "Institutional Development in the Black Community of Atlantic City, New Jersey: 1850–1930". In *The Black Experience in Southern New Jersey,* papers presented at a symposium, February 11 and 12, 1984. Camden, N.J.: Camden Historical Society, 1985.

——. "The Urban Experience of Blacks in Atlantic City, New Jersey: 1850–1915." Ph.D. diss., Rutgers University, 1981.

Funnell, Charles E. *By the Beautiful Sea: The Rise and High Times of That Great American Resort, Atlantic City.* New Brunswick, N.J.: Rutgers University Press, 1983.

Fussell, Paul. *Class.* New York: Ballantine Books, 1983.

Gans, Herbert J. *Middle American Individualism: The Future of Liberal Democracy.* New York: Free Press, 1988.

Gilbert, James. *A Cycle of Outrage: America's Reaction to the Juvenile Delinquent in the 1950s.* New York: Oxford University Press, 1986.

Goodman, Paul. *Growing Up Absurd.* New York: Vintage, 1960.

Hammond, John Y. "Yuppies." *Public Opinion Quarterly* 50 (1986): 488–501.

Hart, Peter, and Associates. "Portrait of a Generation." *Rolling Stone,* April 7, 1988.

"History of Channing." Atlantic County Historical Museum Archives, n.d.

Hochchild, Arlie Russell. *The Second Shift: Working Parents and the Revolution at Home.* Berkeley and Los Angeles: University of California Press, 1989.

Hollingshead, A. B. *Elmtown's Youth*. New York: John Wiley, 1961.

Illick, Joseph I. *At Liberty: The Story of a Community and a Generation: The Bethlehem, Pennsylvania, High School Class of 1952*. Knoxville: University of Tennessee Press, 1989.

Inglehart, Ronald. *Culture Shift in Advanced Industrial Society*. Princeton: Princeton Univesity Press, 1990.

Jackson, Kenneth T. *Crabgrass Frontier: The Suburbanization of the United States*. New York: Oxford University Press, 1985.

Jennings, M. Kent, and Richard G. Niemi. *Generations and Politics: A Panel Study of Young Adults and Their Parents*. Princeton: Princeton University Press, 1981.

Katz, Donald. *Home Fires: An Intimate Portrait of One Middle-Class Family in Postwar America*. New York: Harper Perennial, 1993.

Kenniston, Kenneth. *Youth and Dissent: The Rise of a New Opposition*. New York: Harcourt Brace Jovanovich, 1971.

Lasch, Christopher. *The Culture of Narcissism: America Life in an Age of Diminishing Expectations*. New York: W. W. Norton, 1978.

———. Review of Yankelovich's *New Rules*. *New York Review of Books*, December 3, 1981, 22–24.

Levy, Frank. *Dollars and Dreams: The Changing American Income Distribution*. New York: Russell Sage Foundation, 1987.

Lynd, Robert S., and Helen M. Lynd. *Middletown: A Study in Modern American Culture*. New York: Harcourt, Brace & World, 1956.

Lyons, Paul. *Philadelphia Communists, 1936–1956*. Philadelphia: Temple University Press, 1982.

———. "Yuppie: A Contemporary American Keyword." *Socialist Review* 19 (January–March 1989): 111–22.

McAdam, Doug. *Freedom Summer*. New York: Oxford University Press, 1988.

MacPherson, Myra. *Long Time Passing*. New York: Signet Books, 1984.

Mailer, Norman. *Miami and the Seige of Chicago.* New York: Bantam Books, 1969.

May, Elaine Tyler. *Homeward Bound: American Families in the Cold War Era.* New York: Basic Books, 1988.

Morrow, Lance. Introduction to "Pictorial History of 1968: The Year That Shaped a Generation." *Time,* special collector's edition, spring, 1989.

Mueller, John. *War, Presidents, and Public Opinion.* New York: John Wiley, 1973.

Newfield, Jack. *A Prophetic Minority.* New York: Signet, NAL, 1966.

Newman, Katherine S. *Declining Fortunes: The Withering of the American Dream.* New York: Basic Books, 1993.

Public Broadcasting System (PBS). *Making Sense of the Sixties.* (Six part series) 1991.

Ravitch, Diane. *The Troubled Crusade: American Education, 1945–1980.* New York: Basic Books, 1983.

Reiff, Philip. *Triumph of the Therapeutic: Uses of Faith After Freud.* New York: Harper & Row, 1966.

Reinarman, Craig. *American States of Mind: Political Beliefs and Behaviors Among Private and Public Workers.* New Haven, Conn.: Yale University Press, 1987.

Reisman, David, Nathan Glazer, and Reuel Denney. *The Lonely Crowd: A Study of Changing American Character.* New Haven, Conn.: Yale University Press, 1950.

Rieder, Jonathan. *Canarsie: The Jews and Italians of Brooklyn Against Liberalism.* Cambridge: Harvard University Press, 1985.

Schneider, William. "The Dawn of the Suburban Era in American Politics." *Atlantic,* July 1992, 33–44.

"Short History of Wilbur." Atlantic County Historical Museum Archives, n.d.

"Short History of South Bay." Atlantic County Historical Museum Archives, n.d.

Slater, Philip. *The Pursuit of Loneliness.* Boston: Beacon Press, 1970.

Stacey, Judith. *Brave New Families: Stories of Domestic Upheaval in Late Twentieth Century America.* New York: Basic Books, 1990.

Susman, Warren I. *Culture as History: The Transformation of American Society in the Twentieth Century.* New York: Pantheon Books, 1984.

"U.S. Military Personnel Who Died . . . in the Vietnam War, 1957–1986." Reprint from "Combat Area Casualties, 1957–1986." Records of the Office of the Secretary of Defense, Record Group 330, National Archives, Washington, D.C.

Vanneman, Reeve, and Lynn Weber Cannon. *The American Perception of Class.* Philadelphia: Temple University Press, 1990.

Varenne, Herve. *Americans Together: Structured Diversity in a MidWestern Town.* New York: Teachers College Press, Columbia University, 1977.

Warren, Donald. *The Radical Center: Middle Americans and the Politics of Alienation.* South Bend, Ind.: University of Notre Dame Press, 1976.

Whalen, Jack, and Richard Flacks. *Beyond the Barricades: The Sixties Generation Grows Up.* Philadelphia: Temple University Press, 1989.

Webb, James. *Fields of Fire.* Englewood Cliffs, N.J.: Prentice-Hall, 1978.

"Will We Ever Get Over the Sixties?" *Newsweek,* September 5, 1988.

Wills, Garry. *Reagan's America: Innocents at Home.* Garden City, N.Y.: Doubleday, 1987.

Wolfe, Alan. *America's Impasse: The Rise and Fall of the Politics of Growth.* New York: Pantheon Books, 1981.

Yankelovich, Daniel. *New Rules: Searching for Self-Fulfillment in a World Turned Upside Down.* New York: Bantam Books, 1982.

Young, Michael, and Peter Willmot. *The Symmetrical Family.* London: Penguin, 1973.

Zaroulis, Nancy, and Gerald Sullivan. *Who Spoke Up?* Garden City, N.Y.: Doubleday, 1984.

Index